Traditional
CHRISTMAS
Cooking, Crafts & Gifts

Reader's
Digest

CONTENTS

Decorating the Tree

Around the House

The Holiday Table

Gift Wrapping

Copyright © 1994
Cy DeCosse Incorporated
5900 Green Oak Drive
Minnetonka, Minnesota 55343
1-800-328-3895
All rights reserved
Printed in U.S.A.

Traditional Christmas Cooking, Crafts & Gifts
draws pages from the individual titles of The
Home Decorating Institute®, The Hunting &
Fishing Library®, and the Microwave Cooking
Library®.

CANADIAN CATALOGUING-IN-PUBLICATION DATA
Main entry under title:
Traditional Christmas cooking, crafts & gifts

ISBN 0-88850-231-1

1. Christmas cookery. 2. Christmas decorations.
I. Reader's Digest Association (Canada).
TX839.C45T73 1994   641.5'68   C94-900113-9

Published in Canada in 1994 by
The Reader's Digest Association (Canada) Ltd.
215 Redfern Avenue
Montreal, Quebec H3Z 2V9

READER'S DIGEST and the Pegasus Logo
are registered trademarks of
The Reader's Digest Association (Canada) Ltd.

CY DECOSSE INCORPORATED
Chairman Emeritus: Cy DeCosse
Chairman & CEO: James B. Maus
Executive V.P. Creative: William B. Jones

Created by: The Editors of Cy DeCosse
Incorporated.
Printed on American paper

How to Use This Book

Planning for the holiday season includes a variety of activities, many of which revolve around decorating, gift giving and entertaining. This book helps with that planning. The first part of the book suggests many decorating ideas and projects to be done step-by-step. The later sections include menu planning ideas and recipes, as well as decorations and ornaments that come from your kitchen. Many or these projects make great gifts, too. So, start right in, and fill your home with the sights and smells of Christmas.

Decorating for Christmas

The first section includes detailed instructions for many tree ornaments, as well as for a traditional treetop angel. Finish the tree with a special tree skirt. The Holiday Table section shows how to make a variety of placemats, table runners and centerpieces. Choose a quilted holiday wreath table runner or placemats for an easy quilting project that is great for a gift or for your holiday entertaining. A variety of other placemats, using specialty trims, mitered borders and strip piecing, are also included. Make a festive gift box centerpiece and colorful table accessories, or try your hand at floral centerpieces and ensembles.

Around the House includes instructions for basic evergreen and eucalyptus wreaths, as well as a variety of ways to embellish them. Learn how to make garlands and bows to enhance the mantel, stairs and even the table. Stockings cannot be forgotten; you'll find a pattern for a basic stocking and wonderful ideas for variations. Cone trees and topiaries add to any room, and many styles are shown. Create Santa Sacks and Father Christmas figures from prestarched fabric, for gifts to be proud of. The winter village, a miniature snow village made from milk cartons, can become part of the family's annual holiday traditions.

The Gift Wrapping section shows you how to transform gift boxes into reuseable heirlooms, and how to create your own Victorian gift cards, gift tags and package trims, for that finishing touch.

Materials for the decorating projects, such as Styrofoam®, hot glue, prestarched fabric and polymer clay, can be found at craft stores. Foliage, twine and other materials for wreaths and garlands, cone trees and topiaries can be found in most florist's shops.

Holiday Ideas from the Kitchen

Cooking for the holidays is the way many of us give gifts that are truly from the heart. In the Holiday Ideas section, you can use your microwave to create a wide variety of kitchen treats and save time doing it. Make edible place cards and baskets for a special touch at your dinner table. If your time is limited, treat your guests to our quick cookies and candies. Fill your house with the smells of the season with a Woods-scent Potpourri or Aromatic Dough Ornaments. Also in this section are complete instructions for creating a Graham Cracker Village for display in your home.

Holiday Dinner Menus helps you put together complete meals that feature such meats as turkey, goose, ham and rib roast. Hunters in your family can find tips and recipes for a variety of game birds, too. Following the menus are recipes for all your holiday dinner trimmings, right down to the Orange Pumpkin Pie and Easy Yule Log Cake for dessert.

The Holiday Events section highlights a few of the parties or gatherings you might be hosting this season. For easy planning of a brunch, skating party or bowl game, follow our special collections of recipes. There are even some easy, prepare-ahead meals for those days spent shopping, when you just don't have time to cook.

Step-by-Step Guidance

From beginning to end, the step-by-step instructions in this book make decorating and cooking for the holiday easy and understandable. Whatever your level of expertise, this book can be a help and an inspiration. Use it for a successful, well-planned holiday season.

Decorating The Tree

TREETOP ANGEL

The traditional angel can be the crowning touch on a Christmas tree or the focal point on a mantel or side table. Made from crocheted doilies that are shaped with fabric stiffener, the angel shown here has a delicate, Victorian look. Select doilies with a center motif that can be clipped away, leaving a heading area for gathering as in step 4.

HOW TO MAKE A TREETOP ANGEL

MATERIALS

- Porcelain head, about 1¼" (3.2 cm) high; pearlescent white paint, if desired.
- Crocheted doilies, one each of 6", 12", and 14" (15, 30.5, and 35.5 cm) diameter.
- Liquid fabric stiffener.

- 18" (46 cm) length of ribbon, ⅛" (3 mm) wide, or narrow cording.
- Styrofoam® cone, 8" to 10" (20.5 to 25.5 cm) high.
- 24-gauge brass wire.
- Plastic wrap; wax paper; hot glue gun and glue sticks.

1 Trim the base of the cone so the height is about 7½" (19 cm). Shape peak of the cone, trimming sides if necessary, so head will rest on cone. Apply pearlescent white paint to the head, if desired; this softens hair coloring and skin tone. Set head aside, and cover cone with plastic wrap.

2 Place the 14" (35.5 cm) doily on plastic wrap. Apply the fabric stiffener to doily until saturated, using rag or fingers. Place plastic wrap on top of doily; apply pressure with hands to distribute stiffener and squeeze out excess. Remove top layer of plastic; dab any excess stiffener from doily, using rag.

3 Remove doily from plastic wrap; place center of doily on peak of cone. Shape doily into a scalloped, flared skirt; place sheets of folded wax paper between doily and cone to support skirt. Push head onto cone, over doily, securing it with small amount of fabric stiffener.

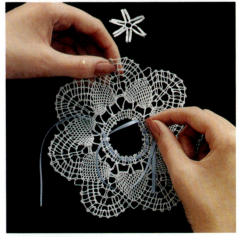

4 Cut away center portion of 6" (15 cm) doily; discard. For collar, weave ribbon through heading on remaining outer portion of doily.

(Continued)

9

5 Place collar on plastic wrap; apply fabric stiffener to collar, except heading and ribbon, using rag or fingers. Place collar over porcelain head, and draw up heading to fit neck; secure ribbon in a bow.

6 Shape collar into soft scallops, supporting shape with crumpled plastic wrap as necessary; keep collar flat at center back to allow space for wings. Allow skirt and collar to dry thoroughly.

7 Apply fabric stiffener to 12" (30.5 cm) doily. Fold doily in half, and place on clean sheet of wax paper. Shape doily into wings, pinching center area and fanning the doily upward. Separate layers toward top of wings; stuff with crumpled plastic wrap to hold shape. Press center area flat. Allow wings to dry.

8 Remove angel from cone form. Secure collar in place with dots of hot glue. Secure the wings at center back of angel, using hot glue.

9 Cut a short length of brass wire, and shape into circle for halo, hooking ends together; secure to head, using hot glue.

MORE
IDEAS FOR
TREE TOPPERS

Unique tree toppers can be created quickly, using a variety of items. For a tree topper that holds fond memories, search through old toys or Christmas decorations for items. For an elegant yet simple look, choose silk or dried greens, spraying them with metallic paint for added glitz. Or position a bow with streamers at the top of the tree, using a special ribbon to make the bow showy and glamorous.

Twisted dried naturals, *shooting out from the top of the tree, accent a contemporary decor.*

Special toys *or stuffed animals, secured with wire to the top of the tree, personalize a toy-theme tree.*

(Continued)

Silk foliage adds a dramatic touch to the treetop.

Several stars, *instead of the traditional single star, are secured to the upper branches of the tree.*

Cluster bows *(page 74), wired back-to-back, make a quick tree topper. The streamers from the bows can be spiraled around the tree or tucked loosely into the branches.*

Ornaments clustered on the treetop create a focal point.

A collection of Santas adds special charm to a Christmas tree.

A single wooden toy is prominently displayed at the top of the Christmas tree.

TRADITIONAL LACE ORNAMENTS

Lace ornaments are ever popular for a romantic holiday decor. The traditional Christmas decorations, angels and stockings, can be created in a variety of lace to make each ornament different. Cutwork lace doilies become angel ornaments with simple folding techniques, and touches of lace trim the stocking ornaments.

HOW TO MAKE A LACE ANGEL ORNAMENT

MATERIALS

- One 4" (10 cm) and one 6" (15 cm) square lace doily.
- One 12" (30.5 cm) and two 18" (46 cm) lengths of double-sided satin ribbon, ⅛" (3 mm) wide.
- One 1" (2.5 cm) satin ball.
- 2½" (6.5 cm) strand of pearls.
- Large-eyed needle, such as chenille needle.
- Hot glue gun and glue sticks.

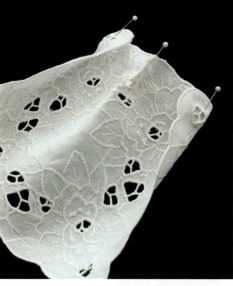

1 Fold 6" (15 cm) doily in half, right sides together; place pin ¼" (6 mm) from foldline to form tuck at center fold at one end. At sides of doily, fold ¾" (2 cm) to wrong side.

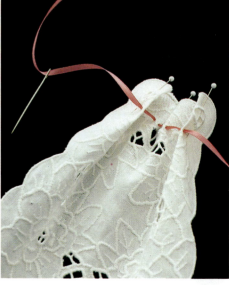

2 Bring folded sides to center on right side of doily. Thread large-eyed needle with 18" (46 cm) length of ribbon. Stitch into one fold, 1" (2.5 cm) down from upper edge; then stitch through center tuck and back up through other fold.

(Continued)

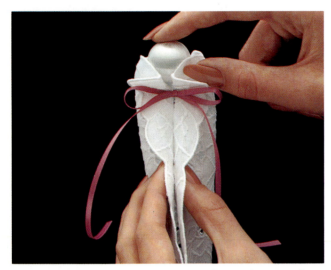

3 Tie ribbon in bow. Glue satin ball for head at top of doily, as shown, using hot glue.

4 Apply hot glue to pearls at each end of strand. Form into halo; press down onto top of head.

5 Fold 4" (10 cm) doily into ¼" (6 mm) accordion pleats; tie 18" (46 cm) ribbon around center. Tie again to knot the ribbon; tie into bow on right side of wings.

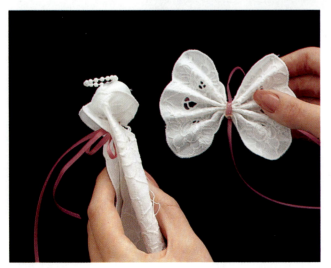

6 Apply wings to back of angel at point where doily was stitched with ribbon, using hot glue.

7 Fold 12" (30.5 cm) ribbon in half; tie ends together to make loop. Place ribbon around wings for hanger.

HOW TO MAKE A LACE STOCKING ORNAMENT

MATERIALS

- ⅛ yd. (0.15 m) fabric, such as batiste, velvet, or taffeta.
- One lace doily or handkerchief, 6" (15 cm) square or larger.
- 9" (23 cm) length of ribbon, ⅛" or ¼" (3 or 6 mm) wide.
- Hot glue gun and glue sticks.
- Embellishments as desired, such as silk rosebuds or beads.

CUTTING DIRECTIONS

- Cut two stocking pieces, using pattern on page 311.

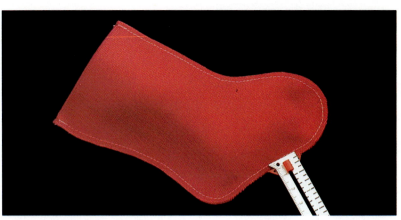

1 Place stocking pieces right sides together. Stitch ⅛" (3 mm) seam around stocking, leaving top open.

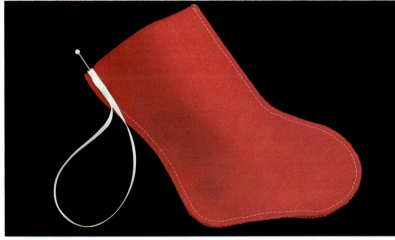

2 Fold ribbon in half; pin to wrong side of stocking, at back seam, matching raw edges of ribbon to upper edge of stocking.

3 Mark a diagonal line measuring 6½" (16.3 cm) long across corner of doily. Cut on marked line.

4 Pin corner piece of doily to the stocking, raw edges even, with right side of doily to wrong side of stocking; center ends of doily on back of stocking and corner of doily on front. Stitch ¼" (6 mm) seam.

5 Turn stocking right side out, folding doily down. Secure raw edges at center back, using hand stitching. Embellish the ornament, if desired; secure items with hot glue, or hand-stitch in place.

VICTORIAN
ORNAMENTS

Victorian ornaments, such as paper fans and potpourri balls, bring a touch of nostalgia to the tree. The elegant paper fans, made from paper lace or wrapping paper, and the potpourri balls, made from bridal illusion, are trimmed with embellishments for romantic appeal.

HOW TO MAKE A PAPER FAN ORNAMENT

MATERIALS

- 12" (30.5 cm) length of paper lace, 2½" to 4" (6.5 to 10 cm) wide; or 12" (30.5 cm) length of wrapping paper, 4" (10 cm) wide.
- Metallic or pearlescent acrylic paint, optional; craft glue; clothespins.
- 9" (23 cm) length of narrow ribbon, for hanging ornament.
- Embellishments as desired, such as dried rosebuds, statice, pearl strands, and ribbon.

1 Apply a light coat of metallic or pearlescent paint to right side of paper, if desired; thin paint as necessary, for a transparent effect. Fold paper in ½" to ⅝" (1.3 to 1.5 cm) accordion pleats, making first fold to back side of paper. Trim excess paper at end, if necessary.

2 Glue pleats together at lower edge; clamp glued ends together with clothespin until dry. Open pleats into fan.

3 Lace ribbon through a hole in top of fan; knot ends together to form hanger. Glue embellishments at lower end of fan.

HOW TO MAKE A POTPOURRI BALL ORNAMENT

MATERIALS

- Bridal illusion, or tulle; 5" (12.5 cm) length of pregathered lace, about 1" (2.5 cm) wide.
- Potpourri, 1 c. (2.50 mL) for each ornament.
- 3" (7.5 cm) length of 24-gauge brass wire.
- 9" (23 cm) length of narrow ribbon, for hanging ornament; craft glue.
- Embellishments as desired, such as dried rosebuds, statice, pearl strands, and ribbon.

1 Place potpourri in center of 12" (30.5 cm) circle of bridal illusion. Gather illusion around potpourri to form ball; secure by twisting wire around gathers.

2 Push one end of wire into center of gathered illusion; fold over and twist to form loop. Trim excess wire.

3 Insert ribbon through wire loop; tie ends together. Glue lace around potpourri ball, overlapping ends. Add embellishments as desired.

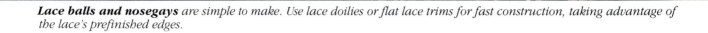

Lace balls and nosegays *are simple to make. Use lace doilies or flat lace trims for fast construction, taking advantage of the lace's prefinished edges.*

HOW TO MAKE A LACE BALL ORNAMENT

MATERIALS

- 12" (30.5 cm) round lace doily.
- 3" or 3½" (7.5 or 9 cm) clear, luminescent, or colored ball ornament.
- 9" (23 cm) length of narrow cord or ribbon, for hanging ornament.
- One or two 22" (56 cm) lengths of narrow ribbon.
- Hot glue gun and glue sticks.
- Embellishments as desired, such as baby's breath, berries, and pinecones.

1 Insert cord into ornament hanger; tie ends. Wrap doily around ball, with center of doily at bottom of ball. Tie ribbon around doily at top of ball; if two ribbons are used, tie them as one bow, and separate loops.

2 Pull edges of doily and adjust ribbons so doily is stretched to fit around ball. Embellish ornament as desired; secure items with hot glue.

HOW TO MAKE A LACE NOSEGAY ORNAMENT

MATERIALS

- 18" (46 cm) length of flat lace trim or 12" (30.5 cm) length of pleated lace trim, 1¾" to 2¾" (4.5 to 7 cm) wide.
- 9" (23 cm) length of narrow ribbon or cord, for hanging ornament.
- Hot glue gun and glue sticks.
- Embellishments as desired, such as ribbons, pearl strands, ribbon roses, and silk flowers.

1 Single-layer ornament. Remove heading from lace, if pleated lace is used. Join ends of lace, right sides together, in ¼" (6 mm) seam. Then stitch ⅛" (3 mm) from upper edge of lace, using short running stitches.

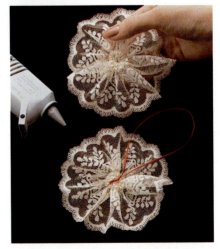

2 Pull thread, gathering lace into a tight circle; secure thread. Flatten the lace circle by pressing it gently with hand.

3 Fold ribbon in half; tie ends together to make loop for hanger. Glue loop to right side of lace at center. Add embellishments as desired.

Double-layer ornament. Make two lace circles as in steps 1 and 2; add ribbon loop to one circle as in step 3. Glue lace circles together, with loop between circles.

GILDED ORNAMENTS

Add a touch of glitz to your tree with a variety of golden and jewel-tone ornaments. Fill clear or luminescent balls with glittery tinsel. String clusters of small sleigh bells on wire and tie them with gold-trimmed bows. Or cover Styrofoam® balls with fabric and trim them with braids to coordinate with the room decor.

MATERIALS

- Clear or luminescent glass ball with removable top.
- Shredded tinsel.
- Hot glue gun and glue sticks.

- 9" (23 cm) length of gold cord, for hanging ornament.
- Embellishments as desired, such as ribbon, statice, berries, and sprigs of greenery.

HOW TO MAKE A TINSEL-FILLED ORNAMENT

1 Remove top of ornament. Insert desired amount of shredded tinsel into ball; replace top. Tinsel may be curled, as for curling ribbon, if desired.

2 Insert gold cord through wire holder; tie ends. Attach embellishments to top of ornament, if desired, using hot glue.

23

HOW TO MAKE A SLEIGH BELL ORNAMENT

MATERIALS

- Nine ⅝" (1.5 cm) sleigh bells.
- 8" (20.5 cm) length of 24-gauge brass wire.
- 10" (25.5 cm) length of ribbon, ⅝" (1.5 cm) wide.
- 8" (20.5 cm) length of ribbon, ¼" (6 mm) wide.
- 9" (23 cm) length of gold cord, for hanging ornament.
- Fabric glue.

1 Insert about 1" (2.5 cm) of wire through hanger of bell; twist to secure.

2 Insert other end of wire into remaining bells. First bell will be at bottom of ornament.

3 Make bow by folding ⅝" (1.5 cm) ribbon back and forth, forming a loop on each side; secure above top bell by wrapping wire around center of bow several times.

4 Form wire loop above bow, twisting wire to secure; trim excess wire.

5 Insert gold cord through the wire loop; tie ends. Tie ¼" (6 mm) ribbon in small bow; glue at center of looped bow, concealing the wire.

HOW TO MAKE A FABRIC-WRAPPED ORNAMENT

MATERIALS

- 3" (7.5 cm) Styrofoam® ball.
- ¼ yd. (0.25 m) fabric.
- 12" (30.5 cm) length of gold braid, ½" (1.3 cm) wide.
- 22" (56 cm) length of gold braid, ¼" (6 mm) wide.
- 9" (23 cm) length of gold cord and decorative cap, for hanging ornament.
- One tassel.
- Fabric glue; hot glue gun and glue sticks.

1 Cut two fabric circles, 4¾" (12 cm) in diameter; pin-mark center of each circle. Pin one circle to Styrofoam ball, distributing fullness evenly at raw edge. Glue edge of fabric to ball, making small tucks to ease in fullness.

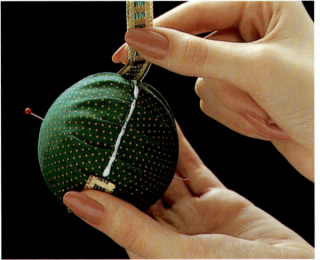

2 Repeat for opposite side of ball, using remaining fabric circle. Glue ½" (1.3 cm) gold braid around middle of ball, covering raw edges of fabric.

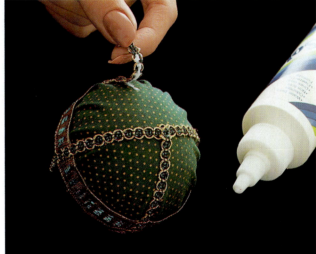

3 Cut ¼" (6 mm) gold braid in half; glue around ball in opposite directions, dividing ball into four sections. Use center pin marks as guide for centering braid.

4 Insert gold cord in decorative cap; knot ends. Shape cap to fit top of ornament; secure with hot glue.

5 Attach tassel to bottom of ornament, using hot glue.

These handcrafted snowmen are easily made by applying an artificial snow paste over a Styrofoam® form. Their features are shaped from polymer clay, a modeling compound that can be oven-baked. These tree ornaments can also be used to decorate packages and wreaths.

TIPS FOR SHAPING POLYMER CLAY

Work with the clay on a smooth, clean, flat surface. If the surface is porous, protect it with a sheet of wax paper or aluminum foil, secured to the surface with tape. Wipe the work surface and tools with petroleum jelly to prevent the clay from sticking.

Knead the clay to soften it with the warmth of your hands before shaping it.

Mix a dab of petroleum jelly into the clay if it seems dry. Keep your hands moist with petroleum jelly or hand lotion.

Roll the clay into balls of the desired size; use a circle gauge, available from stationery stores, to measure the balls.

Roll out the clay, using a rolling pin, to flatten it. Cut the clay with scissors or a mat knife.

HOW TO MAKE A SNOWMAN ORNAMENT

MATERIALS

- One 1½" (3.8 cm) Styrofoam ball; one 2½" (6.5 cm) Styrofoam egg.
- Polymer clay, such as Fimo® or Sculpey®, in orange, black, tan, red, and green.
- Artificial snow paste, such as Snow Accents™; palette knife.
- Small forked twigs; scrap of plaid wool; other accessories as desired.
- 24-gauge brass wire, for hanging ornament.
- Aerosol clear acrylic sealer.
- Toothpicks; wax paper; foam cup; baking sheet.
- Scissors or mat knife.
- Craft glue; hot glue gun and glue sticks.

1 Roll small end of Styrofoam egg, on smooth, hard surface to taper sides slightly. For snowmen with hats, trim a small amount from Styrofoam ball to flatten top. Insert toothpick halfway into the tapered end of the egg; place craft glue at base, and secure ball on top of egg, pushing it onto remainder of toothpick.

2 Form carrot by rolling ¼" (6 mm) ball of orange clay into tapered shape. Using scissors, cut buttons, eyes, and mouth from black clay that has been flattened; cut three larger pieces for buttons and six smaller ones for eyes and mouth.

3 Form hat by flattening ½" (1.3 cm) ball of black clay into round brim. Roll ¾" (2 cm) ball into a cylinder; flatten the ends, and place on brim, pressing gently.

4 Roll the clay for red hatband and green holly leaves to 1/16" (1.5 mm) thickness; cut, using scissors. Roll small berries from red clay. Gently press the hatband around the hat, and position holly and berries.

5 Form pipe by rolling ¼" (6 mm) ball of tan clay into cylinder; insert a piece of toothpick for pipe stem. Hollow out pipe and add texture, using toothpick. Press small amount of clay around toothpick near pipe bowl. Bake clay pieces on a baking sheet until hardened, following the manufacturer's instructions; hats may require more time.

6 Apply a thin coat of snow paste to Styrofoam, using palette knife; for ease in handling, mount on an inverted foam cup, using a toothpick.

7 Press clay features in place on wet snow surface. Allow snowman to dry thoroughly.

8 Make holes for twig arms, using toothpick or blunt needle. Apply craft glue to ends of twigs; insert into holes. Repeat to insert pipe.

9 Cut fabric 1" × 9" (2.5 × 23 cm) for the neck scarf. Fringe edges, and glue scarf in place. For woman, make head scarf from 5" (12.5 cm) square. Glue on additional accessories as desired.

10 Form 8" (20.5 cm) piece of wire into loop; twist ends together. Make hole in back of head. Apply glue to wire; insert in hole. Spray the entire snowman with a light coat of acrylic sealer. Remove snowman from cup, and touch up bottom of snowman with snow paste.

DRUM ORNAMENT

This drum ornament is cleverly crafted by forming prestarched fabric over the cap of an aerosol can. Paint drums in subdued colors for a realistic look or in an array of colors for a theme Christmas tree. An oil-based stain applied over the paint gives an antiqued look.

TIPS FOR USING PRESTARCHED FABRIC

Dip fabric pieces quickly in cool water; begin shaping immediately.

Work quickly, and do not handle the fabric any more than necessary. If the fabric is overworked, it becomes limp and does not hold its shape.

Keep your fingers wet during shaping to prevent the fabric from sticking to them.

Adjust the folds of the fabric with T-pins to avoid overworking the fabric.

Allow the fabric to dry overnight, and apply two light coats of acrylic sealer before painting.

Apply two coats of paint to the fabric for good coverage, allowing the first coat to dry before applying the second coat.

HOW TO MAKE A DRUM ORNAMENT

MATERIALS

- Prestarched fabric, such as Dip 'n Drape®, Drape 'n Shape, and Fab-U-Drape®.
- Cylinder-shaped plastic cap from aerosol can, about 2½" (6.5 cm) in diameter by 2" (5 cm) high; rubber band to fit around cap.
- Acrylic paints and brushes; ivory paint for top of drum and desired color for base of drum.
- Two ⅜" (1 cm) wooden beads and two round toothpicks, for drumsticks.
- 15" (38 cm) length of cord or leather lacing; sprig of artificial holly.
- Oil-based stain; aerosol clear acrylic sealer.
- Hot glue gun and glue sticks; wax paper.
- Permanent marking pen for personalizing ornament, optional.

CUTTING DIRECTIONS

From prestarched fabric, cut one 7" (18 cm) and one 4½" (11.5 cm) square of fabric for each ornament.

1 Dip 7" (18 cm) square of fabric in cool water for 5 to 10 seconds; center fabric over top of the plastic cap. Pull fabric down over sides, smoothing folds flush against cap; fold and finger-press raw edges to inside of cap. Turn cap over; allow to dry on wax paper.

2 Wet 4½" (11.5 cm) square of fabric as in step 1; center it over cap opening. Place rubber band around cap, about ¼" (6 mm) from edge; gently pull fabric taut.

3 Fold under raw edges, working with wet fingers; leave edges scalloped. When dry, remove the rubber band.

4 Apply acrylic sealer to drum. Paint top of drum ivory; paint base of drum desired color. When dry, apply second coat; allow to dry. Apply the stain to the drum, using old brush and following the manufacturer's instructions; wipe off excess stain with soft rag. If stain reappears while drying, rewipe as necessary.

5 Tie cord or lacing around drum, and tie ends together to make a loop for hanging ornament. Glue holly sprig to drum at knot.

6 Cut off pointed ends of two round toothpicks; dip one end of each in glue, and insert into beads to make drumsticks. Glue drumsticks to drum.

7 Apply a light coat of acrylic sealer for protective finish. If desired, personalize ornament, using permanent marking pen.

29

MORE IDEAS FOR ORNAMENTS

Bundles of cinnamon sticks, glued together and tied with ribbon, make quick, fragrant ornaments. Embellish the ribbon with a sprig of greenery.

Miniature dried rosebuds make delicate ornaments. Secure the rosebuds to a 2" (5 cm) Styrofoam® ball, following the instructions for a rosebud topiary on page 91; leave space for pinning and gluing a ribbon hanger in place.

Paper twist and raffia make quick country ornaments. Wrap a 10" (25.5 cm) length of untwisted paper twist around a 2" (5 cm) Styrofoam ball, securing it with several pieces of raffia. Also secure raffia for the hanger, using hot glue.

Simple designs, applied with paint pens, can add extra sparkle to glass ornaments. Replace the wire hangers with bows of gold cording and ribbon.

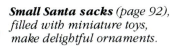

Small Santa sacks (page 92), filled with miniature toys, make delightful ornaments.

Bundles of twigs, tied with jute or ribbon, make simple, rustic ornaments. Embellish the ornament with greenery and a small bird; then spray it with an acrylic sealer.

Cinnamon sticks and clothespins, painted like Santas, are fun for all ages. Use nontoxic acrylic paints for the simple Santa faces; secure strings for hangers, using a drop of hot glue.

Clear plastic balls that snap together can be filled with cherished mementos to make special keepsake ornaments.

TRIMMING THE TREE

Trimmings, such as garlands and bows, are available in an endless variety. These finishing touches unify the tree, even when several styles of ornaments are used together. Choose items that are in keeping with the color scheme and theme of the tree. Some trimmings work better for Victorian decorating styles, while others may be either whimsical, glitzy, or rustic.

Ribbon is wrapped loosely around the tree, spiraling from top to bottom.

Bows (page 74) secured to branches with wire unify a tree with color and repetition.

Purchased trims, such as the ruched paper trim shown here, can be strewn on branches as garlands.

Ornaments clustered in groups of three have more impact than single ornaments.

Streamers are made by wiring five strands of ribbon together, looping them at one end. Attach the wire to the top of the tree, letting the streamers fall freely, or tuck them lightly into the branches. The dried fruits may either be purchased or made, using a food dehydrator.

Tassels hung on the tips of branches have the look of traditional elegance.

Bridal illusion, English netting, or other types of net can be tucked between branches to fill in any bare areas.

TREE SKIRTS

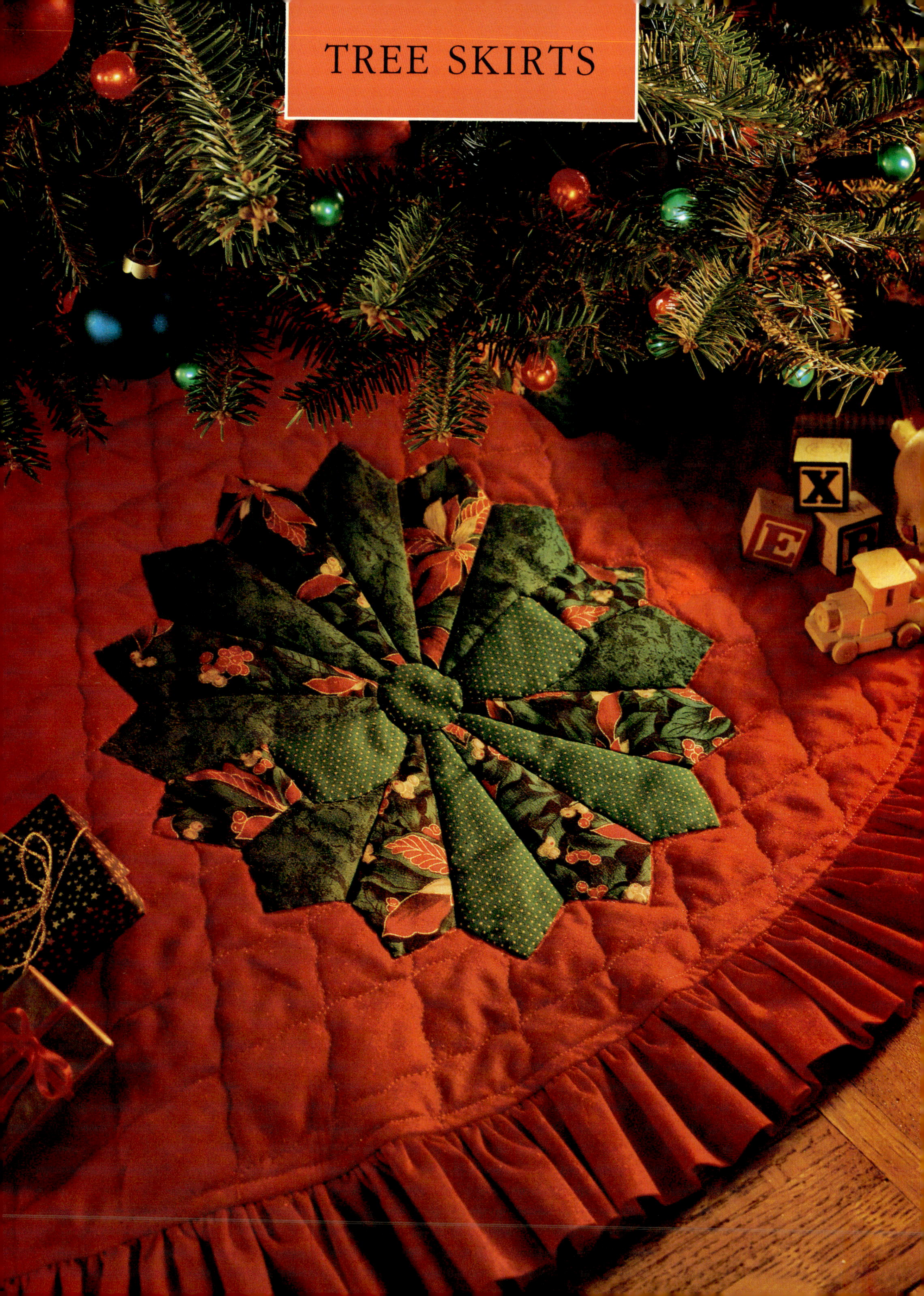

Tree skirts can be fast and easy to sew. An unlined tree skirt (opposite), made from prequilted fabric, is especially quick to make. A pregathered ruffle trim is a simple way to add detailing to the edge of the unlined skirt. Or for a wider ruffle with more fullness, you can make your own from coordinating fabric.

Lined tree skirts (right) are made using a stitch-and-turn method. Low-loft batting adds body to the tree skirt, and optional welting defines the outer edge. A ruffle may be added to the outer edge instead of welting, if desired.

For extra embellishment, appliqués can be added to either of these tree skirts.

Holiday wreath appliqués *(page 44) trim the unlined tree skirt, opposite. The wreaths are a variation of the traditional Dresden Plate quilt design.*

Heart appliqués *(page 38) embellish this lined tree skirt. The hearts may be used as pockets to hold sprigs of greenery, candy, or small gifts.*

HOW TO SEW AN UNLINED TREE SKIRT

MATERIALS

- 1¼ yd. (1.15 m) prequilted fabric.
- 1½ yd. (1.4 m) single-fold bias tape, to match the prequilted fabric.
- 1⅛ yd. (1.05 m) fabric for 2" (5 cm) ruffle, 2 yd. (1.85 m) fabric for 3" to 4" (7.5 to 10 cm) ruffle, or 4 yd. (3.7 m) pregathered ruffle trim.

CUTTING DIRECTIONS

Cut prequilted fabric as in steps 1 to 3, below. If you are making your own ruffle, cut eight fabric strips, across the width of the fabric, two times the desired finished width of the ruffle plus 1" (2.5 cm) for seam allowances.

1 Fold 1¼ yd. (1.15 m) of fabric in half lengthwise, then crosswise. Using a straightedge and pencil, mark an arc on fabric, measuring 21" to 22" (53.5 to 56 cm) from folded center of fabric. Cut on marked line through all layers.

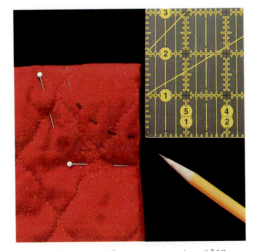

2 Mark a second arc, measuring 1¾" (4.5 cm) from folded center of fabric. Cut on marked line.

3 Cut along one folded edge; this will be the center back of tree skirt.

(Continued)

4 Pin bias tape to back edges and center opening of tree skirt, with right sides together and raw edges matching; stitch along the first foldline of the bias tape. Clip seam allowances around the center circle; trim corners.

5 Press bias tape to wrong side of skirt; pin in place, mitering tape at corners. Stitch close to folded edge. If pregathered ruffle trim is used, omit steps 6 to 8.

6 Stitch short ends of fabric strips for ruffle together in ¼" (6 mm) seams, right sides together. Fold pieced strip in half lengthwise, right sides together; stitch across ends in ¼" (6 mm) seam. Turn right side out, and press.

7 Zigzag over a cord a scant ½" (1.3 cm) from raw edges of ruffle.

8 Divide ruffle strip and curved outer edge of tree skirt into eighths; pin-mark. Place strip on curved edge, right sides together, matching raw edges and pin marks; pull cord, gathering ruffle to fit.

9 Stitch ruffle to lower edge of skirt, right sides together. If pregathered ruffle trim is used, fold over ends of ruffle ½" (1.3 cm) at back edges of skirt.

10 Turn seam allowances to wrong side of skirt; topstitch the ruffle in place, stitching through all layers. Apply the holiday wreath appliqués (page 44) or heart appliqués (page 38), if desired.

MATERIALS

- 1¼ yd. (1.15 m) face fabric, 45" (115 cm) wide.
- 1¼ yd. (1.15 m) lining fabric, 45" (115 cm) wide.
- 45" (115 cm) square low-loft quilt batting.
- 4 yd. (3.7 m) purchased welting; ruffle trim may be used instead of welting, as for unlined tree skirt.

1 Cut face fabric as on page 35, steps 1 to 3; cut the lining, using face fabric as pattern. Make and apply heart appliqués (page 38) or holiday wreath appliqués (page 44) to tree skirt, if desired.

2 Stitch welting, if desired, to curved outer edge on right side of lining, using a zipper foot and matching raw edges; ease welting to fabric as you sew. Curve end of welting into seam allowance at center back.

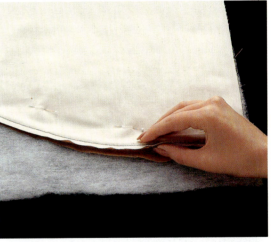

3 Place the face fabric and the lining right sides together, matching raw edges. Place fabrics on batting, lining side up; pin or baste layers together.

4 Stitch ¼" (6 mm) seam around all edges, leaving 8" (20.5 cm) opening on one straight edge. If the tree skirt has welting, use a zipper foot and stitch just inside the previous stitches, crowding stitches against the welting. Cut batting to the same size as fabric. Clip seam allowances around center circle; trim corners diagonally.

5 Turn fabric right side out; stitch opening closed. Lightly press edges, taking care not to flatten batting. Restitch around appliqués through all layers.

HOW TO MAKE & APPLY HEART APPLIQUÉS

MATERIALS (for five hearts)

- ⅓ yd. (0.32 m) each, red and green printed fabrics, 45" (115 cm) wide.
- ⅔ yd. (0.63 m) lining fabric, 45" (115 cm) wide.
- Embellishments, such as sleigh bells and pinecones.

CUTTING DIRECTIONS

Cut two 2" (5 cm) strips across the width of each fabric. For the top of each heart, cut one green and one red piece, using the heart appliqué pattern on page 312.

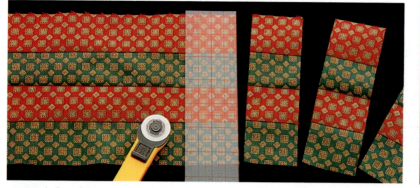

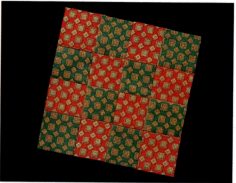

1 Stitch four fabric strips together lengthwise, stitching ¼" (6 mm) seams and alternating colors. Press seam allowances in one direction. Cut 2" (5 cm) strips across pieced strip.

2 Stitch the pieced strips together into five checkerboards, each 6½" (16.3 cm) square, stitching ¼" (6 mm) seams.

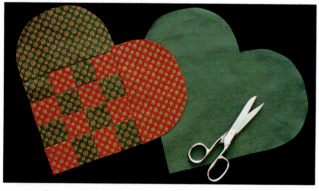

3 Stitch one red and one green heart top to each square, stitching ¼" (6 mm) seams. Cut five hearts from lining fabric, using pieced heart as a guide.

4 Place pieced heart and lining right sides together; pin. Stitch around the edges, stitching ¼" (6 mm) seams and leaving a 2" (5 cm) opening on one side of the checkboard. Trim seam allowances on curves; clip inner corner. Turn heart right side out; press.

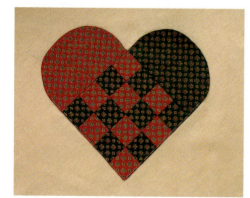

5 Arrange hearts on the tree skirt; pin. Edgestitch the sides of hearts in place, starting and ending 1" (2.5 cm) above the checkerboard. Edgestitch inner corner in place for 1" (2.5 cm) on each side.

6 Stitch or glue the desired embellishments at the inner corners of hearts on completed tree skirt. Fill heart pockets with small gifts, candy canes, or pine sprigs.

MORE
IDEAS FOR
TREE SKIRTS

Crazy quilting *made from scraps of wool, corduroy, and velveteen adds an old-fashioned appeal to this lined tree skirt (page 37). Quilt the fabric for the tree skirt as on page 81, steps 1 to 3.*

Twisted decorative welting *defines the edge of this gold lamé lined tree skirt (page 37) for a rich, elegant look.*

Radiating trims *are stitched on this lined tree skirt (page 37) for an old-world look. The trims are applied to the face fabric before the lining is stitched.*

Wide ruffling *on this unlined tree skirt (page 35) is bunched and tied with satin bows. The prequilted fabric, eyelet ruffles, and bows are all in ivory to unify the design.*

The Holiday Table

a

b

c

Enhance holiday table settings with table runners for the dining table as well as for side tables and buffets.

The holiday wreath table runner **(a)** features the traditional Dresden Plate quilt block, modified to make a wreath with a bow. For easy appliqués, the wedge-shaped pieces for the wreath are stitched together with ¼" (6 mm) seams, and the wreath is appliquéd to the project as one circular piece. The wedge pattern (page 311) includes the necessary seam allowances. For the bow loops and knots, fabric pieces are pressed over cardboard templates, ensuring that the shapes are pressed accurately. Seam allowances are not included in the template patterns; add ¼" (6 mm) when cutting the fabric for the loops and knots. This table runner has five quilt blocks and measures 16" × 70" (40.5 × 178 cm). Matching placemats are on page 51.

Two other styles for table runners include a table runner with a mitered hem **(b)** and another with a contrasting mitered band **(c)**. Both of these styles are unquilted and are variations of the placemats with mitered hems and mitered bands on page 48. These table runners may be custom-made to any size. The yardages required and cutting directions are based on the desired finished size.

HOW TO SEW A HOLIDAY WREATH TABLE RUNNER

MATERIALS

- ⅞ yd. (0.8 m) background fabric.
- 1 yd. (0.95 m) fabric for sashing, borders, and binding.
- 1¼ yd. (1.05 m) backing fabric.
- Low-loft quilt batting.
- Materials for wreath appliqués, listed on page 44.

CUTTING DIRECTIONS

Cut five 13" (33 cm) squares from background fabric. Cut one 20" × 74" (51 × 188 cm) rectangle each from quilt batting and backing fabric, piecing the backing fabric. Cut one 1½" (3.8 cm) strip and ten 2½" (6.5 cm) strips, to be used for sashing, borders, and binding, cutting the strips across the width of the fabric. From the 1½" (3.8 cm) strip, cut three pieces, each 13" (33 cm) long. From one of the 2½" (6.5 cm) strips, cut two pieces, each 13" (33 cm) long; from the remainder of this strip, cut a piece 1½" × 13" (3.8 × 33 cm). Cut five wreath appliqués as on page 44.

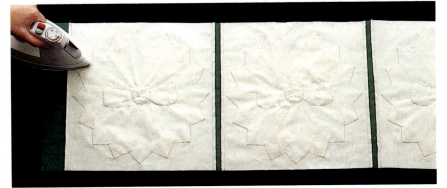

1 Make and apply wreath appliqués as on pages 44 and 45, steps 1 to 7; in step 6, center wedge circle on 13" (33 cm) squares of fabric. Stitch blocks together with 1½" × 13" (3.8 × 33 cm) sashing strips between them, stitching ¼" (6 mm) seams. Stitch 2½" × 13" (6.5 × 33 cm) border strips at ends of table runner. Press seam allowances toward sashing strips.

2 Measure length of pieced block strip down the middle. Cut two border strips to this measurement from 2½" (6.5 cm) strips; piece strips as necessary.

3 Mark centers of border strips and pieced block strip. Pin one border strip along edge of block strip, right sides together, matching ends and center. Stitch; press seam allowances toward border strip. Repeat for other side.

4 Place backing fabric right side down; place batting over backing fabric. Place pieced block strip, right side up, over batting; baste layers together. Trim backing and batting even with raw edges of pieced block strip.

(Continued)

5 Piece remaining 2½" (6.5 cm) strips together as necessary for four binding strips. Press binding strips in half lengthwise, wrong sides together. Place binding strip for one long edge of table runner on pieced block strip, matching raw edges; stitch binding ¼" (6 mm) from raw edges. Trim ends of binding strip even with ends of runner.

6 Wrap binding strip around the edge, covering stitching line on backing side; pin. Stitch in the ditch from the right side, catching binding strip on backing side.

7 Stitch binding strip on remaining long edge as in steps 5 and 6. Stitch binding strips on short ends as in step 5, leaving ends of binding extending ½" (1.3 cm) beyond finished edges; secure binding as in step 6, folding ends over finished edges.

8 Quilt table runner by stitching around appliqués and border, using monofilament nylon thread in needle, and thread to match backing fabric in bobbin. (Contrasting thread was used to show detail.)

HOW TO SEW A HOLIDAY WREATH APPLIQUÉ

MATERIALS (for five or six appliqués)

- Scraps of fabrics in desired prints or solid colors.
- ¼ yd. (0.25 m) fabric for bow of wreath, in a dominant color.
- Small bowl of spray starch.
- Cardboard, for templates.
- Monofilament nylon thread.

CUTTING DIRECTIONS

Transfer bow loop and bow knot templates (page 311) onto cardboard; cut. Using templates, cut one knot and two loops for each block, adding ¼" (6 mm) seam allowances when cutting; turn loop template over for second loop. Transfer wedge pattern (page 311) onto paper. Cut two wedges from bow fabric and fourteen wedges from fabric scraps in desired prints or solid colors for each appliqué; seam allowances are included on wedge pattern.

1 Add lace overlays to some of the fabrics, if desired, by placing right side of wedge face down on wrong side of lace; machine-baste scant ¼" (6 mm) from edges. Trim lace to size of wedge.

2 Fold wide end of one wedge in half, right sides together; stitch ¼" (6 mm) seam across end. Turn right side out, forming point. Press wedge, with seam centered on wrong side of wedge. On light-colored and lightweight fabrics, trim excess fabric from back of the wedge, leaving ¼" (6 mm) seam allowances. Repeat for remaining wedges.

3 Arrange wedges in a circle, with wedges for tails of bow (arrows) separated by one wedge.

4 Stitch two wedges together, right sides together, stitching ¼" (6 mm) seam along adjoining side. Continue to stitch wedges together until circle is completed. Press seams to one side. Repeat steps for remaining holiday wreath appliqués.

5 Center bow loop and bow knot templates on wrong side of fabric pieces. Spray starch into small bowl; dab starch on section of seam allowance. Using tip of dry iron, press seam allowance over edge of template. Continue around appliqués, except do not press under small ends of bow loops. Remove templates. Repeat for the remaining knot and loop pieces. Press all the pieces right side up.

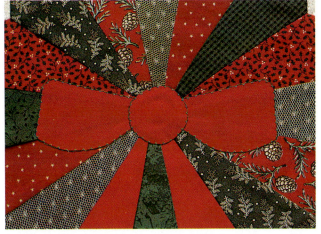

6 Arrange wreaths on right side of fabric; pin in place. Blindstitch around outer edge, using monofilament nylon thread in the needle; stitch as close to edge as possible, just catching appliqué with widest swing of blindstitch. (Contrasting thread was used to show detail.)

7 Pin or glue-baste bows and knots in place on wreaths; blindstitch in place, as in step 6.

HOLIDAY PLACEMATS

Placemats can be made in a variety of styles for any holiday table setting, from formal to casual. They can be used alone or coordinated with table runners (page 42). Made from fine linens, a placemat with a mitered hem **(a)** is a simple yet elegant style for formal dining. The placemat with a contrasting mitered band **(b)** is a bordered variation of this style. The braid-trimmed placemat **(c)** uses lavish trims for another elegant style.

For more casual table settings, the package placemat **(d),** ribbon-trimmed at the corners, is both practical and fun. The quilt-as-you-go placemat **(e),** made with a quick piecing and quilting method, is also embellished at the corners. The holiday wreath placemat **(f),** another quilted style, uses a wreath variation of the traditional Dresden Plate quilt design.

a

b

c

HOW TO SEW A PLACEMAT WITH A MITERED HEM

MATERIALS (for six placemats)

- Fabric, yardage depending on size of project; for size given below, you will need 1½ yd. (1.4 m).

CUTTING DIRECTIONS

Determine the desired finished size. To this measurement, add twice the desired depth of the hem plus ½" (1.3 cm) for turning under the edges. A good finished size for a placemat suitable for a formal table setting is 14" × 18½" (35.5 × 47.3 cm) with a 1¼" (3.2 cm) hem; cut the fabric 17" × 21½" (43 × 54.8 cm).

1 Stitch a scant ¼" (6 mm) from edges of fabric. Fold the edges to wrong side; press just beyond the stitching line. Press under desired hem depth on each side of fabric.

2 Open out corner; fold diagonally so pressed folds match. Press diagonal fold.

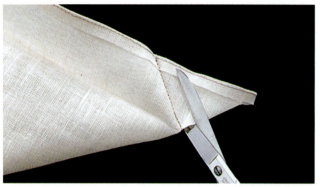

3 Open out corner. Fold through center of corner, right sides together. Stitch on diagonal foldline from step 2. Trim fabric from corner to ¼" (6 mm) from stitching. Press seam open.

4 Press the hem in place, turning corners right side out. Stitch hem, pivoting at corners; use decorative thread, such as rayon or metallic thread, if desired.

HOW TO SEW A PLACEMAT WITH A MITERED BAND

MATERIALS (for six placemats)

- Fabric for contrasting insert, yardage depending on size of project; for size given above, you will need 1¼ yd. (1.15 m).
- Fabric for mitered band, yardage depending on size of project; for size given above, you will need 1½ yd. (1.4 m).
- Fusible interfacing.

CUTTING DIRECTIONS

For each placemat, cut one rectangle from insert fabric equal to the desired *finished* size of the placemat. Cut the fabric for mitered band as for a placemat with mitered hem, above.

1 Follow steps 1 to 3, above. Press band in place, turning corners right side out. Fuse interfacing to wrong side of insert fabric. Place insert on mitered placemat, tucking edges under mitered band; pin.

2 Stitch around the band, securing insert; pivot at corners.

HOW TO SEW A BRAID-TRIMMED PLACEMAT

MATERIALS (for six placemats)

- 2¼ yd. (2.1 m) fabric.
- 2¼ yd. (2.1 m) fusible interfacing.
- 4½ yd. (4.15 m) braid trim.
- Liquid fray preventer, optional.

CUTTING DIRECTIONS

For each placemat, cut two 13" × 19" (33 × 48.5 cm) rectangles from fabric and one from fusible interfacing. Cut two 13" (33 cm) lengths of braid trim; if the trim ravels easily, seal the raw edges with liquid fray preventer.

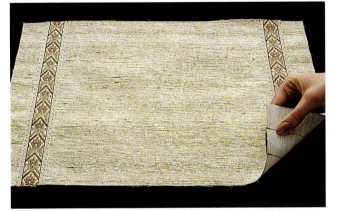

1 Fuse interfacing to the wrong side of placemat top. Position braid trim as desired at sides; pin in place, and edgestitch.

2 Pin placemat pieces right sides together. Stitch around placemat, ¼" (6 mm) from raw edges; leave 4" (10 cm) opening for turning. Trim corners. Turn right side out; press. Slipstitch opening closed.

HOW TO SEW A PACKAGE PLACEMAT

MATERIALS (for six placemats)

- 2¼ yd. (2.1 m) fabric.
- 2¼ yd. (2.1 m) fusible interfacing.
- 7½ yd. (6.9 m) ribbon, about 1" (2.5 cm) wide.
- Liquid fray preventer, optional.

CUTTING DIRECTIONS

For each placemat, cut two 13" × 19" (33 × 48.5 cm) rectangles from fabric and one from fusible interfacing. Cut ribbon into two 10" (25.5 cm) lengths and one 25" (63.5 cm) length.

1 Fuse interfacing to wrong side of placemat top. Pin 10" (25.5 cm) lengths of ribbon across opposite corners of placemat top, keeping ribbon in relaxed position; baste ends in place a scant ¼" (6 mm) from raw edges of placemat top. Trim excess ribbon even with raw edges.

2 Pin placemat pieces right sides together. Stitch around placemat, ¼" (6 mm) from raw edges; leave 4" (10 cm) opening for turning. Trim corners. Turn right side out; press. Slipstitch opening closed. Using 25" (63.5 cm) length of ribbon, tie bow around ribbon at upper corner. Trim ends of ribbon; seal with liquid fray preventer.

HOW TO SEW A QUILT-AS-YOU-GO PLACEMAT

MATERIALS (for six placemats)

- 1¼ yd. (1.5 m) solid-color fabric for background.
- 1¼ yd. (1.5 m) backing fabric.
- Scraps of solid-color and printed fabrics.
- ⅞ yd. (0.8 m) fabric for binding.
- Low-loft quilt batting.

CUTTING DIRECTIONS

Cut six 12½" × 18½" (31.8 × 47.3 cm) rectangles from background fabric. Cut six 13½" × 19½" (34.3 × 49.8 cm) rectangles from the backing fabric and batting.

Cut 1½" (3.8 cm) strips and twelve 3" (7.5 cm) squares from the fabric scraps; cut the squares diagonally to make triangles for corners.

Cut 2½" (6.5 cm) strips from fabric for binding, cutting the strips across the width of the fabric.

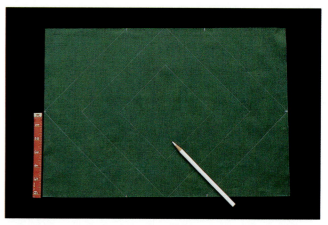

1 Mark right side of background fabric, 6¼" (15.7 cm) from corners, using chalk. Mark diagonal lines across corners, connecting marks. Mark a second set of lines 2" (5 cm) inside marked lines. Mark a square 2" (5 cm) inside second set of lines.

2 Place batting on wrong side of backing fabric; center background fabric on batting, right side up. Pin layers together; quilt the placemat by stitching along the two inside squares.

3 Place a fabric strip on background fabric, right sides together, with one raw edge extending ¼" (6 mm) to the outside of marked line. Stitch through all layers, ¼" (6 mm) from raw edge; stitching will be on marked line.

4 Fold strip right side up; finger-press, and pin in place. Place second strip over first, with right sides together and raw edges even.

5 Stitch ¼" (6 mm) from raw edges of strips. Fold second strip right side up; finger-press, and pin in place. Repeat for the third strip and for the corner triangle.

6 Trim backing fabric and batting to size of pieced top, trimming ends of strips. Apply binding as on page 44, steps 5 to 7, using four binding strips for each placemat.

HOW TO SEW A HOLIDAY WREATH PLACEMAT

MATERIALS (for six placemats)

- ⅞ yd. (0.8 m) background fabric.
- ½ yd. (0.5 m) border fabric.
- 1¼ yd. (1.15 m) backing fabric.
- Low-loft quilt batting.
- Materials for wreath appliqués, listed on page 44.

CUTTING DIRECTIONS

For each placemat, cut one 13" (33 cm) square from background fabric, two 3½" × 13" (9 × 33 cm) strips from border fabric, one 13" × 19" (33 × 48.5 cm) rectangle from backing fabric, and one 15" × 21" (38 × 53.5 cm) rectangle from batting. Cut one wreath appliqué, following the cutting directions on page 44.

1 Make and apply wreath appliqués as on page 44, steps 1 to 7; in step 6, center wedge circle on 13" (33 cm) square of fabric. Stitch border strips to sides of appliquéd block, stitching ¼" (6 mm) seams; press seam allowances toward border strips.

2 Place backing and placemat top right sides together. Place fabrics on batting, backing side up; pin or baste layers together.

3 Stitch around placemat, ¼" (6 mm) from raw edges of placemat top; leave 4" (10 cm) opening for turning. Trim batting to ⅛" (3 mm); trim corners.

4 Turn placemat right side out; press. Slipstitch opening closed. Quilt placemat by stitching around appliqué and along border strips, using monofilament nylon thread in needle and thread that matches backing fabric in bobbin. (Contrasting thread was used to show detail.)

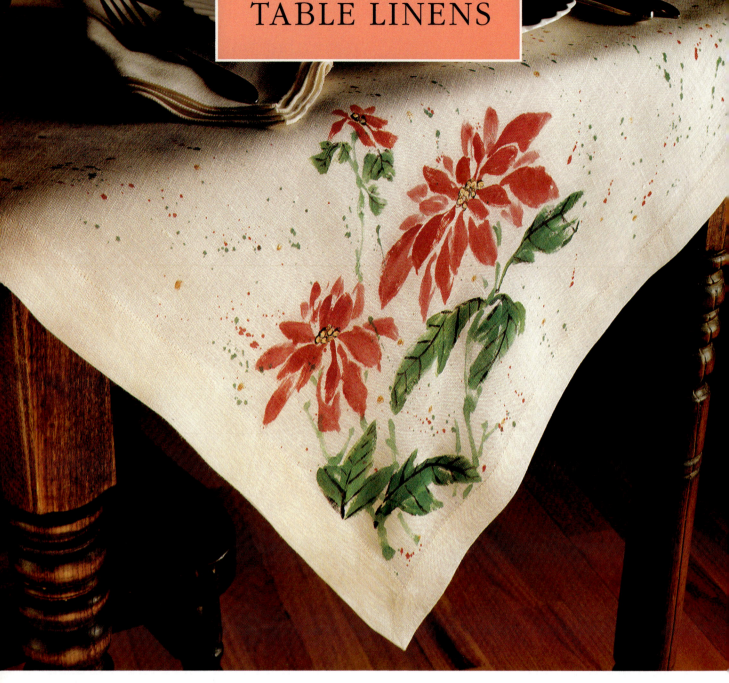

Tablecloths, placemats, table runners, and napkins provide a simple backdrop for hand-painted embellishments. Select purchased table linens, or sew your own linens, following the instructions for placemats with mitered hems on page 48; by varying the size, these instructions can be used for tablecloths, table runners, and napkins as well as for placemats.

Trace designs from stencils, adapt artwork from greeting cards or pictorial books, or paint original designs. For a unified table, coordinate the painted designs with your china, or create a design to enhance a centerpiece.

Practice the painting techniques on fabric scraps or paper before painting the linens. When painting, protect the work surface by covering it with plastic. Heat-set the paints according to the manufacturer's instructions, and when laundering the linens, use the care method recommended for the fabric.

MATERIALS

- Purchased tablecloth, placemats, table runner, or napkins; or fabric for table linens with mitered hems (page 48).

- Textile paints, including metallic paints, if desired.

- Artist's brushes.

- Pictorial design book or stencils, if desired.

TIPS FOR PAINTED TABLE LINENS

Dilute paint that will be used for a spattered effect. Wet brush with paint, and tap the brush to spatter the paint.

Use stencils for marking designs, if desired. Apply paint to small design areas, using artist's brushes.

Use artwork in pictorial books for design ideas like this geometric design. Mark lines on fabric, using pencil or permanent-ink pen and straightedge.

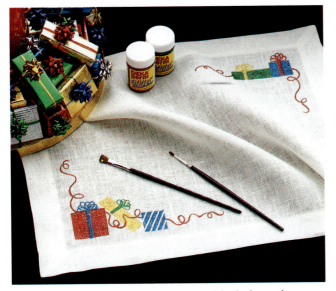

Customize a design to coordinate a tablecloth or placemat with a holiday centerpiece.

Adapt a design from holiday dinnerware by painting a coordinating tablecloth or placemat.

GIFT BOX CENTERPIECES

Miniature gift boxes, stacked and mounted on a circular base, create this candle-ring centerpiece.

For best results, select wrapping papers in solid colors or tiny patterns. Purchase the miniature bows at craft stores. Or make them with a bow maker, available at stores specializing in miniatures.

HOW TO MAKE A GIFT BOX CENTERPIECE

MATERIALS

- Foam board, ⅜" (1 cm) thick.
- Styrofoam® board, ⅜" (1 cm) thick; 18 match boxes can be substituted for part of the ⅜" (1 cm) Styrofoam.
- Styrofoam board, 1" (2.5 cm) thick; 27 snack-size candy boxes can be substituted.
- Assorted wrapping papers.

- 45 miniature bows.
- 1½-yd. (1.4 m) length of ribbon, ⅜" (1 cm) wide.
- Wax adhesive, such as Mini-Hold©
- Mat knife; cellophane tape; craft glue; hot glue gun and glue sticks.
- One 4" (10 cm) candle or three tapered candles.

54

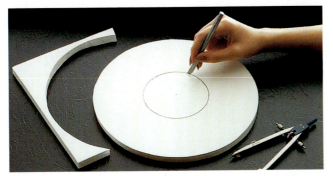

1 Draw a circle with 5½" (14 cm) radius on foam board, using compass. Keeping compass at same center point, draw another circle with radius of 2⅛" (5.3 cm). Cut on marked lines, using mat knife, to make centerpiece base.

2 Trace base on wrong side of wrapping paper; cut, adding ¼" (6 mm) at inner and outer edges. Glue in place to top and sides of base, slashing as necessary.

3 Cover edges of base with ribbon, securing it with craft glue.

4 Cut 9 rectangles from ⅜" (1 cm) Styrofoam board, each measuring 1" × 2¾" (2.5 × 7 cm). Use 18 match boxes and 27 snack-size candy boxes for remaining boxes; or cut 18 rectangles from ⅜" (1 cm) Styrofoam, each 1½" × 2½" (3.8 × 6.5 cm), and 27 rectangles from 1" (2.5 cm) Styrofoam, each 1" × 1½" (2.5 × 3.8 cm).

5 Wrap boxes in assorted papers. Attach bows, using hot glue, to all 1" × 2¾" (2.5 × 7 cm) wrapped boxes and to 9 of the wrapped match boxes. Attach bows to wrapped candy boxes, placing 18 on box ends and 9 on box sides.

6 Arrange boxes without bows on base, placing short sides of boxes at inside of base; secure temporarily with wax; once positioned, secure with hot glue.

7 Arrange 2 candy boxes and 1 match box on top of match boxes from step 6; place inside candy box on end, middle candy box on its side, and the match box in front. Secure with wax.

8 Place remaining candy boxes as shown, positioning each box on its side; secure with wax. Adjust as necessary, so boxes are evenly spaced. Secure with hot glue.

9 Stack 1" × 2¾" (2.5 × 7 cm) boxes on candy boxes, as shown; secure with hot glue. Place candle in the center of the ring.

MORE IDEAS FOR CENTERPIECES

A wreath, *propped against the wall, provides a centerpiece for a side table and does not interfere with the serving space. Position a cluster bow (page 77) at the top of the wreath, and add long streamers to flow onto the table.*

Tinsel-filled ornaments *(page 23), clustered in a basket and surrounded with greens, make a simple centerpiece. The ornaments are set aglow with miniature battery-operated lights.*

Fresh evergreen sprays, *placed end-to-end and topped with a bow, make a quick and attractive centerpiece. Candles are placed in the greens.*

An artificial garland, *arranged in an S shape and embellished with golden artichokes and gilded pinecones and pomegranates, creates an easy and elegant centerpiece. This style is especially suited for long tables.*

HOW TO MAKE A FRESH EVERGREEN SPRAY CENTERPIECE

MATERIALS

- Fresh tips from various evergreens; cedar greens work well for the base.
- 22-gauge or 24-gauge wire; wire cutter; floral tape.
- Embellishments as desired, such as candles, ribbon, and berries.

1 Layer fresh greens, and secure stems with wire. Wrap wired stems with floral tape to protect the table, stretching the tape as it is applied. Repeat to make two garlands.

2 Overlap and wire stems of layered greens together; cover with floral tape.

3 Make bow with long streamers (page 74), and secure to greens, concealing wired stems. Twist and loop the streamers among the greens. Arrange candles and other embellishments as desired.

HOW TO MAKE AN ARTIFICIAL GARLAND CENTERPIECE

MATERIALS

- Artificial garland, 18" to 24" (46 to 61 cm) longer than desired length of centerpiece.
- French ribbon, about 18" (46 cm) longer than garland.
- Artichokes; dried pomegranates; pinecones; cinnamon sticks.
- Gold aerosol paint; gold wax-based paint.
- 26-gauge wire; wire cutter; floral tape.

1 Arrange garland in S shape on the table; adjust length, if necessary. Twist ribbon loosely throughout garland.

2 Apply gold aerosol paint to artichokes; spray the pinecones, if desired. Rub gold wax-based paint on pomegranates to add highlights. Wire pinecones and cinnamon sticks as on page 66.

3 Place artichokes near the center of the arrangement. Secure pinecones and cinnamon sticks to garland. Arrange the pomegranates between pinecones and cinnamon sticks. Arrange the candles as desired.

TABLE ACCESSORIES

Small accessories, like napkin rings and etched glassware, add charm to each place setting. Easy to make, these finishing touches make a holiday table festive.

Ornaments, such as French horns and wreaths, make inexpensive napkin rings that can double as favors for guests.

Lace napkin rings (opposite) complement a table setting with a Victorian theme.

A garland sprig napkin ring (opposite), embellished with artificial holly, is quick to make.

Sheer and pleated ribbons, tied around napkins and stemware, add a festive touch.

Etching (below), done using a rub-on etching stencil and etching cream, turns inexpensive glassware into holiday goblets and plates.

HOW TO MAKE TABLE ACCESSORIES

Lace napkin rings. Cut 20" (51 cm) length of flat lace with a heading; stitch short ends together. Using a tapestry needle, weave 32" (81.5 cm) length of ⅛" (3 mm) ribbon through the lace heading. Gather lace around napkin; tie ribbon in a bow.

Garland sprig napkin rings. Cut individual sprigs from an artificial garland. Wrap sprigs around a cylinder, such as cardboard tube, for shape; twist ends of sprigs together. Secure holly with hot glue.

1 **Etched glassware.** Use rub-on etching stencil and etching cream, available from craft stores. Apply a border of masking tape around stencil, overlapping the edges. Cover area of glass that will not be etched with plastic and masking tape.

2 Apply a thick layer of etching cream over entire design area, using a soft-bristle brush; allow etching cream to remain on design for 1 minute. Rinse design thoroughly to remove all etching cream; pat area dry. Remove stencil, plastic, and masking tape.

TABLE ENSEMBLES

Whether you are planning a casual get-together with friends for cookies and hot chocolate, a formal dinner party for coworkers, or a family gathering for Christmas dinner, holiday table settings can have a special flair. For a party that will be remembered, coordinate the table appointments down to the last detail.

A Victorian setting is used for this formal dinner party. Victorian cards (page 117) at each place setting establish the theme; place cards are made to match. Tassels accent the candlesticks, and a fresh evergreen spray centerpiece (page 57) is trimmed with a lavish gold bow. Lace napkin rings (page 59) add to the romantic look.

A casual Santa theme is set with Santa sacks (page 92). Filled with tiny gifts, small sacks are favors for the guests, and larger sacks create the centerpiece. Placemats with contrasting mitered bands (page 48) and garland sprig napkin rings (page 59) add to the festive look. Santa cinnamon sticks (page 31), painted at one end, are used for stirring the cider.

A festive table setting starts with star-studded china and gold-rimmed glassware. The table linens are painted with metallics to coordinate with the china (page 52), and sheer metallic ribbon makes elegant napkin rings.

A centerpiece of tinsel-filled ornaments (page 23) is aglow with miniature battery-operated lights. Small presents for the guests in decoupaged gift boxes (pages 114-115) accent each place setting.

Around The
House

WREATHS

Nothing echoes a Christmas tradition more than wreaths. You can make your own from fresh, preserved, or artificial greens. Or purchase ready-made wreaths and add your own embellishments. Fresh evergreen and eucalyptus wreaths, both easy to make, add fragrance to a room. Other wreath styles, including grapevine and twig wreaths, are available at craft and floral stores.

You may choose to embellish an entire wreath, use a third of the wreath as the design area, or add a single

embellishment. It is usually more attractive if the focal point of the design is slightly offset.

Choose embellishments that are in scale with the size of the wreath, and vary the size of the embellishments so there will be a dominant focal point, with smaller items that complement it. Choose items that are harmonious in style, yet provide some contrast in color and texture. Several suggestions for embellishing wreaths are shown on pages 66 to 69.

HOW TO MAKE A FRESH EVERGREEN WREATH

MATERIALS

- Fresh greens.
- 22-gauge or 24-gauge paddle floral wire; wire cutter; pruning shears.
- Coat hanger.
- Ribbon and embellishments as desired.

1 Shape coat hanger into circle. Cut greens into sprigs. Wire three sprigs to hanger, with tips facing up, placing two in front and one in back; wrap wire at base of sprigs.

2 Continue wrapping clusters of greens with wire, overlapping each cluster to conceal wire. When coat hanger is covered, cut some full tips of greens and wire them to hanger, concealing ends of sprigs.

HOW TO MAKE A EUCALYPTUS WREATH

MATERIALS

- Ready-made straw wreath.
- Eucalyptus with fine stems; two or three bunches will be sufficient for most wreath sizes.
- 22-gauge or 24-gauge paddle floral wire; wire cutter; pruning shears.
- Ribbon and embellishments as desired.

1 Cut eucalyptus in half or in thirds, so each sprig is 6" to 7" (15 to 18 cm) long. Secure the bottom 1" (2.5 cm) of several sprigs to wreath with wire, wrapping the wire around wreath; cover front and sides of wreath.

2 Continue adding sprigs to front and sides of wreath; layer sprigs and wrap with wire, working in one direction. Stagger the length of the tips randomly.

3 Lift tips of sprigs at starting point, and secure last layer of sprigs under them. Make a wire loop for hanging; secure loop to back of the wreath. Embellish as desired.

TIPS FOR EMBELLISHING WREATHS

Secure ribbon tails with hot glue, arranging twists and loops.

Make picks by grouping items together. Attach wire to items as necessary. Wrap stems and wires with floral tape.

Separate bunches of dried flowers by holding them over steam for 1 to 2 minutes; remove from steam and pull stems apart gently.

Attach wire to pinecone by wrapping wire around bottom layers of pinecone.

Add wire as necessary to fragile stems of dried flowers, to strengthen them. Wrap stem and wire with floral tape.

Attach wire to cinnamon stick by inserting it through the length of the stick; wrap the wire around the stick, twisting ends at middle. Trim wire, leaving 6" (15 cm) ends for attaching to wreath.

Create a base for anchoring embellishments by wiring a piece of floral foam, which has been covered with moss, to the wreath. Attach embellishments to moss-covered base.

Shape an artificial wreath made on a single wire into a candy cane or swag. Cut the wreath apart where the wire was joined.

Add luster to pinecones by applying glossy brown aerosol paint.

Spray artificial snow on wreath for a lightly flocked appearance.

Highlight twigs and vines with frost or glitter aerosol paint.

Keep a balanced look when embellishing an entire wreath by dividing wreath into three or four sections; distribute items evenly within each section.

Display wreath over a length of wide ribbon for added color. Embellish the top of the ribbon with a sprig.

MORE IDEAS FOR WREATHS

Snowman ornaments (page 26) add a whimsical touch to this artificial wreath. The light misting of artificial snow, the tiny purchased sleds, and the candy canes carry out the wintery holiday theme.

A Victorian wreath made from eucalyptus (page 65) features a pearlescent cherub on a pastel satin bow. Statice and clustered pastel embellishments are used throughout the wreath.

The musical theme on this fresh evergreen wreath (page 65) was created using purchased instrument ornaments and paper fans (page 19) made from sheet music.

Dried naturals are the primary embellishments for this ready-made twig wreath. The bird's nest, slightly off-center on the wreath, becomes the focal point.

Silver and gold *are combined for this wreath. Silver aerosol paint is used to highlight the greens, and a sheer silver ribbon becomes a strong focal point. Touches of gold are introduced in the smaller embellishments.*

The evergreen bouquet *of mixed greens and pinecones is wired asymmetrically onto a ready-made grapevine wreath for a quick embellishment. The narrow French ribbon is wrapped loosely around the wreath.*

Gold and red metallics *are used for a dramatic effect, and the embellishments are offset for even more impact. The ready-made straw wreath used as the base was concealed with metallic ribbon and tiny garland.*

Apples and popcorn *are used as the dominant embellishments for this fresh wreath of mixed greens (page 65). To carry out the natural look, nuts and pinecones are also used.*

69

GARLANDS

Graceful swags of garland add a dramatic touch to a room. Whether the garlands are made from fresh, preserved, or artificial greens, they can be embellished for an impressive statement.

Fresh garlands are quick and easy to make, and handmade fresh garlands have a fuller shape than purchased ones. When making your own, mix different varieties of greens for added color and texture. Fresh cuttings can often be purchased by weight from nurseries. Cedar greens work especially well for indoor use; they do not shed, and they keep their color longer than most varieties.

For the realistic look of fresh garlands, use dried or preserved greens. They last longer than fresh garlands and can be used for more than one season. For a garland that can be used year after year, use artificial greens. To add the fragrance of evergreen, embellish the garland with scented pinecones or tuck in a few sprigs of fresh greens.

HOW TO MAKE A FRESH GARLAND

MATERIALS

- Fresh greens.
- Lightweight rope or twine.
- 22-gauge paddle floral wire or chenille stems.
- Pruning shears.
- Wire cutter.

2 Continue wiring greens around rope, overlapping them to conceal the wire. At desired length, wire full tips of greens to bottom of garland, concealing ends of sprigs.

1 Tie rope to solid overhead object, such as ceiling-mounted plant hook. Cut fresh greens into sprigs. Wire three sprigs to rope, with tips facing up, placing two in front and one in back; wrap wire at the base of the sprigs.

3 Cut the wire and rope at ends of garland; knot ends, forming loops for hanging, if desired.

MORE IDEAS FOR GARLANDS

A garland is used traditionally to dress the mantel. To secure the garland without nailing into the mantel itself, cut a 1 x 1 board the length of the mantel. Stain or paint the board to match the mantel, and pound nails into the board for securing the garland.

A swag is draped high above a fireplace, and sprays are displayed on each side. To make a pair of sprays from an artificial garland, cut a 9-ft. (2.75 m) garland in half. Fold each piece in half, creating two sprays, and embellish them as desired.

Safety note: Do not leave any open flame, including candles, unattended. For fireplaces, always use a fire screen. (Screen was removed for photo effect.)

A bow-shaped garland is hung over the fireplace instead of a wreath. Tie a wide ribbon to the ends of the garland, and hang the garland from the ribbon.

A fresh garland is used to decorate a bannister. To protect wood surfaces, use chenille stems instead of wire when making the garland.

HOLIDAY BOWS

Lavish bows and streamers are often a finishing touch for holiday decorations. Use ribbons in the traditional red and green, or in colors to match the decor of the room.

The key to achieving a luxurious look is to be generous with the ribbon. The size of the bow should be in proportion to the project being embellished. For example, large garlands require large, full bows with long streamers; for large bows, use wide, stiff ribbons.

Craft ribbon is available in several fabric types, including taffeta, moiré, satin, and velvet. French ribbon, sometimes called wired ribbon, makes beautiful bows. The fine wires that run along the edges of the ribbon can be bent into curves and folds, giving bows an old-world look that is distinctly elegant. For a more homespun or country look, bows can be made from paper twist.

Two styles of bows are so versatile that they meet most holiday decorating needs: the cluster bow and the traditional bow.

The cluster bow can easily be made in any size. To estimate the ribbon yardage, multiply the desired diameter of the bow times the number of loops desired. Add 6" (15 cm) to this measurement for the center loop plus the desired amount for tails and extra streamers.

The traditional bow is commonly used for wreaths, but also works well for elegant packages. For a 7" to 8" (18 to 20.5 cm) bow, you will need 2½ yd. (2.3 m) of ribbon.

Plaid taffeta ribbon is used for the large cluster bow on this spray of greens. For added embellishment, pinecones surround the bow.

Two layers of French ribbon, treated as one, are used for the cluster bow on this tiered plate stand.

Sheer metallic ribbon in cluster bows adorns a pair of candlesticks.

Taffeta French ribbon, tied into a traditional bow, embellishes this Christmas package.

Paper twist is used instead of ribbon for the traditional bow on a fruit basket.

French ribbon makes the cluster bow for this ivy plant. For an ivy wreath, secure the vines to a wire wreath base.

MATERIALS

- 2½-yd. to 3-yd. (2.3 to 2.75 m) length of ribbon, 2" to 2½" (5 to 6.5 cm) wide.

- 22-gauge or 24-gauge floral wire; or chenille wire for bows that will be wired to packages or around woodwork.

1 Cut 18" (46 cm) length of ribbon; set aside for center tie. Starting 8" to 12" (20.5 to 30.5 cm) from end of remaining length of ribbon, fold 3½" to 4" (9 to 10 cm) loop with right side of ribbon facing out.

2 Fold a loop toward the opposite side, bringing ribbon underneath the tail to keep the right side of the ribbon facing out.

3 Continue wrapping the ribbon, making loops that fan slightly, until there are three or four loops on each side with a second tail extending.

4 Bend wire around ribbon at center; twist wire tightly, gathering ribbon. Hold wire firmly at the top, and turn the bow, twisting wire snug.

5 Fold width of 18" (46 cm) ribbon into thirds through the middle portion of ribbon. Tie ribbon around center of the bow, knotting it on the back of the bow.

6 Separate loops. Trim tails as desired.

MATERIALS

- Ribbon in desired width; calculate yardage as on page 74.

- 22-gauge or 24-gauge floral wire; or chenille wire for bows that will be wired to packages or around woodwork.

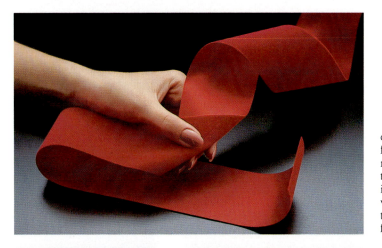

1 Place thumb and index finger at determined length for tail, with ribbon right side up. Fold the ribbon back on itself at a diagonal, with wrong sides together, so ribbon forms a right angle.

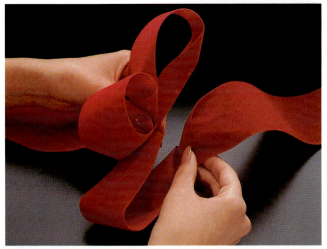

2 Wrap ribbon over thumb to form center loop; secure with fingers. Twist ribbon one-half turn at underside of loop, so the right side of the ribbon faces up.

3 Form first loop. Twist ribbon one-half turn, and form loop on opposite side.

4 Continue forming loops under the previous loops, alternating sides and twisting ribbon so right side always faces up; make each loop slightly larger than the loop above it.

5 When final loop has been formed, insert wire through center of bow. Bend wire around ribbon at center; twist wire tightly, gathering ribbon. Hold wire firmly at the top and turn the bow, twisting wire snug. Separate and shape the loops.

Christmas stockings often have sentimental value if they are handmade. They need not be time-consuming projects to be special. Simple stockings can become heirlooms when they are embellished with family keepsakes, such as lace handkerchiefs or sections from tea towels or doilies. Or, use scraps of your favorite fabrics to make a crazy-quilt stocking; these stockings take on special meaning when made from old fabrics or scraps from cherished garments.

For stockings that are dramatic and elegant, select fabrics like velvets, moirés, and tapestries. Or for stockings that look rustic, select corduroys and wools. Pad the stocking with lightweight batting or fleece to add body.

HOW TO SEW A LINED STOCKING

MATERIALS

- ½ yd. (0.5 m) face fabric.
- ½ yd. (0.5 m) lining fabric.
- Low-loft quilt batting or polyester fleece.
- Ribbon, cording, or plastic ring, for hanging stocking.

CUTTING DIRECTIONS

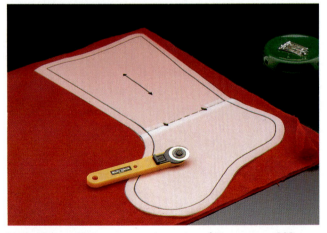

Transfer stocking pattern pieces A and B on pages 309 and 310 to paper. Tape pieces together, matching notches and dotted lines; add ½" (1.3 cm) seam allowances on all sides to make full-size stocking pattern. Cut two stocking pieces, right sides together, from face fabric and two from lining. Also cut two stocking pieces from batting or fleece.

1 Pin lace embellishments, if desired, right side up on right side of stocking front. Trim lace even with raw edges of stocking; baste in place. Baste batting or fleece to wrong side of stocking front and back.

(Continued)

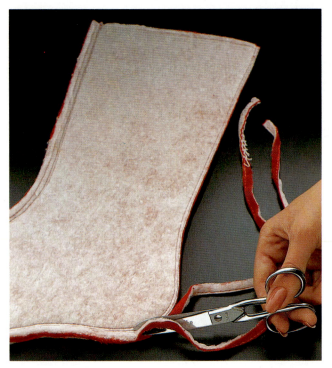

2 Pin the stocking front to the stocking back, right sides together. Stitch ½" (1.3 cm) seam around stocking, leaving top open; stitch again next to first row of stitching, within seam allowances. Trim seam allowances close to stitches. Turn stocking right side out; lightly press.

3 Pin lining pieces, right sides together. Stitch ½" (1.3 cm) seam around lining, leaving top open and bottom unstitched 4" to 6" (10 to 15 cm); stitch again next to first row of stitching, within seam allowances. Trim seam allowances close to stitches.

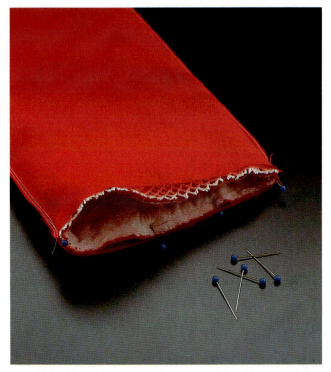

4 Place outer stocking inside lining, right sides together. Pin upper edges, raw edges even; stitch. Turn right side out through opening in foot of lining.

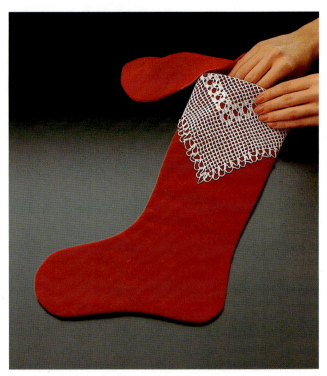

5 Stitch lining opening closed. Insert lining into the stocking; lightly press upper edge. Handstitch ribbon, cording, or ring at upper edge of stocking for hanger. Edgestitch around upper edge, if desired.

HOW TO SEW A CRAZY-QUILT STOCKING

MATERIALS

- Scraps of fabric for stocking front.
- ⅝ yd. (0.6 m) coordinating fabric for stocking back.
- ⅝ yd. (0.6 m) lining fabric.
- ⅝ yd. (0.6 m) fusible interfacing.
- Low-loft quilt batting or polyester fleece.
- Tear-away stabilizer.

CUTTING DIRECTIONS

Make stocking pattern (page 78), using stocking pattern pieces A and B on pages 309 and 310. Cut two stocking pieces from the lining, right sides together, and two from the batting or fleece. Cut one stocking front from fusible interfacing, with fusible side of interfacing up. Cut fabric scraps into a variety of shapes. Cut one stocking back from coordinating fabric, with right side of fabric down.

1 Place interfacing piece on ironing board, fusible side up. Arrange fabric scraps, right side up, on interfacing, overlapping edges. Fuse pieces in place.

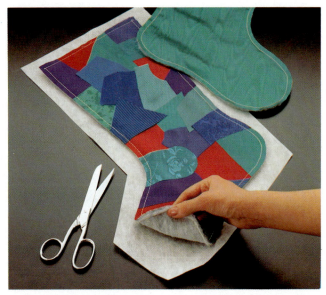

2 Trim fabric edges even with interfacing, from wrong side. Baste batting or fleece to wrong side of stocking front and back pieces; place tear-away stabilizer on batting side of stocking front.

3 Stitch around fabric scraps on stocking front, stitching through all layers with decorative machine stitches, using wide stitches that cover raw edges well. If necessary, trim raw edges of the fabric close to stitches. Remove the tear-away stabilizer.

4 Add embellishments, such as ribbons, lace, or buttons, if desired, gluing or stitching them in place. Complete stocking as in steps 2 to 5, opposite.

MORE IDEAS FOR STOCKINGS

Old buttons and lavish streamers turn a simple tapestry stocking into a treasured keepsake.

Beadwork and gold braid elegantly trim this stocking. The trims, hand-stitched in place, create the appearance of a cuff.

A crazy-quilt stocking made from scraps of wool has a rustic appearance. Metallic thread adds sparkle.

Hand-crocheted overlay *creates an heirloom stocking. Cut the overlay from undamaged sections of old table linens.*

Ruffled lace and specialty ribbons *are added to a Christmas stocking for romantic flair.*

Galloon lace *on moiré taffeta makes a distinctive, elegant stocking. Silky ribbons complete the look.*

CONE TREES

Cone trees are stunning arrangements for buffet tables and side tables. A wide selection of suitable embellishments is available at craft stores and floral shops. Choose from dried naturals, pinecones, fruits, preserved greens, ribbon, and other items, depending on the look you want. Use an inverted basket as a base for the cone tree.

The lemon cone tree (left) may be made with either fresh or artificial lemons. The tree is embellished with gold pinecones, statice, eucalyptus, and cinnamon sticks; a bird perched near the top of the tree adds the finishing touch. To vary the look, apples, pears, or other fruit may be substituted for the lemons.

For a dried-natural cone tree (page 86), make a tree from preserved evergreens, using two types of greens for added depth and texture. Embellish the tree with pinecones, berries, and ribbon, adding statice to give the tree a more delicate look. Artificial greens and berries may be substituted for the natural items.

For either tree, use a Styrofoam® cone as the form, covering it with Spanish moss for the background. The desired embellishments are inserted into the cone using wire or wooden picks, making it easy to rearrange the items until you achieve a balanced look. Add the embellishments, distributing them evenly but not in rows. Work from the bottom of the tree toward the top; trim the pick length as necessary at the top of the tree. Frequently stand back to view the arrangement from all sides. This allows you to check the balance and look for any bare areas that need embellishments.

HOW TO MAKE A LEMON CONE TREE

MATERIALS

- Styrofoam® cone, about 18" (46 cm) high with 5" (12.5 cm) base.
- Woven basket with 5" (12.5 cm) base.
- Spanish moss.
- 18 to 20 small lemons, fresh or artificial.
- Statice and green eucalyptus, about 5 stems of each.
- 10 to 12 cinnamon sticks, 3" (7.5 cm) in length.

- 20 or more pinecones in various sizes; gold metallic aerosol paint.
- Decorative bird, optional.
- 4" (10 cm) wooden floral picks; 3" (7.5 cm) wooden floral picks with wire.
- 18-gauge wire; wire cutter.
- Hot glue gun and glue sticks.

1 Apply hot glue to the top of the inverted basket; secure cone to the basket. Puncture each fresh lemon at stem end with point of 4" (10 cm) wooden pick; insert flat end of pick into punctured lemon for about 2" (5 cm).

2 Secure lemons to the cone by inserting the picks, arranging lemons in a spiral around cone. Wrap cone with a string to use as a guide. Arrange the Spanish moss around the lemons, pulling the moss apart so it loosely covers Styrofoam; secure with hot glue.

3 Break the statice into small sprigs ranging from 2" to 6" (5 to 15 cm) long. Insert sprigs into cone, placing longer sprigs at bottom of cone and shorter sprigs toward top. Secure as necessary, using hot glue.

4 Attach a wooden pick with wire to the bottom of each pinecone by wrapping the wire around bottom layers of pinecone. Apply gold paint to the pinecones; for easier application, insert picks into a piece of Styrofoam. When dry, place the pinecones in the arrangement.

5 Attach 18-gauge wire to each cinnamon stick by inserting it through the length of the stick. Wrap the wire around the stick, twisting ends at the middle. Cut off one end of wire, using wire cutter; cut the other end to 2" or 3" (5 to 7.5 cm). Insert wired cinnamon sticks into cone.

6 Cut eucalyptus into sprigs ranging from 3" to 4" (7.5 to 10 cm) long; break leaves off as necessary to make stem. Insert the sprigs, placing longer pieces at the bottom of the tree. Attach wooden pick to bird; insert near top of arrangement.

HOW TO MAKE A DRIED-NATURAL CONE TREE

MATERIALS

- Styrofoam® cone, about 18" (46 cm) high with 5" (12.5 cm) base.
- Woven basket with 5" (12.5 cm) base.
- Spanish moss.
- Preserved or artificial greens, such as spruce, cedar, and boxwood.
- 20 or more pinecones in various sizes.

- 11 yd. (10.1 m) ribbon, ⅜" (1 cm) wide.
- Several stems of small berries.
- Dried naturals, such as statice or baby's breath.
- 3" (7.5 cm) wooden floral picks with wire.
- Pruning shears; wire cutter.
- Craft glue; hot glue gun and glue sticks.

1 Apply hot glue to the top of the inverted basket; secure cone to basket. Arrange Spanish moss on cone, pulling moss apart so it loosely covers Styrofoam; secure with dots of hot glue, using glue sparingly.

2 Cut greens into sprigs ranging from 3" to 6" (7.5 to 15 cm) long, making angled cuts. Insert the stems into cone, angling the sprigs so they point downward; place longer sprigs at the bottom of the cone and shorter ones toward the top.

3 Cut boxwood into pieces ranging from 3" to 6" (7.5 to 15 cm) long; intersperse other greens with boxwood.

4 Wire pinecones as on page 85, step 4. Insert pinecones, placing larger ones at the bottom and smaller ones at the top.

5 Cut berries into about 20 clusters; wire them to picks, and arrange on cone. Or attach stemmed clusters by inserting stems directly into cone.

6 Cut 15 to 20 clusters of statice; wire them to picks. Insert picks into cone, angling clusters so they point downward.

7 Cut ribbon into 1-yd. (0.95 m) lengths. Fold ribbon, forming three or four loops on each side; leave two tails, with one tail about 2" (5 cm) longer than the other. Attach to a wooden pick with wire, wrapping the wire around the center of the bow several times.

8 Wrap longer tail of bow twice around center, concealing the wire; secure with the remaining wire, and twist wire around pick.

9 Attach bows to cone tree, inserting picks. Attach one bow to the top of the tree; shorten the pick on this bow, if necessary, and secure with glue.

TOPIARY TREES

A topiary tree is a classic floral arrangement. The size of topiary trees can be varied, making them suitable for side tables, desks, or end tables. Group several trees of various sizes together for an eye-catching centerpiece on a mantel or buffet table.

For most topiary trees, the base is a Styrofoam® ball secured to a branch or dowel and set into a pot with plaster of Paris. Make the base yourself, following the easy steps below. Or purchase a ready-made base at a floral or craft store; on some purchased bases, the ball is wire mesh instead of Styrofoam. Decorate the topiary with preserved boxwood, grapevine, dried rosebuds, dyed pistachios, or other embellishments, as shown opposite and on the following pages.

HOW TO MAKE A TOPIARY TREE

MATERIALS

- Clay pot or ceramic vase.
- Self-adhesive felt, optional.
- Styrofoam ball.
- Branch or stained dowel for the trunk; additional twigs, if desired.
- Plaster of Paris; disposable container for mixing.
- Heavy-duty aluminum foil.

- Hot glue gun and glue sticks; masking tape.
- Aerosol paint to match embellishments, if portions of the Styrofoam ball will be exposed between the embellishments.
- Saw, pruning shears, floral wire, and wire cutter may be needed for some projects, depending on materials selected.
- Spanish moss; embellishments as desired.

1 Line clay pot or vase with two layers of aluminum foil. Crumple foil loosely to shape of pot, to allow room for plaster to expand as it dries; edge of foil should be about ¾" (2 cm) below top of pot. If desired, trace bottom of pot or vase onto self-adhesive felt. Cut felt circle, cutting inside marked line; affix to bottom of pot.

2 Apply paint to Styrofoam ball, if desired. Insert trunk of tree into ball to one-half the diameter of ball. Place trunk in pot and adjust height of topiary by cutting trunk to the desired length. Remove the ball from the trunk.

3 Mix plaster of Paris, following the manufacturer's instructions. Pour plaster into the pot, filling pot to edge of foil. When the plaster has started to thicken, insert trunk, making sure it stands straight. Support the trunk, using tape as shown, until plaster has set.

4 Apply hot glue into hole in Styrofoam ball; place ball on trunk. Conceal plaster with Spanish moss or items used to decorate tree. Embellish ball as desired (page 91).

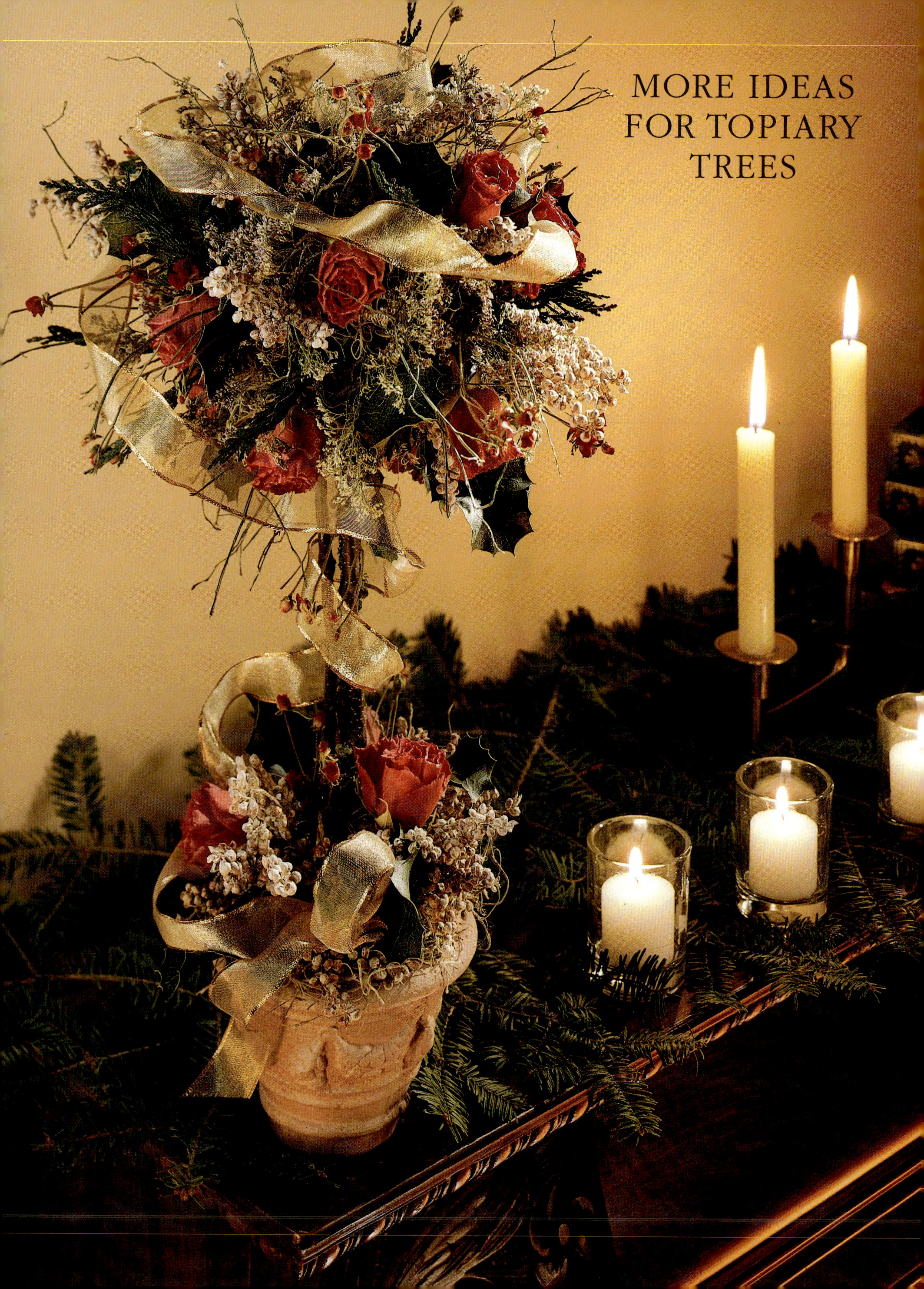
MORE IDEAS
FOR TOPIARY
TREES

Dyed pistachios *are used for casual topiaries that are inexpensive. On one small area at a time, apply hot glue to a painted Styrofoam® ball and quickly secure the pistachios with the unopened end down.*

Tiny dried rosebuds *are delicate and elegant for small topiaries. For easier insertion of the rosebud stems, make holes in the painted Styrofoam ball, using a toothpick, and dip the stems in craft glue before inserting them.*

Flowers and berries *have appealing color and texture. The selections for this topiary tree are hydrangea florets and pepper berries.*

Double topiary trees *are a variation of the basic tree. A ready-made topiary base, purchased at a floral shop, was used for this large floor tree. Pomegranates, oranges, and pinecones, secured with hot glue, are the primary embellishments.*

Sheer French ribbon *coils gently around the topiary tree opposite. Rosebuds and other embellishments are either secured with hot glue or inserted directly into the ball.*

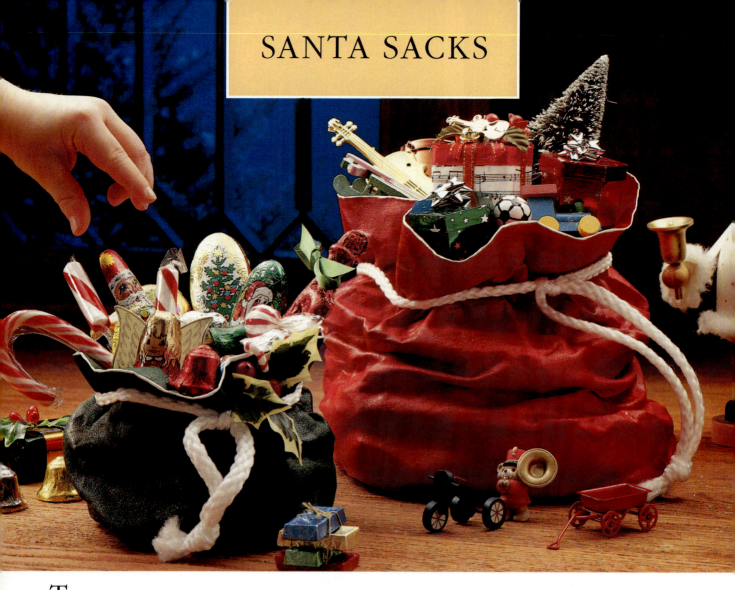

These Santa sacks are made quickly and easily from prestarched fabric. Made in the largest size, they hold almost anything, from poinsettia plants to baked goods. Filled with fingertip towels, medium-size sacks become bathroom accessories. Filled with miniature toys, the smallest sacks make whimsical party favors for the dinner table or ornaments for trees and wreaths. For ease in handling prestarched fabric, place a sheet of wax paper on the work surface and follow the tips on page 28 for shaping the fabric.

HOW TO MAKE A SANTA SACK

MATERIALS

- Prestarched fabric, such as Dip 'n Drape®, Drape 'n Shape, and Fab-U-Drape®.
- Acrylic paint of desired color for sack, in aerosol or liquid form; liquid acrylic paint for contrasting edging; artist's brush.
- Aerosol clear acrylic sealer.
- Cording or leather lacing; sprig of greenery, optional.
- Wax paper; sponge.

CUTTING DIRECTIONS

From prestarched fabric, cut two 15" × 30" (38 × 76 cm) rectangles for the large sack, two 10" × 20" (25.5 × 51 cm) rectangles for the medium sack, or one 5" × 10" (12.5 × 25.5 cm) for the small sack.

1 Large or medium sack. Place the fabric rectangles together; fold over 1" (2.5 cm) on one long edge, and open flat

2 Dip top layer of fabric quickly into cool water. Lay it back down on the other layer. Smooth layers together, and refold hem for top of sack. Wipe along all edges, using a dampened sponge.

3 Lift fabric at the folded edge, using wet fingers. Form into a cylinder with folded edge facing out. Overlap sides 1" (2.5 cm); press along overlap to close seam.

5 Set sack on wax paper; press inside of sack flat. Stuff crumpled wax paper in the sack, so it holds its shape until dry. Wet fingers, and gather opening of sack slightly; do not overwork fabric. Allow sack to dry thoroughly.

4 Support cylinder with one hand inside, and fold in lower one-third of fabric to form closed bottom of sack.

6 Apply acrylic sealer to entire sack. Paint the sack; to keep fabric from softening, paint inside of sack first and allow it to dry before painting outside. Apply two coats, if necessary. Paint upper edge a contrasting color. Apply acrylic sealer to entire sack.

7 Tie cord around sack; glue sprig of greenery over knot, if desired.

1 **Small sack.** Fold over ½" (1.3 cm) on one long edge, and open flat. Dip fabric quickly into cool water; press fold in place. Wipe along all the edges, using a dampened sponge.

2 Complete the sack, following steps 3 to 7, above. If desired, fill sack with miniature toys and gifts, securing them with hot glue.

FATHER CHRISTMAS

A popular symbol of the holiday season is the legendary Father Christmas. This one is handcrafted from prestarched fabric and is embellished for old-world charm. Prestarched fabric, available at craft stores, is dipped in cool water, then shaped while it is wet, following the tips on page 28. Experiment with samples of prestarched fabric to become familiar with the technique. Oil-based stain, applied to the fabric after it is painted, gives the Father Christmas an antiqued look.

The traditional colors of this Father Christmas are bright and festive. Standing upright, he is holding a small Christmas tree.

Decorator colors from your home may be used instead of the traditional colors. This Father Christmas leans on a walking stick and carries kindling wood.

MATERIALS

- Prestarched fabric, such as Dip 'n Drape®, Drape 'n Shape, or Fab-U-Drape®.
- One 3¼" (8.2 cm) Styrofoam® egg; one 1½" (3.8 cm) Styrofoam ball.
- 12" × 4" (30.5 × 10 cm) Styrofoam cone.
- Floral clay; 18-gauge floral wire; wire cutter.
- Natural or white unspun wool.

- Oil-based stain; 1" (2.5 cm) soft brush.
- Aerosol clear acrylic sealer.
- Acrylic paints; artist's brushes.
- Rubber bands; straight pins; T-pins; craft glue; wax paper; old baking sheet or plastic tray; knife; round toothpicks.
- Hot glue gun and glue sticks.
- Desired accessories.

CUTTING DIRECTIONS

From prestarched fabric, cut one 9" (23 cm) square for the base, one 5" (12.5 cm) square for the face, two 4" (10 cm) squares for the hands, one 14" × 16" (35.5 × 40.5 cm) rectangle for the gown, one 16" × 18" (40.5 × 46 cm) rectangle for the robe, two 6" × 7" (15 × 18 cm) rectangles for the sleeves, one 8" × 13" (20.5 × 33 cm) rectangle for the hood, and one 5" × 7" (12.5 × 18 cm) rectangle for the pouch.

HOW TO MAKE A FATHER CHRISTMAS

1 Trim ¼" (6 mm) from top of cone, using knife; set aside for the nose. Trim another 1½" (3.8 cm) from top of cone; discard. For Father Christmas with an angled stance, cut a wedge from bottom of the cone, measuring ½" (1.3 cm) on one side and tapering to nothing on opposite side. Wet fabric for base and wrap around bottom of cone; when dry, secure base with floral clay to center of tray. (Extra cone is shown for clarity.)

2 Press center of 3¼" (8.2 cm) Styrofoam® egg for head against edge of table; gently roll egg from side to side, creating an indentation halfway around the egg.

3 Press with thumbs along edges of indentation to soften cheekline. Roll forehead area lightly on table to soften the line.

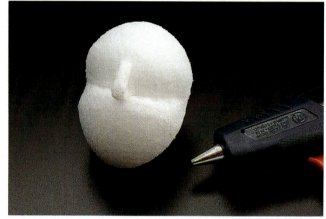

4 Compress sides of Styrofoam reserved for nose into a triangle; soften edges. Turn triangle sideways and glue in place at crest of cheekline, using hot glue.

5 Cut 1½" (3.8 cm) Styrofoam ball in half, using knife. Remove an oblong wedge, measuring ½" × ¾" (1.3 × 2 cm), from one half to form separation between thumb and fingers. Place halves together; cut same shape from other half.

6 Press firmly with finger into palm of Styrofoam hand to make curvature. Soften all cut edges of each hand by rolling on hard, smooth surface and pressing with thumb. Compress Styrofoam for smaller hands.

7 Wet fabric for the face; center over the face, with corners of fabric at top and bottom of the head. Gently pull the side corners of the fabric toward back of head, allowing fabric to cup over features; pull taut over eye area and secure with small pins to prevent wrinkles from occurring when fabric dries. Smooth excess fabric to back of head. Allow to dry on wax paper.

8 Wet fabric for one hand; center over back of hand, with corners at fingertip and wrist areas. Wrap and fold fabric over fingers and press into palm; extend excess fabric down toward wrist area. Keep fabric as smooth as possible on back of hand and between fingers and thumb. Twist fabric at wrist area.

9 Press three parallel lines into back of hand to form fingers, using blade of knife in rocking motion. Repeat for the remaining hand. Allow to dry on wax paper.

10 Apply two coats of acrylic sealer to face and hands; then paint them flesh color. Apply small amount of coral-tone paint to cheeks and nose, blending color. Using pencil, mark placement of eyes, spacing them as indicated in step 11.

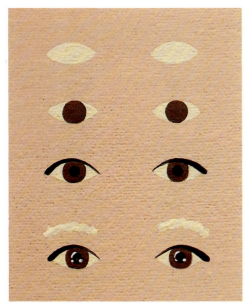

11 Paint eyes and eyebrows as shown. (Photo shows actual size and spacing.)

12 Wet the gown piece. Hand-gather one short side; place on front of cone at the neck, securing with rubber band. Arrange fabric halfway around the cone, turning under raw edge at base. Adjust the folds as necessary, using a T-pin. Place rubber band around cone about 4" (10 cm) from top of cone to define waistline. Allow to dry; remove rubber bands. Apply two coats of acrylic sealer to gown, then paint it desired color.

(Continued)

13 Wet the robe piece. Hand-gather one short side; place on back of cone at neck, securing with rubber band. Turn under sides of robe as they overlap gown piece; turn under the lower raw edges of the robe. Adjust folds as necessary, using a T-pin.

14 Insert two round toothpicks into top of cone, then into base of the head, applying hot glue to secure head to cone.

15 Insert an 18" (46 cm) length of wire through peak of cone, from side to side, for shoulders; secure with hot glue. Shape wire for the shoulders and elbows, with bend of elbows about 3" (7.5 cm) from shoulders. Position wire for arms to hold desired accessories; trim wire so forearm and upper arm are same length.

16 Push wire into Styrofoam® at back of hand near wrist; secure wire with hot glue.

17 Fold ½" (1.3 cm) hem on one short side of sleeve piece; unfold. Wet fabric, refold hem, and fold fabric for elbow. Form sleeve loosely around arm, overlapping hand slightly. Close sleeve at hand to conceal wire; hand-gather fabric at neck. Adjust folds as necessary, using a T-pin; pull fabric away from cone to create shoulder line.

18 Fold ½" (1.3 cm) hem on one long side of hood piece; unfold. Wet fabric, and refold hem. Place hood on head with hemmed edge around face; turn under front corners of hood, pinning in place with T-pins. Stuff small amount of wax paper between hood and top of head to allow space for hair.

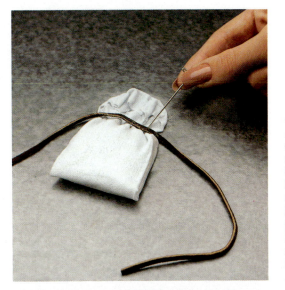

19 Turn under the raw edge at back of hood; pin in place. Remove pins and wax paper when hood is dry.

20 Wet the pouch fabric; place on wax paper. Fold a paper towel into 2" (5 cm) square. Fold long sides of fabric over paper towel. Fold in opposite ends, inserting 16" (40.5 cm) length of cording; shape top of pouch into rounded flap. Allow to dry.

21 Apply two coats of acrylic sealer to robe and pouch. Paint them desired color; paint inside edges of hood and sleeves. Allow to dry.

22 Apply two coats of acrylic sealer to Father Christmas and pouch. Apply the stain, using an old brush. When items are completely covered with stain, wipe off excess with clean rag, leaving the stain in the recessed areas to maintain dark contrast. If the stain reappears while drying, rewipe as necessary. Allow to dry thoroughly.

23 Arrange wool for desired effect for hair, beard, and moustache; glue in place, using hot glue.

24 Drape pouch over shoulder, tying ends together. Attach a belt and additional accessories, securing them with hot glue. Apply light coat of acrylic sealer for protective finish.

WINTER VILLAGE

Memories of old can be captured in this small re-creation of a winter village. A fascination for children and adults, this village is aglow with its own lighting. The buildings get their basic shape from milk cartons and can be crafted to achieve a variety of exterior finishes. The village can be accessorized with any quarter-scale figures and embellishments and can be displayed with a model train.

HOW TO MAKE A CAPE COD COTTAGE

MATERIALS

- 1-qt. (1 L) milk carton.
- Balsa or bass wood: ⅛" (3 mm) clapboard siding; corner molding; ¹⁄₁₆" x ¼" (1.5 x 6 mm) strips for shingles and shutters; ¹⁄₁₆" x ⅛" (1.5 x 3 mm) flat trim for gable; wood board, ¹⁄₁₆" (1.5 mm) thick, for door; wood strip, ⅛" (3 mm) thick, for steps.
- Acrylic paints; artist's brushes.

- Clear plastic film and ¹⁄₃₂" (0.8 mm) white graphic chart tape for windows.
- Polymer clay for chimney, such as Sculpey® or Fimo®; small bead for doorknob.
- Masking tape; fine sandpaper; metal straightedge; mat knife.
- Thick craft glue; hot glue gun and glue sticks.

1 Open top of milk carton; cut out areas as shown. Mark lines on all sides of carton 2" (5 cm) from top foldline of carton; cut on marked lines.

2 Tape top and sides of carton together to form gables, trimming upper edges of top as necessary so edges meet at peak. Sand all sides lightly.

(Continued)

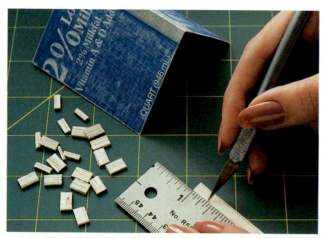

3 Cut two pieces for roof from remainder of carton, each measuring 2⅜" × 3⅛" (6.2 × 7.8 cm); tape pieces together along long side. Sand roof pieces lightly. Cut 1/16" × ¼" (1.5 × 6 mm) balsa into ⅜" (1 cm) lengths, using mat knife. Cut a few pieces in half lengthwise to use as needed at ends of rows.

4 Glue shingles in place on roof, starting at bottom edges, using thick craft glue; bottom rows should overhang the roof ⅛" (3 mm). Continue to glue rows of shingles up to top of each piece, staggering shingles and overlapping rows ⅛" (3 mm).

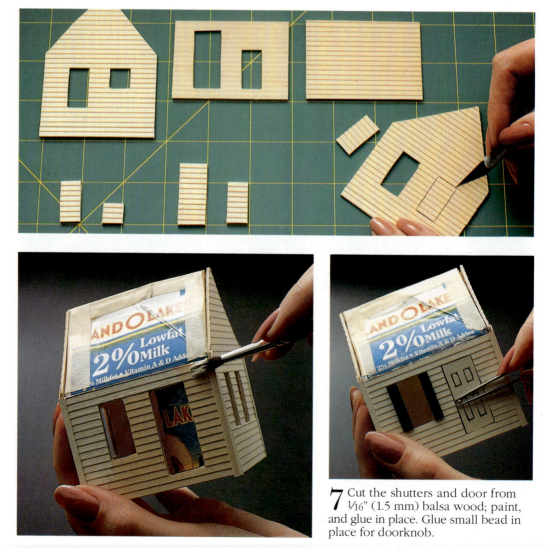

5 Trace shape of walls and gable on the back of the clapboard siding; cut pieces, using mat knife and metal straightedge. Cut openings in siding for windows and doors as desired, cutting the door ¼" (6 mm) from the bottom edge, to allow room for steps.

6 Glue siding on house, using hot glue. Cut the corner moldings to fit the corners of the house; glue in place. Cut out milk carton in window areas; for the door, cut along three sides and fold on remaining side. Paint the house as desired, using an acrylic paint.

7 Cut the shutters and door from 1/16" (1.5 mm) balsa wood; paint, and glue in place. Glue small bead in place for doorknob.

8 Cut clear plastic film slightly larger than each window. Outline windows and make mullions with graphic chart tape. Tape windows in place from inside of box, using masking tape.

9 Cut two $1/16$" × (1.5×6 mm) strips of balsa wood to the length of roof top. Paint roof and strips with thinned acrylic paint so wood grain shows through; paint edges on the underside of roof. Weight roof while drying to prevent warping.

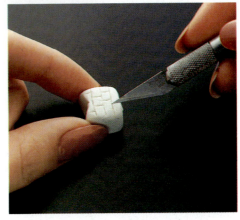

10 Glue the roof in place. Glue the strips of balsa wood to the length of roof top over top rows of shingles. Cut flat trim to fit peak; paint and glue in place.

11 Shape polymer clay into chimney shape, cutting bottom of chimney to fit roof. Use mat knife to score brick pattern on chimney.

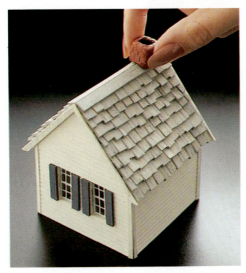

12 Bake the chimney, following the manufacturer's instructions. Paint chimney, and glue to roof.

13 Cut one $3/4$" x $3/4$" (1.9×1.9 cm) and one $1/2$" x $3/4$" (1.3×1.9 cm) piece from $1/8$" (3 mm) wood; glue together for steps. Paint as desired; glue in place beneath door.

VARIATIONS FOR VILLAGE HOUSES

To add variety to the winter village, the sizes and shapes of some of the houses may be changed. Stucco and brick may be used for the exterior finishes instead of clapboard siding. Asphalt and wood-shingle roofs may be used on some of the houses instead of wood shakes.

HOW TO VARY THE SIZE & SHAPE OF HOUSES

Tape portions of cartons together for houses of various sizes and shapes. To add dormers, use the pattern on page 311. Vary the exterior finishes, as shown below and opposite.

HOW TO MAKE A STUCCO EXTERIOR

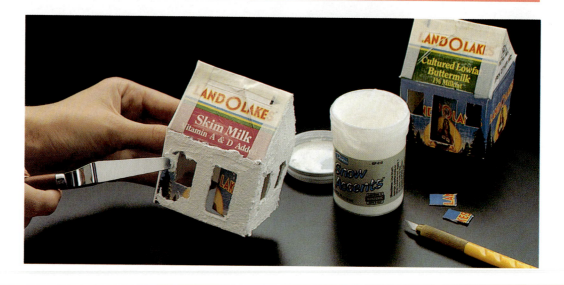

Apply one or two coats of artificial snow paste to the sides of the house after the windows and doors have been cut.

HOW TO MAKE A BRICK EXTERIOR

1 Roll polymer clay on a sheet of heavy aluminum foil to ⅛" (3 mm) thickness; to ensure even thickness, support sides of rolling pin with ⅛" (3 mm) strips of wood.

2 Mark the dimensions of house on clay. Cut on marked lines, using mat knife; do not cut through foil. Remove excess clay. Mark placement of doors and windows by scoring the clay. Score clay, marking horizontal rows ⅛" (3 mm) apart; score clay vertically for individual bricks.

3 Cut out doors and windows. Transfer the foil to a baking sheet, and bake according to manufacturer's instructions.

4 Glue the brick pieces to sides of house, using hot glue. Cut out doors and windows in milk carton. Glue corner moldings at corners of house. Paint the brick and moldings desired color.

HOW TO MAKE WOOD-SHINGLE & ASPHALT ROOFS

Wood-shingle roof. Mark roof measurements from carton on back of ¼" (6 mm) clapboard; add ⅜" (1 cm) width and length for overhangs and eaves. Cut pieces, using mat knife and metal straightedge. Cut corner molding the length of roof. Paint roof and corner molding with thinned paint. Mark staggered lines for shingles, using mat knife. Weight roof while drying to prevent warping. Glue roof in place. Glue corner molding along roof top.

Asphalt roof. Cut #60 coarse sandpaper into ¼" (6 mm) strips; from strips, cut ¼" × ⅜" (6 mm × 1 cm) shingles. Cut a few pieces in half lengthwise to use as needed at ends of rows. Attach shingles as on page 102, step 4. Fold ¼" (6 mm) strip of sandpaper in half; glue in place over top rows of shingles.

VILLAGE CHURCH

A red brick church, with its bell tower, pillared entryway, and stained glass windows, is an important part of the village. The basic construction of the church is the same as for the houses on page 101.

MATERIALS

- Three 1-qt. (1 L) milk cartons.
- Balsa or bass wood: ⅛" (3 mm) clapboard for siding of tower; ¼" (6 mm) clapboard for roof; corner molding for corners of church and top of roof; 1⁄16" × ⅛" (1.5 × 3 mm) flat trim for gable and tower back; wood strip, 3⁄16" (4.5 mm) thick, for steps; wood strip, 1⁄16" (1.5 mm) thick, for doors; dowel, for pillars.
- 6 oz. (170 g) Sculpey® polymer clay for brick; aluminum foil; rolling pin; baking sheet.
- Acrylic paints; artist's brushes; clear plastic film; 1⁄32" (0.8 mm) black graphic chart tape; stained glass paints or permanent marking pens.
- Two small beads for doorknobs; small bell and bead for steeple.
- Masking tape; fine sandpaper; thick craft glue; hot glue gun and glue sticks; mat knife.

HOW TO MAKE A VILLAGE CHURCH

1 Follow steps 1 and 2 on page 101, marking the lines 3½" (9 cm) from top foldline; repeat for second carton. Tape the two cartons together securely.

2 Cut piece for bell tower, 6½" high × 5" wide (16.3 × 12.5 cm), from remaining carton; position fold of carton on the lengthwise center of rectangle. Mark and score a line 1¼" (3.2 cm) from each long edge.

3 Fold tower, and tape together. Cut piece for steeple from carton, using pattern on page 311; score on dotted lines. Fold steeple, and tape together.

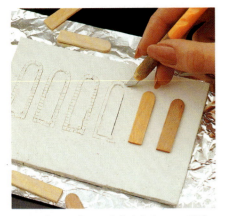

4 Make and attach brick (page 105) to sides of church, using a 1½" (3.8 cm) portion of popsicle stick for window pattern; if desired, score brick around windows as shown.

5 Make and attach windows as on page 103, step 8, using black chart tape. If desired, paint windows, using stained glass paints or permanent marking pens.

6 Attach wood-shingle roof (page 105). Paint flat trim, and glue to front and back of church, with lower edge 3½" (9 cm) from bottom of church; cut ends to fit roof angle. Cut flat trim for peak; paint, and glue in place.

7 Cut clapboard and doors for the tower and steeple according to patterns on pages 311 and 312. Glue clapboard in place, using hot glue.

8 Cut corner moldings to fit corners of tower and steeple; glue in place. Cut away carton for windows. Cut flat trim, and attach to top and bottom of windows. Cut two 3½" (9 cm) strips of flat trim; attach to back of tower at bottom of corner moldings.

9 Paint tower and steeple. Score roof for shingles, if desired. Attach bell to a length of wire, and insert wire through top of steeple; adjust height of bell, and glue in place. Trim excess wire. Glue steeple to tower; glue bead at peak of steeple.

10 Paint and attach the doors, with lower edge ⅝" (1.5 cm) from bottom of tower. Glue beads for doorknobs in place. Cut one 1½" x 1½" (3.8 x 3.8 cm) piece, one 1¼" x 1½" (3.2 x 3.8 cm) and one 1" x 1½" (2.5 x 3.8 cm) from ³⁄₁₆" (5 mm) wood; glue together for steps. Paint the steps as desired, and glue in place.

11 Cut two 1" (2.5 cm) squares from the clapboard for the awning roof; cut awning front, using pattern on page 311. Glue awning pieces together; paint. Score roof for shingles, if desired. Cut two pillars from dowel, each 1¾" (4.5 cm) long; paint. Glue awning and pillars in place; position pillars on top step. Glue tower to front of church.

TIPS FOR LANDSCAPING THE VILLAGE

Landscape base.
Cut foam board to desired size. Wrap the board with polyester fleece or quilt batting; tape in place on underside.

Skating pond. Cut away the fleece or batting to desired shape of skating pond. Apply sheet of silver Mylar® to foam board, using spray adhesive. Use white paint pen to simulate tracings from skate blades, if desired.

1 Hill. Shape a hill, using a box and crumpled foil. Battery packs for lighting can be stored in box.

2 Cover hill with fleece or batting. Add small stones or polymer clay stones (opposite), moss, and twigs as desired; attach, using hot glue.

1 Lighting. Use battery-operated lights, concealing battery packs in hill (above). Cut slit in fleece or batting; run wiring to buildings.

2 Cluster light bulbs; tape together. Tape to ceiling inside house.

Hedges and shrubs.
Use sprigs of artificial garland for hedges. For the shrubs, wind the garland sprigs around finger, or trim the tops from miniature pine trees, using wire cutter.

Stonework. Roll polymer clay to 1/8" (3 mm) thickness. Cut out paving stone shapes with a knife. Use a toothpick to make paving patterns in clay. Bake clay, following the manufacturer's instructions; paint as desired. Place the stonework on fleece or batting to create walkways.

Snow and icicles.
Sprinkle artificial snow to conceal lighting wires and add finishing touch to roofs, hedges, and other items. Glue purchased icicles designed for miniature villages to the eaves of the buildings.

Gift Wrapping

KEEPSAKE GIFT BOXES

For memorable gift giving, create spectacular packages. The gift boxes themselves can become keepsakes for storing mementos like your favorite Christmas cards and letters. Or they may be used again for wrapping next year's presents.

Bandboxes can be transformed into gift boxes that resemble antiqued drums. Or use wicker baskets with lids as gift boxes; embellished with special trims, the baskets themselves become an extra gift.

Decoupaged boxes, embellished with cutouts from special Christmas cards, antique reproduction cutouts, and metallic trims have old-fashioned appeal. The beautifully wrapped boxes are preserved for years to come by applying a decoupage medium to the wrapping paper. For best results, use sturdy, noncollapsible gift boxes and wrapping papers that are heavier in weight. Lightweight papers can be strengthened by spraying them with aerosol clear acrylic sealer. For shallow boxes, it may only be necessary to cover the lid of the box. On deeper boxes with shallow lids, cover both the box and the lid.

Paper lace fans can adorn decoupaged gift boxes for a dimensional effect. For easier storage of gift boxes with paper lace fans, make the fans detachable by using self-adhesive hook and loop tape.

HOW TO MAKE A DRUM GIFT BOX

MATERIALS

- Wooden bandbox; extra lid from a second bandbox, optional.
- Acrylic paints; oil-based stain; artist's brushes.
- Braids and trims to simulate detailing of drums.
- Craft glue.
- Two large wooden beads and two wooden dowels to fit into beads, for drumsticks; length of dowels depends on diameter of bandbox lid.

1 Glue extra lid, if desired, on bottom of box. Glue wooden bead to one end of each dowel to make drumsticks; allow to dry. Paint bandbox and drumsticks. When dry, apply stain, following manufacturer's instructions.

2 Glue trim to sides of box to simulate detailing of drum. Glue drumsticks in place on top of lid. Glue braid to lower edge of box and upper edge of lid; cover ends of braid with a trim for a neater finish.

HOW TO MAKE A BASKET GIFT BOX

MATERIALS

- Wicker basket with lid.
- Acrylic paint and oil-based stain, if desired; artist's brushes.
- Craft glue.
- Embellishments as desired, such as dried naturals or miniatures.

1 Apply paint and stain to wicker basket, if desired.

2 Embellish gift box as desired; secure items with hot glue.

HOW TO MAKE A DECOUPAGE GIFT BOX

MATERIALS

- Gift boxes.
- Wrapping paper.
- Decoupage medium; brush or sponge applicator.
- Metallic or pearlescent acrylic paint, optional.
- Embellishments as desired, such as dried naturals, decorative cutouts, ribbons, braids, doilies, and glitter glue.

1 Cut wrapping paper so it extends 1" to 2" (2.5 to 5 cm) beyond the edges of the box or lid.

2 Spread decoupage medium on the wrong side of the wrapping paper; allow to set about 1 minute to prevent paper from bubbling when mounted.

3 Center the box or lid on the wrong side of wrapping paper. Turn over, and smooth the paper in place, removing any bubbles.

4 Turn box over, and smooth paper onto two long sides. Cut paper from upper edge to corner; wrap paper to inside of box. Trim remaining paper at sides even with edge of box.

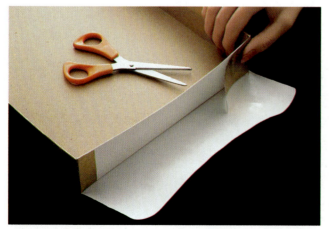

5 Cut paper at ends into the corner; fold flaps, trimming excess paper, if desired. Secure the flaps to the short sides of the box.

6 Smooth paper in place on short sides of box and around to inside. Allow box to dry thoroughly.

7 Use decoupage medium to affix embellishments, such as cutouts, to box; allow to dry.

8 Highlight the cutouts with glitter glue or with pearlescent or metallic paint, if desired; apply paint with brush and circular strokes, or dab paint on with small piece of natural sponge.

9 Brush a thin coat of decoupage medium onto entire outside surface; allow to dry. Additional coats may be applied, if desired; to eliminate brush strokes, sand lightly between coats, using fine sandpaper.

10 Apply heavier trims, such as dried naturals, with craft glue. Apply acrylic sealer.

HOW TO MAKE A PAPER FAN GIFT BOX

MATERIALS

- Gift boxes.
- Wrapping paper.
- Decoupage medium; brush or sponge applicator.
- Circles of light-duty hook and loop tape.
- Materials for paper fans, listed on page 19.
- Ribbon for bow, if desired.

1 Make decoupage box, following steps 1 to 6, opposite, and step 9, above. Make paper fans as on page 19.

2 Secure loop side of hook and loop tape to bottom edges of paper fans and bow; secure hook side to package.

VICTORIAN CARDS

Paper doilies, either round or square, can be folded and embellished to create unique cards, gifts tags, and package trims. For an old-fashioned look, use antique reproduction cutouts and stickers, available in stationery stores and gift shops. Or create your own cutouts from Christmas cards and wrapping paper. Decorative doilies and medallions are available from stationery stores and cake decorating suppliers.

MATERIALS

- Round paper doilies in 8", 10", or 12" (20.5, 25.5, or 30.5 cm) sizes.
- Square paper doilies in 8" or 10" (20.5 or 25.5 cm) sizes; doilies should have solid square area at center.

- Cutouts or stickers.
- Glue stick or liquid craft glue.
- Embellishments as desired, such as ribbon, feathers, foil leaves and medallions, foil papers, and glitter glue.

FOUR WAYS TO FOLD VICTORIAN CARDS

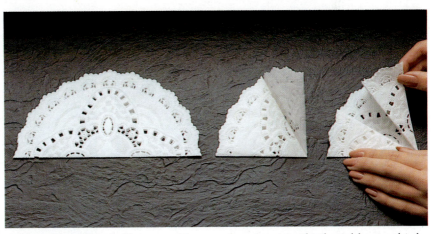

Fold round doily in half, wrong sides together; then fold right and left sides so edges meet in center.

Fold round doily in half, wrong sides together, then into thirds. Fold outer thirds in half so folded edges meet in center.

Fold opposite corners of square doily along solid area. Fold back points, if desired, so folded edges meet.

Fold all four corners of square doily along solid area, envelope-style.

117

TIPS FOR EMBELLISHING VICTORIAN CARDS

Glue 6" to 8" (15 to 20.5 cm) lengths of silk ribbon to doily, with glued ends facing away from center, for ties. Glue cutout, which has been cut in half, on doily over ribbons.

Strengthen wrapping paper by spraying four or five coats of acrylic sealer on both sides. Cut design from wrapping paper; glue to doily.

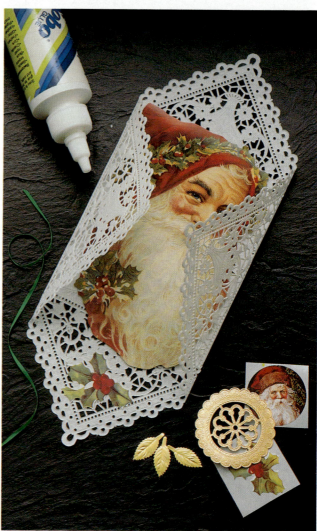

Cut decorative foil paper, and glue in center of square doily for colorful background under motif.

Embellish cards with gold leaves and medallions, gluing them in place. Or add small stickers to cards.

118

Create pop-up designs by mounting them on heavy strips of paper, folded into M or Z shapes.

Highlight designs with glitter.

Sign the card on a small "banner" of paper or ribbon. Or add gift tags to the embellishments.

Glue medallions or portions of doilies under cutout motifs for added interest. Tuck feathers behind designs, if desired.

MORE IDEAS FOR GIFT WRAPPING

Embossed gift cards are made using a stamp and embossing ink and powder. Cut around the top portion of the design with a mat knife, if desired, before folding the gift card.

Gift bags can be personalized with appliqués cut from fabric and applied with spray adhesive. Perforated bags designed for use with candles may also be used for gift bags.

Ornaments, used instead of bows, become an extra keepsake gift. This package is embellished with a lace nosegay ornament (page 21).

Santa sacks (page 92) make creative packaging for gifts of food or plants.

Stamps can be used to create your own wrapping paper. Use permanent marking pens to add detailing to the stamped designs.

Tassels and medallions add an elegant touch to tailored bows.

Creative napkin rings (page 58) can decorate the neck of a bottle or the handle of a basket.

Small artificial wreath, cut and attached to the rim of a gift basket, adds a festive touch.

A Blizzard of
Holiday Ideas

QUICK COOKIES & CANDY CREATIONS

N̄o time for baking? Packaged or bakery cookies give you a head start. Dip them in melted candy coating, then be creative with colored sugars, chopped nuts or multicolored shot. For an afternoon of family fun, enlist the children's help. Create the easy, festive candies from nuts, caramels, microwave-melted chocolate and candy coating.

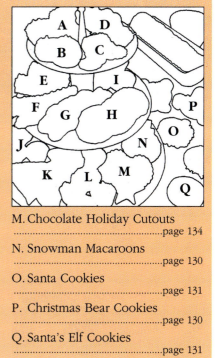

CANDY COATING MELTING CHART

Amount	Container	Microwave at 50% (Medium)
⅛ lb. (60 g)	Small mixing bowl	2-3 min.
¼ lb. (125 g)	Small mixing bowl	2-4 min.
½ lb. (250 g)	Small mixing bowl	2½-5 min.
¾ lb. (375 g)	Medium mixing bowl	2½-5½ min.
1 lb. (500 g)	Medium mixing bowl	4-8 min.

BUTTER COOKIE WREATHS ↑

- ⅛ lb. (60 g) white or chocolate-flavored candy coating
- 12 butter cookies, (2"/5 cm) with hole in center

- Red or green colored sugar
- Red cinnamon candies
- 12 pieces shoestring licorice (4"/10 cm lengths)

1 dozen cookies

Christmas Jewel Kiss: *Follow recipe left, except omit cinnamon candies and shoestring licorice. Place a chocolate kiss in the center of each dipped cookie.*

1 Line a baking sheet with wax paper. Set aside. Melt candy coating as directed in chart, page 125.

2 Dip the top of each cookie into coating. Place cookies dipped-side-up on prepared baking sheet.

3 Decorate each cookie with colored sugar and cinnamon candies. Tie licorice into bows, and use coating to attach to each cookie. Let stand, or chill, until set. Store in cool, dry place.

QUICK HOLIDAY COOKIES ↑

- ¼ lb. (125 g) white or chocolate-flavored candy coating
- 12 cookies (2½"/6 cm)
- Multicolored shot

1 dozen cookies

1 Line a baking sheet with wax paper. Set aside. Melt candy coating as directed in chart, page 125.

2 Dip half of each cookie into coating. Place cookies on prepared baking sheet. Sprinkle dipped portion of each cookie with shot. Let stand, or chill, until set. Store in cool, dry place.

HOLIDAY NUT CRISPS

- ⅛ lb. (60 g) white or chocolate-flavored candy coating
- 12 vanilla wafer cookies (1½"/4 cm)
- ⅓ cup (75 mL) chopped walnuts or pecans

1 dozen cookies

1 Line a baking sheet with wax paper. Set aside. Melt candy coating as directed in chart, page 125.

2 Dip half of each cookie into coating. Place cookies on prepared baking sheet. Sprinkle dipped portion of each cookie with chopped nuts. Let stand, or chill, until set. Store in cool, dry place.

CHOCOLATE-DIPPED PRETZELS ↑

- ⅛ lb. (60 g) chocolate-flavored candy coating
- 36 small pretzel twists
- Multicolored shot
- ⅛ lb. (60 g) white candy coating

3 dozen pretzels

1 Line a baking sheet with wax paper. Set aside. Melt chocolate-flavored coating as directed in chart, page 125. Dip half of each pretzel into coating. Place pretzels on prepared baking sheet. Sprinkle dipped portion of each pretzel with shot. Let stand, or chill, until set.

2 Repeat with white coating, dipping undecorated half of each pretzel into coating. Omit shot. Store in cool, dry place.

WAFER COOKIE ← PRESENTS

- ¼ lb. (125 g) white candy coating
- 1 pkg. (10 oz./284 g) cream-filled wafer cookies (2½"/6 cm)
- Food color paste*
- 24 silver balls

2 dozen cookies

1 Line a baking sheet with wax paper. Set aside. Melt candy coating as directed in chart, page 125. Spoon a small amount of coating onto 24 cookies. Top each cookie with another cookie. Press gently to sandwich together. Place cookies on prepared baking sheet. Set aside.

2 Tint remaining coating with food color paste. Spoon coating into 1-quart (1 L) sealable freezer bag. Squeeze coating to one corner of bag. Seal bag. Using scissors, snip corner of bag slightly to form writing tip. Pipe coating across cookie to make ribbon and bow. Place silver ball in center of each bow. Let stand, or chill, until set. Store in cool, dry place.

Food color paste is available at most food specialty stores. Do not use liquid food coloring.

APPLIQUÉD HOLIDAY COOKIES

- 12 sugar cookies (2½"/6 cm)
- 4 chewy fruit rolls (0.5 oz./15 g each)

1 dozen cookies

1 Arrange 6 sugar cookies on a plate. Set aside. Unroll 2 fruit rolls. Cut out holiday shapes, using cookie cutter or scissors. Place 1 cutout on each cookie.

2 Microwave cookies at High for 30 seconds to 1 minute, or just until warm, rotating plate once. (Watch closely to prevent burning.) Pat appliqués gently so they adhere to surface of warm cookies. Repeat with remaining cookies and fruit rolls. Cool completely. Store in cool, dry place.

FANCY FILLED COOKIES →

- 1 cup (250 mL) ready-to-spread frosting
- 1 pkg. (5½ oz./156 g) pirouette cookies
- ⅛ lb. (60 g) white or chocolate-flavored candy coating
- Red or green colored sugar (optional)
- Multicolored shot (optional)

2 dozen cookies

1 Line a baking sheet with wax paper. Set aside. Place frosting in 1-quart (1 L) sealable freezer bag. Squeeze frosting to one corner of bag. Seal bag. Using scissors, snip corner of bag slightly to form tip. Pipe frosting into both ends of each cookie. Place cookies on prepared baking sheet. Set aside.

2 Melt candy coating as directed in chart, page 125. Spoon coating into another 1-quart (1 L) sealable freezer bag. Squeeze coating to one corner of bag. Seal bag. Using scissors, snip corner of bag slightly to form writing tip. Pipe coating over filled cookies in zigzag or other decorative pattern. Sprinkle with colored sugar and shot. Let stand, or chill, until set. Store in cool, dry place.

GINGER MAN SANDWICH COOKIES

- ¼ lb. (125 g) white candy coating
- Red or green food color paste* (optional)
- 1 pkg. (5 oz./142 g) ginger man cookies
- 10 pieces shoestring licorice (4"/10 cm lengths)
- Red cinnamon candies

10 cookies

1 Line a baking sheet with wax paper. Set aside. Melt candy coating as directed in chart, page 125. Add food color paste. Mix well.

2 Spoon a small amount of coating onto the back of 10 cookies. Place cookies coated-side-up on prepared baking sheet. Fold licorice pieces in half to form loops. Place 1 loop at head end of each cookie, with cut ends in coating on cookie.

3 Top each cookie with another cookie, right-side-up, and press gently to sandwich together. Decorate one side, using remaining coating to attach cinnamon candies for eyes, nose and buttons. Let stand, or chill, until set. Store in cool, dry place.

*Food color paste is available at most food specialty stores. Do not use liquid food coloring.

SNOWMAN MACAROONS ↑

- ¼ lb. (125 g) white candy coating
- 12 macaroon cookies (2"/5 cm)
- Flaked coconut
- 12 red cinnamon candies
- 12 raisins, cut in half

- 12 pieces red shoestring licorice (¾"/2 cm lengths)
- 12 pieces black shoestring licorice (½"/1 cm lengths)
- ¼ cup (50 mL) sugar, divided
- 24 large black gumdrops

1 dozen cookies

1 Line a baking sheet with wax paper. Set aside. Melt candy coating as directed in chart, page 125. Dip the top of each cookie into coating. Place cookies dipped-side-up on prepared baking sheet.

2 Sprinkle each cookie with coconut. Use remaining coating to attach cinnamon candy for nose, raisin halves for eyes and red licorice for mouth. Use black licorice for stem of pipe.

3 For hat and bowl of pipe, sprinkle 1 teaspoon (5 mL) sugar on piece of wax paper. Place 2 large black gumdrops on sugar. Top with another piece of wax paper. Roll gumdrops between wax paper to ¼" (5 mm) thickness. Cut flattened gumdrops into shape of hat and pipe bowl. Attach with coating. Repeat for remaining snowmen. Let stand, or chill, until set. Store in cool, dry place.

CHRISTMAS BEAR
← COOKIES

- ¼ lb. (125 g) white candy coating
- 12 macaroon cookies (2"/5 cm)
- Flaked coconut
- 12 red cinnamon candies
- 12 miniature marshmallows, flattened
- 24 miniature chocolate chips
- 6 large marshmallows, quartered
- Red colored sugar
- 12 large gumdrops, cut in half lengthwise
- 12 candy-coated plain chocolate pieces

1 dozen cookies

1 Line a baking sheet with wax paper. Set aside. Melt candy coating as directed in chart, page 125. Dip the top of each cookie into coating. Place cookies dipped-side-up on prepared baking sheet.

2 Sprinkle each cookie with coconut. To make nose, use remaining coating to attach a cinnamon candy to the center of each flattened marshmallow and to attach nose to each cookie. Attach chocolate chips for eyes. Attach marshmallow quarter to each side of cookie for ears. Spread small amount of coating on each ear, and sprinkle with colored sugar.

3 Use coating to attach 2 gumdrop halves to make bow tie and to attach candy-coated chocolate piece in center of each bow. Let stand, or chill, until set. Store in cool, dry place.

SANTA COOKIES →

- ¼ lb. (125 g) white or chocolate-flavored candy coating
- 12 sugar cookies (2½"/6 cm)
- Red or green colored sugar
- Flaked coconut
- 6 small gumdrops, cut in half crosswise
- 36 red cinnamon candies

1 dozen cookies

1 Line a baking sheet with wax paper. Set aside. Melt candy coating as directed in chart, page 125. Dip the top of each cookie into coating. Place cookies dipped-side-up on prepared baking sheet.

2 Decorate each Santa with red or green colored sugar to make hat, and coconut to make beard. Use gumdrop half to make pom-pom for hat, and cinnamon candies for eyes and nose. Let stand, or chill, until set. Store in cool, dry place.

SANTA'S ELF COOKIES ↑

- ¼ lb. (125 g) white candy coating
- 12 sugar cookies (2½"/6 cm)
- Red or green colored sugar
- 12 miniature marshmallows

- 24 chocolate chips
- 12 red cinnamon candies
- 12 small red gumdrops, cut in half crosswise

- 12 pieces red shoestring licorice (1"/2.5 cm lengths)

1 dozen cookies

1 Line a baking sheet with wax paper. Set aside. Melt candy coating as directed in chart, page 125. Dip half of each cookie into coating to make hat.

2 Place cookies on prepared baking sheet. Sprinkle hat with colored sugar. Use remaining coating to attach marshmallow for pom-pom of hat, and chocolate chips for eyes.

3 Attach cinnamon candy for nose, gumdrop halves for cheeks and piece of licorice for mouth. Let stand, or chill, until set. Store in cool, dry place.

← CHOCOLATE CHERRY CUPS

- 20 small paper candy cups
- 1 cup (250 mL) chocolate chips or 1 (6 oz./170 g) white baking bar, broken into pieces
- 20 red or green candied cherries

20 candies

1 Place candy cups on a baking sheet. Set aside. Place chocolate chips in small mixing bowl. Microwave at 50% (Medium) for 3½ to 4½ minutes, or until chocolate is glossy and can be stirred smooth, stirring once or twice.

2 Spoon chocolate evenly into candy cups, filling three-fourths full. Top each candy with candied cherry. Let stand, or chill, until set. Cover and store in refrigerator.

← CRUNCHY CARAMEL CHEWS

- 20 small paper candy cups
- 10 caramels, cut into quarters
- 1 cup (250 mL) chocolate chips or 1 (6 oz./170 g) white baking bar, broken into pieces
- ¼ cup (50 mL) crisp rice cereal

20 candies

1 Place candy cups on a baking sheet. Place 2 pieces of caramel in each candy cup. Set aside. Place chocolate chips in small mixing bowl. Microwave at 50% (Medium) for 3½ to 4½ minutes, or until chocolate is glossy and can be stirred smooth, stirring once or twice.

2 Spoon chocolate evenly over caramels, filling candy cups. Sprinkle each candy with cereal. Let stand, or chill, until set. Cover and store in refrigerator.

← RAISIN-PECAN CLUSTERS

- 20 small paper candy cups
- ⅓ cup (75 mL) raisins, divided
- 40 pecan halves, divided
- 1 cup (250 mL) chocolate chips or 1 (6 oz./170 g) white baking bar, broken into pieces

20 candies

1 Place candy cups on a baking sheet. In each candy cup, place about 6 raisins and 1 pecan half. Set aside. Place chocolate chips in small mixing bowl. Microwave at 50% (Medium) for 3½ to 4½ minutes, or until chocolate is glossy and can be stirred smooth, stirring once or twice.

2 Spoon chocolate evenly over raisins and pecan halves, filling candy cups full. Top each candy with 1 pecan half. Let stand, or chill, until set. Cover and store in refrigerator.

Peanut Clusters: *Follow recipe above, except in each candy cup substitute 4 dry-roasted peanuts for raisins and pecan half. Substitute 4 peanut halves for pecan half on top of each candy.*

Macadamia Nut Clusters: *Follow recipe above, except in each candy cup substitute 3 macadamia nuts for raisins and pecan half. Substitute 1 macadamia nut for pecan half on top of each candy.*

JORDAN ALMOND BARK ↑

- 1¼ lbs. (625 g) white candy coating
- ½ lb. (250 g) Jordan almonds
- ½ cup (125 mL) unblanched whole almonds

2 lbs./1 kg

Jelly Bean Bark: Follow recipe above, except substitute 2 cups (500 mL) jelly beans for almonds.

1 Line a baking sheet with foil. Set aside. In 2-quart (2 L) casserole, microwave candy coating at 50% (Medium) for 4 to 6 minutes, or until coating can be stirred smooth, stirring twice. Stir in almonds.

2 Spread to ¼ to ½" (5 mm to 1 cm) thickness on prepared baking sheet. Let stand, or chill, until set. Break into pieces. Store in cool, dry place.

- 3 pkgs. (4 oz./114 g each) German sweet chocolate, broken up
- 2 pkgs. (6 oz./170 g each) white baking bar, broken up
- Colored sugar

1½ lbs./750 g

Mint Chocolate Cutouts: *Follow recipe left, except substitute 12 oz. (340 g) semisweet mint chocolate chips for German sweet chocolate.*

Crispy Cutouts: *Follow recipe left, except sprinkle 1 cup (250 mL) crisp rice cereal evenly over rectangle of melted German sweet chocolate, and omit colored sugar.*

Chocolate-Nut Cutouts: *Follow recipe left, except sprinkle 1 cup (250 mL) chopped pecans evenly over rectangle of melted German sweet chocolate, and omit colored sugar.*

1 Use pencil to trace 14 x 9" (35 x 23 cm) rectangle on wax paper. Place wax paper in 15½ x 10½" (40 x 25 cm) jelly roll pan. Set aside.

2 Place chocolate pieces in 8-cup (2 L) measure. Microwave at 50% (Medium) for 3 to 5 minutes, or until chocolate is glossy and can be stirred smooth, stirring twice.

3 Pour and spread chocolate evenly within 14 x 9" (35 x 23 cm) rectangle on prepared jelly roll pan. Place in freezer 5 minutes, or until set.

4 Place baking bar pieces in 8-cup (2 L) measure. Microwave at 50% (Medium) for 3 to 5 minutes, or until mixture is glossy and can be stirred smooth, stirring twice. Cool slightly. Pour and spread evenly over chocolate layer.

5 Sprinkle baking bar layer with colored sugar. Place in freezer 5 minutes, or until set. Remove from freezer. Let stand about 10 minutes, or until slightly thawed.

6 Cut desired shapes, using metal cookie cutters or sharp knife. Place on plate in single layer. Cover with plastic wrap. Chill until set.

CHOCOLATE PLACE CARDS OR GIFT TAGS ↑

- 1 recipe Chocolate Holiday Cutouts (opposite)
- ⅛ lb. (60 g) chocolate-flavored candy coating

42 cards or tags

1 Prepare Chocolate Holiday Cutouts as directed. Use sharp knife to cut 3 x 1" (8 x 2.5 cm) rectangles or cut into shapes with cookie cutters. For Gift Tags, cut hole in one end with tip of sharp knife. Melt candy coating as directed in chart, page 125. Spoon coating into 1-quart (1 L) sealable freezer bag. Squeeze coating to one corner of bag. Seal bag. Using scissors, snip corner of bag slightly to form writing tip.

2 Pipe names over sugar sprinkles. Let stand, or chill, until set. Wrap each card or tag in small piece of plastic wrap. Use place cards for holiday table setting. Tie gift tags with ribbon and attach to presents.

DECORATING WITH FOOD

For centuries, decorating with food expressed the spirit of holiday bounty. The microwave oven helps you continue this tradition in contemporary style. Create edible decorations to deck your own halls or to give as gifts.

LACY CHOCOLATE BASKET

- ⅛ lb. (60 g) chocolate-flavored candy coating
- ¼ lb. (125 g) white candy coating, divided

1 basket

1 Invert a small shallow dish (about 5"/12 cm). Cover with foil. Smooth foil down tightly to remove large wrinkles. Place foil-covered dish in freezer for at least 30 minutes, or overnight.

2 Place chocolate-flavored candy coating in small bowl. Microwave at 50% (Medium) for 2 to 3 minutes, or until coating can be stirred smooth. Spoon into 1-quart (1 L) sealable freezer bag. Squeeze to one corner of bag. Seal bag.

3 Use scissors to snip corner of bag slightly to form writing tip. Remove foil-wrapped dish from freezer. Pipe melted coating over dish in looping, lacy pattern. Return dish to freezer for 10 minutes.

4 Place ⅛ lb. (60 g) white candy coating in small bowl. Microwave at 50% (Medium) for 2 to 3 minutes, or until coating can be stirred smooth. Spoon into another 1-quart (1 L) sealable freezer bag. Squeeze to one corner of bag. Seal bag.

5 Use scissors to snip corner of bag slightly to form writing tip. Pipe coating over first layer in looping, lacy patterns. Freeze for 10 minutes. Repeat with remaining ⅛ lb. (60 g) white candy coating.

6 Remove dish and then foil carefully from inside of candy basket. Fill basket with jelly beans, gumdrops or cookies. Baskets are fragile, so handle carefully. Store in cool, dry place away from direct heat.

CANDY TREASURE CHEST

- 1 lb. (500 g) white candy coating
- ¼ lb. (125 g) chocolate-flavored candy coating
- Red or green colored sugar (optional)

1 chest

1 Line a 15½ x 10½" (40 x 25 cm) jelly roll pan with wax paper. Set aside. In 8-cup (2 L) measure, microwave white candy coating at 50% (Medium) for 3 to 5 minutes, or until coating can be stirred smooth, stirring once or twice.

2 Pour and spread coating evenly into prepared pan to within ½" (1 cm) of edges. Place in freezer for 10 minutes, or until coating is set. Let stand at room temperature for 30 minutes before cutting.

3 Cut 6 rectangles: two 5 x 6"/12 x 15 cm (bottom and top), two 5 x 2"/12 x 5 cm (short sides), two 6 x 2"/15 x 5 cm (long sides), using 8" (20 cm) chef's knife. Place scraps in 2-cup (500 mL) measure. Microwave at 50% (Medium) for 1 to 2 minutes, or until coating can be stirred smooth.

4 Spoon coating into 1-quart (1 L) sealable freezer bag. Squeeze to one corner of bag. Seal bag. Using scissors, snip corner of bag slightly to form writing tip. Place one 5 x 6" (12 x 15 cm) rectangle on wax paper. Pipe coating along edges. Place sides of chest upright along edges of bottom, piping additional coating between edges to secure sides.

5 Place chocolate coating in 2-cup (500 mL) measure. Microwave at 50% (Medium) for 2 to 4 minutes, or until coating can be stirred smooth. Spoon into another 1-quart (1 L) sealable freezer bag. Squeeze to one corner of bag. Seal bag. Using scissors, snip corner of bag slightly to form writing tip. Pipe coating along top edges of chest. Before set, sprinkle edges with colored sugar.

6 Make lid for chest by piping coating around edges of remaining rectangle. Pipe holiday messages or designs on top. Let stand, or chill, until set. Fill chest with candy. Top with lid. Chests are fragile, so handle carefully. Store in cool, dry place away from direct heat.

DECORATED CONE TREES ↑

1 Line a baking sheet with wax paper. Set aside. In 8-cup (2 L) measure, microwave 1 lb. (500 g) white or chocolate-flavored candy coating at 50% (Medium) for 4 to 6 minutes, or until coating can be stirred smooth.

2 Stand 8 sugar cones on prepared baking sheet. Spoon coating over cones, covering outside. Decorate as directed below. Let stand, or chill, until coating is set.

Popcorn and Red Cinnamon Candy Tree: *Attach pieces of popped popcorn and red cinnamon candies by pressing lightly into candy coating. Top with popped kernel of corn.*

Gumdrop Tree: *Attach small colored gumdrop halves randomly over coated tree cone. Top tree with star cut from flattened gumdrop.*

Silver Ball Tree: *Sprinkle silver balls over coated tree cone. Top tree with shoestring licorice bow or with star cut from flattened gumdrop.*

Drizzled Snow-capped Tree: *Coat cones as directed left. Let stand, or chill, until coating is set. Place 1/4 lb. (125 g) candy coating of a contrasting color in 1-cup (250 mL) measure. Microwave at High for 3 to 4 minutes, or until coating can be stirred smooth. Drizzle contrasting coating over each coated tree. Sprinkle with red or green colored sugar.*

FROSTED FRUITY WREATHS

- ¾ lb. (375 g) white candy coating, divided
- 5 cups (1.25 L) frosted fruit-flavored corn puff cereal
- Red or green colored sugar (optional)
- 12 large gumdrops, cut in half lengthwise
- 12 candy-coated plain chocolate pieces

1 dozen wreaths

1 Line 2 baking sheets with wax paper. Set aside. Place ½ lb. (250 g) coating in large mixing bowl. Microwave at 50% (Medium) for 2½ to 5 minutes, or until coating can be stirred smooth. Add cereal. Stir to coat. Spoon about one-twelfth of mixture onto prepared baking sheet. Shape into 3" (8 cm) wreath. Sprinkle with colored sugar. Repeat with remaining mixture, placing 6 wreaths on each prepared baking sheet.

2 Place remaining ¼ lb. (125 g) coating in small mixing bowl. Microwave at 50% (Medium) for 2 to 4 minutes, or until melted, stirring once. Spoon into sealable freezer bag. Squeeze coating to one corner of bag. Seal bag. Using scissors, snip corner of bag slightly to form writing tip. Drizzle all but small amount of coating over wreaths. Use remaining coating to attach 2 gumdrop halves for bow at base of each wreath. Attach 1 candy-coated chocolate piece in center of each bow. Let wreaths stand, or chill, until set. Hang in cool, dry place.

Chow Mein Wreath Cookies:
Follow recipe above, except substitute ½ lb. (250 g) chocolate-flavored candy coating for ½ lb. (250 g) white candy coating, and 5 cups (1.25 L) chow mein noodles for fruit-flavored corn puff cereal. Omit large gumdrops and candy-coated plain chocolate pieces. Decorate with red cinnamon candies for holly berries, and gumdrop leaves, sliced length-wise, for holly leaves.

141

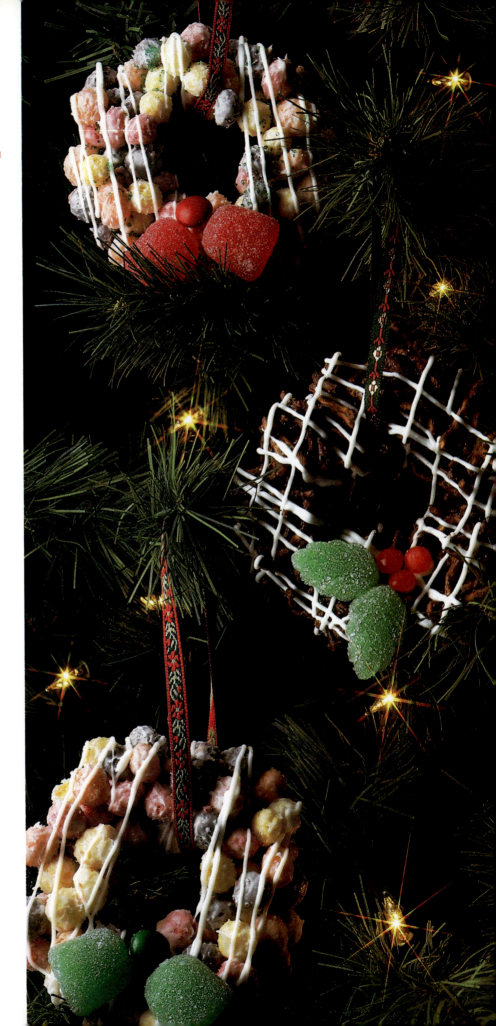

REINDEER
← CENTERPIECE

- 1 lb. (500 g) white candy coating, divided
- 20 homemade gingerbread reindeer cookies (about 2½"/6 cm)
- 10 vanilla wafer cookies
- 1 cup (250 mL) flaked coconut
- 2 pieces (each 38"/95 cm long) red shoestring licorice
- 1 red cinnamon candy

1 Out of heavy cardboard, cut an elongated S-shape base measuring about 24" (60 cm) long and 2½" (6 cm) wide. Cover base with foil. Set aside.

2 Line a baking sheet with wax paper. Melt ¼ lb. (125 g) candy coating as directed in chart, page 125. Spoon a small amount of melted coating onto the back of each of 10 cookies. Place coated-side-up on prepared baking sheet. Top each of these cookies with another and press gently to sandwich. Let stand or chill until set.

3 Use the remaining melted coating to attach each reindeer sandwich to a vanilla wafer cookie. Attach 5 reindeer front-hooves-down, and 5, hind-hooves-down. Hold each reindeer sandwich upright on wafer cookie until coating is set. (This allows reindeer to stand upright.)

4 In a medium mixing bowl, melt remaining ¾ lb. (375 g) coating as directed in chart, page 125. Spoon evenly over foil-covered base. Stand reindeer cookies end to end on base. Sprinkle base with coconut. Let stand until set.

5 Tie shoestring licorice pieces together in a bow. Tuck under chin of lead reindeer and continue crisscrossing licorice between reindeer. Tie at end to secure. Use coating to attach red cinnamon candy to tip of nose of lead reindeer.

GUMDROP CANDLE WREATH ↑

- ½ lb. (250 g) white candy coating
- 2 pkgs. (10¾ oz./305 g each) large gumdrops, divided
- 6 spearmint gumdrop leaves, cut in half lengthwise

1 wreath

1 Line the base of a 10" (25 cm) removable-bottom angel food cake pan with foil. In small mixing bowl, microwave candy coating at 50% (Medium) for 2½ to 5 minutes, or until coating can be stirred smooth. Reserve 1 tablespoon (15 mL) melted coating in small bowl. Set aside.

2 Pour remaining melted candy coating evenly into bottom of prepared cake pan. Reserve 3 gumdrops. Stand remaining gumdrops upright in melted coating, alternating colors. Let stand, or chill, until set. Remove gumdrop wreath from pan. Remove foil. Slice reserved gumdrops in half crosswise.

3 If necessary, microwave reserved candy coating at 50% (Medium) for 30 to 45 seconds, or until coating can be stirred smooth. Use coating to attach 1 gumdrop slice and 2 leaf slices on wreath. Continue attaching remaining gumdrop and leaf slices. Let wreath stand, or chill, until set. Place 2" (5 cm) candle in center and use as holiday centerpiece. Set in cool, dry place away from direct heat.

PRETZEL CANDY CANE

- 1 lb. (500 g) white candy coating, divided
- 20 large pretzel twists
- Red food color paste*
- Green food color paste*

1 candy cane

1 Line a baking sheet with wax paper. Set aside. In medium mixing bowl, microwave ¾ lb. (375 g) candy coating at 50% (Medium) for 2½ to 5½ minutes, or until coating can be stirred smooth. Dip 7 pretzels, one at a time, in coating. On prepared baking sheet, arrange pretzels end to end in candy cane shape.

2 Dip 6 more pretzels, one at a time, in coating. Arrange dipped pretzels over first layer of pretzels at points where 2 pretzels meet. Dip remaining pretzels, one at a time, in coating, and arrange over a second layer.

3 In small bowl, microwave ⅛ lb. (60 g) coating at 50% (Medium) for 2 to 3 minutes, or until coating can be stirred smooth. Tint lightly with red food color paste. Spoon into 1-quart (1 L) sealable freezer bag. Squeeze to one corner of bag. Seal bag. Using scissors, snip corner of bag slightly to form writing tip. Drizzle coating across candy cane. Repeat with remaining ⅛ lb. (60 g) coating and the green food color paste. Let stand, or chill, until set. Tie with bow. Set in cool, dry place away from direct heat and sunlight.

Food color paste is available at most food specialty stores. Do not use liquid food coloring.

GLAZED NUT WREATH

- 6 cups (1.5 L) mixed nuts in the shell (about 1¾ lbs./875 g)
- 2 tablespoons (25 mL) shortening, divided
- 2 cups (500 mL) sugar
- 1 cup (250 mL) corn syrup
- ½ cup (125 mL) water

1 wreath

NOTE: *Placing nuts in mold requires 2 people and must be done very quickly before the syrup sets. Recipe not recommended for ovens with less than 600 cooking watts.*

1 Place nuts in large mixing bowl. Set aside. Line a 6½-cup (1.5 L) ring mold with foil. Grease foil with 1 tablespoon (15 mL) shortening. Set aside. Grease a 14" (35 cm) sheet of foil with remaining 1 tablespoon (15 mL) shortening. Set aside.

2 Combine remaining ingredients in 8-cup (2 L) measure. Inset microwave candy thermometer. Microwave at High for 15 to 20 minutes, or until thermometer registers 310°F/155°C (hard crack stage, page 148).

3 Remove thermometer. Immediately pour syrup over nuts in bowl, tossing quickly to coat. Spoon evenly into prepared ring mold. With buttered fingers, press lightly to pack nuts into mold. Cool 10 minutes.

4 Unmold nut mixture carefully onto prepared sheet of foil. Press into desired wreath shape. Let stand 24 hours before decorating. Attach bow with wire, if desired. Use as centerpiece, or hang in cool, dry place away from direct heat and sunlight.

GIFTS FROM YOUR KITCHEN

Nothing speaks of caring friendship more personally than a gift from your kitchen. This section includes private-label preserves, distinctive candies and flavored nuts, and fragrant potpourri to scent the winter air. Package your present in a pretty or practical container, such as a champagne glass, a mug, a decorative jar or a basket.

Make decorative labels for gift giving by tracing a cookie cutter on heavy paper, such as plain note cards. Use colored markers to decorate labels. Include instructions for storage. Place on paraffin just after final sealing.

CURRIED PEAR CHUTNEY

- 1 cup (250 mL) packed brown sugar
- ¼ cup (50 mL) cider vinegar
- 1½ teaspoons (7 mL) curry powder
- ½ teaspoon (2 mL) salt
- ½ teaspoon (2 mL) ground cinnamon
- 2 large pears, chopped (about 3 cups/750 mL)
- 1 large orange, peeled and chopped (about 1 cup/250 mL)
- ½ cup (50 mL) chopped green pepper
- ½ cup (125 mL) chopped red pepper
- ½ cup (125 mL) golden raisins
- ½ cup (125 mL) slivered almonds

Two ½-pint (250 mL) jars

1 In 2-quart (2 L) casserole, combine brown sugar, vinegar, curry powder, salt and cinnamon. Microwave at High for 1½ to 3 minutes, or until sugar dissolves, stirring once. Stir in remaining ingredients, except almonds. Microwave at High for 30 to 50 minutes, or until liquid is syrupy and fruit is very tender, stirring 2 or 3 times. Stir in almonds. Cool slightly.

2 Spoon chutney into 2 sterilized ½-pint (250 mL) jars. Cover and refrigerate no longer than 2 weeks. Serve as a condiment with lamb, pork or chicken.

3 For gift giving, decorate jar lids with cloth covers and ribbons. Include decorative labels that list contents, serving and storage instructions.

CARROT RELISH

- 2 cups (500 mL) chopped carrots
- 1 cup (250 mL) chopped cucumber, peeled and seeded
- ¾ cup (175 mL) chopped celery
- ¾ cup (175 mL) sugar
- ¾ cup (175 mL) white vinegar
- ½ cup (125 mL) chopped green pepper
- ½ cup (125 mL) chopped onion
- 2 teaspoons (10 mL) pickling salt
- 2 teaspoons (10 mL) mustard seed
- ½ teaspoon (2 mL) ground ginger
- ¼ teaspoon (1 mL) red pepper sauce
- ⅛ teaspoon (0.5 mL) ground cloves

Three ½-pint (250 mL) jars

1 In 2-quart (2 L) casserole, place all ingredients. Mix well. Cover. Microwave at High for 15 minutes, stirring once or twice. Microwave, uncovered, at High for 20 to 25 minutes longer, or until mixture thickens slightly, stirring twice.

2 Spoon relish into 3 sterilized ½-pint (250 mL) jars. Cover and refrigerate for no longer than 1 month. Serve as a condiment with pork roast, ham, sausages and wieners.

3 For gift giving, decorate jar lids with cloth covers and ribbons. Include decorative labels that list contents, serving and storage instructions.

PINK CHAMPAGNE JELLY

- 2¾ cups (675 mL) pink champagne
- 1 pkg. (3 oz./85 mL) liquid fruit pectin
- ½ teaspoon (2 mL) ground cardamom
- ¼ teaspoon (1 mL) ground allspice
- 3½ cups (875 mL) sugar
- Paraffin wax

Nine 4-oz. (125 mL) glasses

1 In 8-cup (2 L) measure, combine all ingredients, except sugar and paraffin. Microwave at High for 8 to 12 minutes, or until boiling, stirring after every 4 minutes. Boil 1 minute. Gradually stir in sugar until blended.

2 Microwave at High for 3 to 6 minutes, or until mixture returns to a boil, stirring every 2 minutes to prevent boil-over. Boil 1 minute. Skim any foam from top.

3 Pour jelly evenly into each of 9 sterilized, straight-sided 4-oz. (125 mL) champagne glasses to within ½" (1 cm) from top.

4 Melt paraffin conventionally in small saucepan over medium heat. (Paraffin is transparent to microwave energy and cannot be melted in the microwave.) While jelly is hot, cover with ⅛" (3 mm) of paraffin. When jelly is cool, add another ⅛" (3 mm) of paraffin for final sealing. Refrigerate jelly no longer than 1 month.

CASHEW TOFFEE ↑

- 1 cup (250 mL) plus 1 tablespoon (15 mL) butter or margarine, divided
- 1¼ cups (300 mL) chopped cashews, divided
- 2 cups (500 mL) sugar
- 2 tablespoons (25 mL) light corn syrup

- 2 tablespoons (25 mL) water
- ⅛ teaspoon (0.5 mL) cream of tartar
- 1 teaspoon (5 mL) vanilla
- 1 pkg. (12 oz./340 g) vanilla milk chips or semisweet chocolate chips

2½ lbs. (1.25 kg)

1 Line a 15½ x 10½" (40 x 25 cm) jelly roll pan with foil. Grease foil with 1 tablespoon (15 mL) butter. Sprinkle 1 cup (250 mL) cashews in an even layer in prepared pan. Set aside.

2 In an 8-cup (2 L) measure, microwave remaining 1 cup (250 mL) butter at High for 1½ to 2 minutes, or until melted. Stir in sugar, corn syrup, water and cream of tartar. Microwave at High for 4 minutes. Mix well. Insert microwave candy thermometer. Microwave mixture at High for 5½ to 7½ minutes, or until thermometer registers 290°F/143°C (soft crack stage, right). Remove thermometer.

3 Stir in vanilla. Pour slowly and evenly over nuts in pan. Immediately sprinkle with vanilla chips. Let stand about 1 minute. Spread chips over toffee mixture. Sprinkle with remaining ¼ cup (50 mL) cashews. Cool completely. Break into pieces. Store in airtight container.

4 For gift giving, place toffee in clear glass candy dish, or arrange on glass plate. Cover with plastic wrap. Decorate with ribbons. Include a decorative label that lists contents.

NOTE: *Recipe not recommended for ovens with less than 600 cooking watts.*

HOW TO TEST CANDY FOR DONENESS

If you don't have a microwave-safe candy thermometer, use cold water test to judge doneness. Fill a cup with very cold water. Drop about ½ teaspoon (2 mL) of mixture into the cup, and let stand for a few seconds. Then test syrup with your fingers.

Soft Crack Stage: *Syrup separates into hard* but not *brittle threads (pictured).*

Hard Crack Stage: *Syrup separates in hard* and *brittle threads.*

FILBERT
← BRITTLE

- 2 tablespoons (25 mL) butter or margarine, divided
- ½ cup (125 mL) granulated sugar
- ½ cup (125 mL) packed brown sugar
- ½ cup (125 mL) light corn syrup
- Pinch of salt
- ¾ cup (175 mL) chopped filberts
- 2 teaspoons (10 mL) lemon extract
- 1 teaspoon (5 mL) baking soda

1 lb. (500 g)

1 Line a baking sheet with foil. Grease foil with 1 tablespoon (15 mL) butter. Set aside. In 8-cup (2 L) measure, combine sugars, corn syrup and salt. Mix well. Microwave at High for 5 minutes. Stir in filberts.

2 Insert microwave candy thermometer. Microwave at High for 3½ to 6 minutes, or until thermometer registers 300°F/150°C (hard crack stage, left), stirring every 2 minutes. Remove thermometer. Quickly stir in remaining 1 tablespoon (15 mL) butter, the lemon extract and baking soda until mixture is light and foamy.

3 Spread to ¼" (5 mm) thickness on prepared baking sheet. Cool completely. Break into pieces. Store in airtight container.

4 For gift giving, arrange brittle in a brandy snifter or clear glass canister. Cover with plastic wrap. Decorate with ribbons. Include a decorative label that lists contents.

Peanut Brittle: *Follow recipe above, except substitute 1 cup (250 mL) shelled raw peanuts for filberts, and 1½ teaspoons (7 mL) vanilla for lemon extract. Microwave as directed above. After stirring in peanuts, microwave at High for 5 to 10 minutes, or until thermometer registers 300°F/150°C, stirring every 2 minutes. Continue as directed.*

MINT SWIRL FUDGE ↑

- 1 tablespoon (15 mL) shortening
- 1 pkg. (3 oz./85 g) cream cheese
- 1 can (14 oz./398 mL) sweetened condensed milk, divided
- ¼ teaspoon (1 mL) mint extract
- 1 to 2 drops green food coloring
- 3 pkgs. (6 oz./170 g each) semisweet chocolate chips
- 1 tablespoon (15 mL) butter or margarine
- ½ teaspoon (2 mL) vanilla
- Green colored sugar

2¼ lbs. (1.125 kg)

1 Line a 9" (23 cm) pie plate with foil. Grease with shortening. Set aside. In medium mixing bowl, microwave cream cheese at High for 15 to 30 seconds, or until softened. Add 2 tablespoons (25 mL) milk, the mint extract and food coloring. Beat at low speed of electric mixer until smooth. Set aside.

2 In an 8-cup (2 L) measure, combine remaining milk, the chocolate chips and butter. Microwave at 50% (Medium) for 2 to 3½ minutes, or until mixture is glossy and can be stirred smooth, stirring twice. Stir in vanilla.

3 Pour into prepared pie plate. Smooth with spatula. Drop cream cheese mixture by spoonfuls over chocolate mixture. Use spatula to swirl decoratively into chocolate. Sprinkle with sugar. Chill until firm. Cut into squares. Store in cool, dry place.

4 For gift giving, leave fudge in pie plate. Cover with plastic wrap. Decorate with ribbons. Include decorative label that lists contents and storage instructions.

RASPBERRY TEA MIX

- 1¼ cups (300 mL) sugar
- 1 cup (250 mL) instant unsweetened tea
- 2 pkgs. (0.17 oz./6 g each) raspberry-flavored unsweetened soft drink mix

For one serving:

- 1 cup (250 mL) hot water
- 2 to 3 tablespoons (25 to 50 mL) tea mix

16 servings

HOW TO GIFT WRAP RASPBERRY TEA MIX

1 Combine all tea mix ingredients in medium mixing bowl. Store in airtight container no longer than 6 months.

2 Place hot water in large mug for 1 serving. Microwave at High for 1 to 2 minutes, or until very hot. Stir in tea mix.

Strawberry Tea Mix: *Follow recipe above, except substitute strawberry-flavored unsweetened soft drink mix for raspberry-flavored unsweetened soft drink mix.*

1 Line 8 to 12-oz. (250 to 375 mL) mugs with small plastic food-storage bags for gift giving. Fill each bag with tea mix. Tie ribbon at top of bag to close.

2 Decorate handle of mug with bow, and attach old-fashioned candy sticks for stirrers. Include decorative label that lists contents, serving and storage instructions.

CARNIVAL DRINK MIX →

- 2½ cups (625 mL) instant nonfat dry milk powder
- 2 cups (500 mL) multicolored miniature marshmallows
- 1 cup (250 mL) strawberry-flavored mix for milk
- ½ cup (125 mL) powdered sugar
- ⅓ cup (75 mL) buttermilk powder
- ⅓ cup (75 mL) powdered nondairy creamer

For one serving:

- ¾ cup (175 mL) hot water
- ⅓ cup (75 mL) drink mix

16 servings

1 In medium mixing bowl, combine all drink mix ingredients. Mix well. Store in airtight container no longer than 6 months.

2 For 1 serving, place hot water in large mug. Microwave at High for 1 to 2 minutes, or until very hot. Stir in drink mix.

3 For gift giving, place drink mix in clear glass canisters. Decorate canisters with ribbons. Include decorative label that lists contents, serving and storage instructions.

Hot Chocolate Malted: *Follow recipe above, except substitute plain miniature marshmallows for multi-colored marshmallows, chocolate-flavored mix for strawberry-flavored mix, and instant malted milk powder for buttermilk powder.*

CINNAMON COCOA COFFEE

- 2 cups (500 mL) sugar
- 1½ cups (375 mL) instant coffee crystals
- 1 cup (250 mL) powdered nondairy creamer
- ½ cup (125 mL) cocoa
- ½ teaspoon (2 mL) ground cinnamon

For one serving:

- 1 cup (250 mL) hot water
- 2 to 3 tablespoons (25 to 50 mL) coffee mix

40 servings

1 In medium mixing bowl, combine all coffee mix ingredients. Store in airtight container no longer than 6 months.

2 For 1 serving, place hot water in large mug. Microwave at High for 1 to 2 minutes, or until very hot. Stir in coffee mix.

3 For gift giving, place coffee mix in clear glass canisters. Decorate canisters with ribbons. Include decorative label that lists contents, serving and storage instructions.

ELEGANT
RASPBERRY SAUCE

- 2 pkgs. (12 oz./340 g each) unsweetened frozen red raspberries
- 1 large orange
- 1 cup (250 mL) sugar
- ¾ cup (175 mL) light corn syrup
- ¼ cup (50 mL) black raspberry liqueur

   Two 1-pint (500 mL) jars

1 Microwave raspberries in 8-cup (2 L) measure at High for 5 to 8 minutes, or until defrosted, stirring gently once. Set aside.

2 Cut long strips (or zest) from orange, using sharp knife and being careful not to remove white membrane with peel. Cut strips into 1" (2.5 cm) lengths. Reserve orange for future use.

3 Place orange peel, sugar and corn syrup in 4-cup (1 L) measure. Mix well. Microwave at High for 4 to 5 minutes, or just until sugar mixture boils, stirring once. Add sugar mixture and liqueur to berries. Stir gently until combined.

4 Pour into 2 sterilized 1-pint (500 mL) jars. Cover and refrigerate no longer than 1 month. Serve over fresh fruit, ice cream or pound cake.

5 Decorate jar lids with cloth covers and ribbons for gift giving. Include decorative labels that list contents, serving and storage instructions.

RUM-BUTTERSCOTCH SAUCE ↑

- 1½ cups (375 mL) packed brown sugar
- ½ cup (125 mL) butter or margarine
- ¼ cup (50 mL) dark corn syrup
- 1½ cups (375 mL) half-and-half
- 2 teaspoons (10 mL) imitation rum extract

Three ½-pint (250 mL) jars

1 In 2-quart (2 L) casserole, combine brown sugar, butter and corn syrup. Microwave at High for 3 to 6 minutes, or until brown sugar dissolves and mixture boils, stirring after every minute. Blend in remaining ingredients.

2 Pour sauce into 3 sterilized ½-pint (250 mL) jars. Cover and refrigerate no longer than 1 month. To reheat 1 cup (250 mL) of sauce, remove lid from jar. Microwave at High for 1 to 1½ minutes, or until mixture is warm and can be stirred smooth, stirring every 30 seconds. Serve over ice cream or pound cake.

3 For gift giving, decorate jar lids with cloth covers and ribbons. Include decorative labels that list contents, serving, heating and storage instructions.

GINGER ORIENTAL SAUCE

- ½ cup (125 mL) finely chopped green pepper
- 2 teaspoons (10 mL) grated fresh gingerroot
- 2 tablespoons (25 mL) vegetable oil
- 1 cup (250 mL) apricot preserves
- 1 cup (250 mL) catsup
- ⅓ cup (75 mL) vinegar
- 2 tablespoons (25 mL) soy sauce
- 2 teaspoons (10 mL) sesame oil

Three ½-pint (250 mL) jars

1 In 2-quart (2 L) casserole, combine green pepper, gingerroot and vegetable oil. Microwave at High for 2 to 3½ minutes, or until pepper is tender, stirring once. Stir in remaining ingredients. Microwave at High for 9 to 12 minutes, or until sauce begins to thicken, stirring twice.

2 Pour sauce into 3 sterilized ½-pint (250 mL) jars. Cover and refrigerate no longer than 1 month. Serve with ribs, chicken or fish.

3 For gift giving, decorate jar lids with cloth covers and ribbons. Include decorative labels that list contents, serving, heating and storage instructions.

MINT CHOCOLATE SAUCE ↑

- 1 cup (250 mL) semisweet chocolate chips
- ¼ cup (50 mL) butter or margarine
- 2 tablespoons (25 mL) light corn syrup
- 1 cup (250 mL) whipping cream
- ½ cup (125 mL) finely crushed peppermint candy

Two ½-pint (250 mL) jars

1 In 2-quart (2 L) casserole, combine chocolate chips, butter and corn syrup. Microwave at 50% (Medium) for 4 to 5 minutes, or until mixture melts, stirring 2 or 3 times. Blend in whipping cream, using whisk. Microwave at High for 1 minute. Stir in candy.

2 Pour into 2 sterilized ½-pint (250 mL) jars. Cover and refrigerate no longer than 1 month. To reheat 1 cup (250 mL) of sauce, remove lid from jar. Microwave at High for 1 to 1½ minutes, or until mixture is warm and can be stirred smooth, stirring every 30 seconds. Serve over ice cream or cheesecake.

3 For gift giving, decorate jar lids with cloth covers and ribbons. Include decorative labels that list contents, serving, heating and storage instructions.

SHERRIED MIXED NUTS ↑

- ¼ cup (50 mL) dry sherry
- 2 tablespoons (25 mL) light corn syrup
- ¼ teaspoon (1 mL) ground allspice
- 1 can (12 oz./340 g) salted mixed nuts

    ¾ lb. (375 g)

1 Line a baking sheet with foil. Set aside. In medium mixing bowl, combine all ingredients, except nuts. Mix well. Add nuts. Toss to coat. Spoon evenly into 10" (25 cm) pie plate. Microwave at High for 6½ to 8½ minutes, or until liquid is absorbed and nuts are glazed, stirring every 2 minutes.

2 Spread nuts on prepared baking sheet. Cool completely. Cover and store in cool, dry place no longer than 2 weeks.

3 For gift giving, place nuts in clear glass container or nut dish. Cover nut dish with plastic wrap. Decorate with ribbons. Include decorative label that lists contents and storage instructions.

ROSEMARY-FLAVORED WALNUTS ↑

- 1 tablespoon (15 mL) butter or margarine
- 2 teaspoons (10 mL) Worcestershire sauce
- ¾ teaspoon (4 mL) dried rosemary leaves, crushed
- ½ teaspoon (2 mL) lemon pepper seasoning
- 1 pkg. (8 oz./227 g) walnut halves

    ½ lb. (250 g)

1 Line a baking sheet with paper towels. In 9" (23 cm) pie plate, microwave butter at High for 45 seconds to 1 minute, or until melted. Add remaining ingredients, except walnuts. Mix well.

2 Add walnuts, stirring to coat. Microwave at High for 4 to 6 minutes, or until butter is absorbed, stirring every 2 minutes. Spread on prepared baking sheet to cool. Cover and store in cool, dry place no longer than 2 weeks.

3 For gift giving, place nuts in clear glass container or nut dish. Cover nut dish with plastic wrap. Decorate with ribbons. Include decorative label that lists contents and storage instructions.

Cheese Spread:

- 4 slices bacon
- ½ cup (125 mL) butter or margarine, cut into cubes
- 1 pkg. (3 oz./85 g) cream cheese, cut into cubes
- 2 cups (500 mL) finely shredded Cheddar cheese
- 2 cups (500 mL) finely shredded Swiss cheese
- 1 teaspoon (5 mL) caraway seed
- ½ teaspoon (2 mL) onion powder
- Pinch of garlic powder

Snowman:

- 2 pretzel sticks
- 3 capers
- 3 black peppercorns
- 1 whole pimiento
- 1 pimiento-stuffed green olive
- 1 round buttery cracker

Santa's Boot:

- Sliced almonds
- 5 black peppercorns
- Pimiento strips

2 cheese spreads
(about ¾ lb./375 g each)

1 Place bacon on roasting rack. Cover with paper towel. Microwave at High for 3 to 6 minutes, or until brown and crisp. Cool slightly. Crumble and set aside.

2 Combine butter and cream cheese in medium mixing bowl. Microwave at 30% (Medium Low) for 1½ to 2½ minutes, or until softened, stirring once. Stir in remaining cheese spread ingredients. Mix well. Divide mixture in half.

3 Make snowman by dividing one-half of cheese mixture into 3 portions. Shape each portion into ball, making balls for head and upper body slightly smaller than base. Stack balls on serving tray.

4 Make snowman's arms by inserting pretzel sticks into cheese. Use capers for buttons, and peppercorns for eyes and nose. Cut small piece of pimiento for mouth.

5 Cut ½" (1 cm) wide strip of pimiento to make scarf. Trim top and bottom from olive, and use wooden pick to secure olive to cracker for hat. Place on snowman's head. Cover and refrigerate no longer than 1 week.

6 Make Santa's boot by forming remaining half of cheese mixture into boot shape. Trim top of boot with sliced almonds for fur. Use peppercorns and pimiento for laces and bow. Cover and refrigerate no longer than 1 week.

CITRUS-SPICE POTPOURRI ↑

- 1 orange
- 1 lemon
- 1 lime
- ⅓ cup (75 mL) water
- ¼ cup (50 mL) whole cloves
- 2 tablespoons (25 mL) whole allspice
- 3 cinnamon sticks, broken up
- 4 bay leaves, crumbled

1 cup (250 mL)

1 Cut long strips (or zest) from orange, lemon and lime, using sharp knife and being careful not to remove white membrane with peel. Cut strips into 1" (2.5 cm) lengths. Reserve fruit for future use.

2 Place peels in single layer on paper-towel-lined plate. Pour water into 1-cup (250 mL) measure. Place water next to plate in microwave oven. Microwave at High for 4 to 5 minutes, or just until peels begin to dry, tossing with fingers after every minute.

WOODS-SCENT
← POTPOURRI

- ½ cup (125 mL) fresh pine needles
- ¼ cup (50 mL) juniper berries
- 2 tablespoons (25 mL) dried rosemary leaves
- 1 tablespoon (15 mL) celery seed
- 1 tablespoon (15 mL) caraway seed
- 6 bay leaves, crumbled

1 cup (250 mL)

1 In small plastic food-storage bag, combine all ingredients. Secure bag. Shake to mix.

2 For gift giving, place dry potpourri in small plastic food-storage bag. Tie ribbon at top of bag to close. Place in small bowl with handle. Include decorative label that lists contents and instructions for use.

3 To scent room, place 1 cup (250 mL) hot water and 1 tablespoon (15 mL) potpourri in small bowl with handle. Microwave at High for 2 to 3 minutes, or until boiling. Remove from oven. Let potpourri stand. When cool, microwave as directed once or twice more.

3 Remove peels to another paper towel. Air dry for 24 hours. Place dried peels in small plastic food-storage bag. Add remaining potpourri ingredients. Secure bag. Shake to mix.

4 Place dry potpourri in small plastic food-storage bag for gift giving. Tie ribbon at top of bag to close. Place in small bowl with handle. Include decorative label that lists contents and instructions for use.

5 Scent room by placing 1 cup (250 mL) hot water and 1 tablespoon (15 mL) dry potpourri in small bowl with handle. Microwave at High for 2 to 3 minutes, or until boiling. Remove from oven. Let potpourri stand. When cool, microwave as directed once or twice more.

The microwave oven accelerates the drying of fresh flowers. Simply bury the flowers in a drying agent like silica gel, microwave briefly and let stand for 12 hours. Silica gel absorbs moisture while supporting the flower in its natural shape. The gel can be reused several times.

Cut flowers in the early morning or late afternoon. Select fresh, dry blossoms that are not fully opened. Avoid flowers that are already in full bloom or have bruised or wilted petals.

Flowers with vivid colors – red, orange, yellow, blue, purple or deep pink – retain their color best. Dark red flowers may appear black when dried; use them in potpourri. Whites and pastels will turn brown.

After drying, spray flowers with hair spray or acrylic spray coating, available at art supply or craft stores. Silica gel, florists' wire and tape are available at craft shops or florists.

Type of Flower	Number	Dish size	Silica gel	Microwave at High
Carnations, large	2	1½-quart (1.5 L)	6 cups (1.5 L)	2 to 3 minutes
Carnations, small	4	1½-quart (1.5 L)	6 cups (1.5 L)	1½ to 2½ minutes
Chrysanthemums, medium	3	1½-quart (1.5 L)	6 cups (1.5 L)	2 to 2½ minutes
Daffodils	1	2-cup (500 mL) measure	2 cups (500 mL)	2 to 2½ minutes
Daisies, large	2	1½-quart (1.5 L)	4 cups (1 L)	1½ to 2 minutes
Daisies, small	4	1½-quart (1.5 L)	4 cups (1 L)	1½ to 2 minutes
Roses, miniature	4	1½-quart (1.5 L)	6 cups (1.5 L)	2 to 2½ minutes
Tulips	1	2-cup (500 mL) measure	2 cups (500 mL)	2½ to 3 minutes

MICROWAVE DRIED FLOWERS

- Flowers (opposite)
- Scissors
- Silica gel
- Small paintbrush
- Hair spray or acrylic spray coating
- Florists' wire
- Florists' tape
- Silk leaves (optional)

1 Trim stems of selected flowers to within ½" (1 cm) of flower base. Place one-third of silica gel in dish.

2 Arrange flowers, blossoms up, in dish. Carefully sprinkle with remaining silica gel, filling spaces between petals and covering flowers completely.

3 Place dish in microwave. Place ½ cup (125 mL) water in 1-cup (250 mL) measure; set next to dish in oven. Microwave at High, as directed in chart (opposite), or until gel feels very warm, rotating dish once.

4 Let flowers stand in silica gel for 12 hours to complete drying. Carefully pour off silica, and lift out dried flowers. Shake gently to remove excess gel. Use fine-bristled paintbrush to remove any remaining gel.

5 Spray flowers with hair spray for protection. Dry flowers completely. Attach florists' wire to stems of the flowers.

6 Wrap wire with florists' tape. Connect silk leaves to wire stem, if desired, and wrap entire wire with florists' tape.

DRIED FLOWER WREATH ↑

- Assorted dried flowers (page 158)
- Baby's breath
- Very thin florists' wire
- Florists' tape
- 1 twig wreath (available at craft stores)
- Hair spray or acrylic spray coating
- Ribbon (optional)

1 wreath

1 Attach florists' wire to dried flowers and to small bunches of baby's breath. Wrap with florists' tape to secure flower to wire. Thread prepared flowers and baby's breath through wreath, with baby's breath below flowers. Twist wires together and wrap or weave around back of wreath.

2 Spray dried flowers with hair spray or acrylic spray. Let dry. Decorate with ribbon. Hang wreath with wire.

DRIED FLOWER BASKET

- Assorted dried flowers (page 158)
- Florists' wire
- Florists' tape
- Floral foam
- Decorative basket
- Hair spray or acrylic spray coating

1 Attach wire to stems of dried flowers with florists' tape. Cut floral foam to fit bottom of decorative basket. Arrange flowers by inserting taped stems into foam.

2 Spray dried flowers with hair spray. Let dry.

POTPOURRI

- 1 large jar with lid
- 3 or 4 small decorative jars or containers, with covers
- ½ cup (125 mL) non-iodized salt
- 1 tablespoon (15 mL) whole allspice
- 1 tablespoon (15 mL) juniper berries
- 1 tablespoon (15 mL) dried grated orange peel
- 4 cinnamon sticks, broken up
- 4 cups (1 L) dried flower petals (use mostly roses; page 158)
- 1 bottle (¼ oz./7 mL) lavender and rose-scented oil (alternative oils available at craft or drugstores)

1 In small mixing bowl, combine salt, allspice, cloves, juniper berries, orange peel and cinnamon sticks. Mix well. Set aside. Layer 2 cups (500 mL) flower petals in large jar. Sprinkle with half the lavender and rose oil. Spoon salt mixture over petals. Layer remaining flower petals over salt mixture and sprinkle with remaining oil. Close jar tightly. Shake gently to mix.

2 Label jar with date. Let potpourri age in covered jar for 4 to 6 weeks, shaking jar once a week. Divide mixture between decorative jars or containers.

3 Let open jar of potpourri stand for 1 to 2 hours, to scent room as desired. Yields about 2½ cups (625 mL).

TIPS: *Display and store dried flowers by layering loosely in a decorative, see-through jar. Cover jar tightly.*

For scented sachet, cut 6" (15 cm) squares of thin cotton fabric and place about 2 teaspoons (10 mL) potpourri in center of each. Bring sides up and tie tightly with narrow ribbon, enclosing potpourri. Use to scent closets or drawers.

161

DOUGH ART

Create distinctive gift tags or decorate an old-fashioned family Christmas tree with ornaments made in the microwave.

ORNAMENT DOUGH

- 3 cups (750 mL) all-purpose flour
- ¾ cup (175 mL) salt
- ¾ teaspoon (4 mL) powdered alum
- 1¼ cups (300 mL) water

1 In large mixing bowl, combine flour, salt and alum. Mix well. Add water. Mix well and shape dough into ball. Knead dough on lightly floured surface for about 5 minutes, or until smooth. If dough is too stiff, sprinkle with water; if too moist, add flour. Work with small portions at a time. Store excess dough in airtight container.

2 Form shapes as desired (pages 164 and 165). Decorate cutouts with bits of dough in the shape of leaves or bows. Use a drinking straw to cut hole, ¼" (5 mm) or larger, near top of cutout for hanging or for tying to gift. Microwave as directed, page 164, for the amount of time specified in the chart, page 165.

1 Spray 10" (25 cm) pie plate with vegetable cooking spray. Prepare ornament dough, page 162. Place ornaments in prepared pie plate.

2 Microwave at 30% (Medium Low) as directed in chart opposite, or until tops of ornaments feel dry, rotating plate and checking ornaments every 2 minutes.

3 Remove ornaments to cooling rack. Set aside for 24 hours to complete drying. Paint with water colors or acrylic colors.

COOKIE CUTTER ORNAMENTS

1 Prepare dough as directed, page 162. Roll dough on lightly floured surface to ¼" (5 mm) thickness. Dip edges of cutters into vegetable oil. Cut out shapes with 2½ to 4" (6 to 10 cm) cookie cutters or with pastry cutter.

2 Decorate cutouts or connect several shapes to make one large 5" (12 cm) ornament. To connect pieces of dough, moisten with water-dipped paintbrush. Yields forty 2½ to 3" (6 to 8 cm) ornaments or twenty-four 3½ to 4" (9 to 10 cm) ornaments.

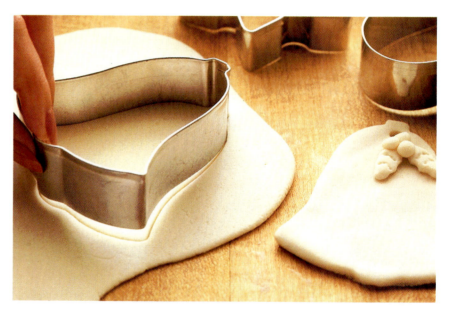

164

MICROWAVE CHART FOR ORNAMENTS

Quantity	Diameter	Microwave Time 30% (Medium High)
4 cookie cutter ornaments	2½-3" (6 to 8 cm)	5-10 min.
3 cookie cutter ornaments	3½-4" (9 to 10 cm)	5-10 min.
1 cookie cutter ornament	5" (12 cm)	5-10 min.
2 twisted or braided ornaments		6-10 min.
2 bear ornaments		6-8 min.

TEDDY BEAR ORNAMENTS

1 Prepare dough as directed, page 162. Roll dough on lightly floured surface to ¼" (5 mm) thickness. Dip edges of cutters into vegetable oil. Cut one 3" (8 cm) circle for body, one 2" (5 cm) circle for head, and seven 1" (2.5 cm) circles for 4 paws, 2 ears and 1 muzzle.

2 Hand-shape fifteen ¼" (5 mm) circles to use for 12 toes on paws, and for eyes and nose. Yields 16 ornaments.

TWISTED OR BRAIDED ORNAMENTS

1 Prepare dough as directed, page 162. Hand-roll small pieces of dough into ¼" (5 mm) round ropes, each about 8" (20 cm) long. Make 2 ropes for twisting, or 3 ropes for braiding.

2 Moisten one end of each rope, and pinch moistened ends together. Twist or braid. Shape into wreath or candy cane. Decorate with small pieces of dough shaped into holly leaves, berries or bows. Yields 16 ornaments.

MICROWAVED AROMATIC DOUGH ORNAMENTS

- Floured board
- Rolling pin
- Cookie cutters
- Whole allspice and cloves
- Small paintbrush
- Garlic press
- Wooden picks

- Drinking straw
- Vegetable cooking spray
- 1 pie plate (10"/25 cm)

Dough:
- 2¾ cups (675 mL) all-purpose flour
- ¾ cup (175 mL) salt

- ¼ cup (50 mL) ground cinnamon
- 1 tablespoon (15 mL) ground allspice
- 1 tablespoon (15 mL) ground cloves
- ¾ teaspoon (4 mL) powdered alum
- 1¼ cups (300 mL) water

1 Combine flour, salt, cinnamon, allspice, cloves and alum in medium mixing bowl. Mix well. Add water. Mix well to form dough. Shape dough into ball. Knead on lightly floured board for about 5 minutes, or until dough is smooth. (If too stiff, sprinkle with additional water; if too moist, add flour.)

2 Work with small portions of dough at a time. Roll dough to ¼" (5 mm) thickness. Cut out shapes with 2½ to 4" (6 to 10 cm) cookie cutters. Decorate tops of cutouts with cloves and allspice, or with bits of dough (moisten dough with water-dipped paintbrush and join to cutout). Store remaining dough in plastic bag.

3 Push small amounts of dough through garlic press for textured "hair" or "fur" for animal or people shapes, or use a wooden pick to texture surface. Using a drinking straw, cut hole (at least ⅜"/8 mm) near top of cutout for hanging.

4 Spray 10" (25 cm) pie plate with vegetable cooking spray. Place four 2½ to 3" (6 to 8 cm), or three 3½ to 4" (9 to 10 cm) cutouts in prepared pie plate. Microwave at 30% (Medium Low) for 5 to 8 minutes, or until tops of cutouts feel dry, rotating plate and checking ornaments after every 2 minutes.

5 Remove ornaments to rack and set aside for 24 hours to complete drying. Insert thin ribbon through holes and tie for hanging. If desired, spray decorations lightly with vegetable cooking spray for a glossier appearance.

SPICED WALL
← HANGING

- 5 aromatic dough ornaments (2½"/6 cm; page 167)
- 5 cinnamon sticks
- 1 yard ribbon (⅝ to ¾"/1 to 2 cm)
- Extra ribbon for bow

1 wall hanging

1 From back side of first ornament, thread ribbon through hole and loop over cinnamon stick. Rethread ribbon back through ornament. Continue threading ribbon through ornaments and looping around cinnamon sticks, leaving about 3" (8 cm) between ornaments.

2 On final ornament, leave ribbon hanging 3 or 4" (8 to 10 cm) below for decoration. Cut bottom of ribbon at an angle or with a decorative notch. Tie extra ribbon in bow and secure at top of wall hanging with needle and thread.

MODELING CLAY →

- 1 box (16 oz./454 g) baking soda
- 1 cup (250 mL) cornstarch
- 1¼ cups (300 mL) cold water
- Food coloring (any color)

1 In large mixing bowl, combine soda and cornstarch. In 2-cup (500 mL) measure, combine water and food coloring. Pour colored water over soda mixture. Stir until smooth.

2 Microwave at High for 4 to 8 minutes, or until mixture is stiff but can still be stirred, stirring after every minute. Cover clay with damp towel until cool. Knead until smooth. Store clay in airtight containers or plastic bags.

Delight the youngsters and the young-at-heart with these charming variations on the traditional gingerbread house. Make one building or a whole village. Use your imagination to create your own designs.

VILLAGE BASICS

Graham Cracker Bricks. Cut each whole graham cracker along perforations to yield 4 bricks, using 8" (20 cm) chef's knife. Patterns call for whole bricks, three-quarter bricks, half bricks and quarter bricks. Cut bricks for desired patterns, pages 174, 176 and 178, before melting mortar.

Microwaved Mortar. Melt white candy coating ⅛ lb. (60 g) at a time, because coating hardens as it cools. Melt as directed in chart, page 125. Spoon coating into 1-quart (1 L) sealable freezer bag. Squeeze coating to one corner of bag. Seal bag. Using scissors, snip corner slightly to form writing tip.

(Continued)

Graham Cracker Base. Arrange 10 whole graham crackers on wax-paper-lined baking sheet, ⅛" (3 mm) apart in 2 rows of 5. Pipe mortar between graham crackers. Press together slightly. Let stand until set. Set aside.

1 **Walls & Roof Panels.** Assemble walls and roof panels, as shown in patterns on pages 174, 176 and 178, by placing bricks ⅛" (3 mm) apart on wax-paper-lined baking sheets. Pipe mortar between bricks. Press together slightly. Let stand until set.

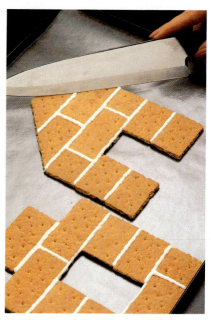

2 Trim tops of end walls as shown in patterns on pages 174, 176 and 178, using a chef's knife. Decorate roof panels by piping mortar designs or attaching multi-colored fruit-flavored gumdrop slices with mortar.

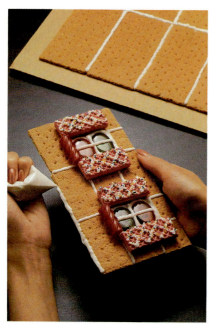

1 **Buildings.** Decorate walls and roof panels before assembling. (See details pages 175, 177 and 179 for decorating ideas.) Place prepared graham cracker base on a piece of sturdy cardboard. Pipe mortar along bottom edge of one side wall. Place on base. Hold in place, or support with heavy object, until set.

2 Pipe mortar along side and base of adjoining wall. Hold in place several minutes until set. Continue with remaining walls. Pipe additional mortar along edges where walls join. Let stand until set.

Roof Supports. Make supports for church and cottage by piping a heavy line of mortar on the inside of each roof panel, the length of supporting wall. Apply about 1½" (4 cm) from bottom for cottage and ½" (1 cm) from bottom for church. Let stand until set.

1 **Attach Roof.** Pipe mortar along top edge and sides of walls. Position decorated roof panels in place, resting piped roof support along top edge of wall. Let stand until set.

2 Pipe mortar along top of roof where panels meet. Attach round peppermint candies, if desired. Let stand until set.

Shrubs & Trees. Use 1 large gumdrop for base. Attach small multicolored gumdrops to base, using colored wooden picks. (Break picks to desired lengths.) Decorate sugar cones as directed, page 140, for trees. Place next to buildings.

1 **Village People.** Use round peppermint candies for faces. Use mortar to attach silver balls for eyes and small pieces of shoestring licorice for mouth. To make hair, press one large gumdrop through a garlic press. Style hair and shape around face. (Hair will be sticky, but hardens when exposed to air.)

2 Cut sugar cone about 2" (5 cm) from pointed end, using serrated knife. Trim pointed end slightly to flatten. Discard large end. Using mortar, attach head to small end of body. Hold in place until mortar begins to set. Allow mortar to set before decorating body.

3 Pipe mortar onto body to make clothing. Before mortar sets, decorate with colored sugar and multicolored shot. Pipe mortar to make arms. Flatten large gumdrops and cut small pieces to make muff, scarf and belt buckle.

173

GRAHAM CRACKER COTTAGE

- 28 whole graham crackers
- About 1½ lbs. (750 g) white candy coating
- Several 1-qt. (1 L) sealable freezer bags
- Multicolored hard candies
- Multicolored fruit-flavored gumdrop slices
- Fruit-flavored bite-size candies

- Red licorice
- Red shoestring licorice
- Red cinnamon candies
- Round peppermint candies
- Green gumdrop wreaths
- Silver balls
- Large multicolored gumdrops
- Small multicolored gumdrops

- Red and green colored sugar
- Cream-filled wafer cookies (2½"/6 cm)
- Multicolored candy-coated licorice pieces
- Multicolored shot

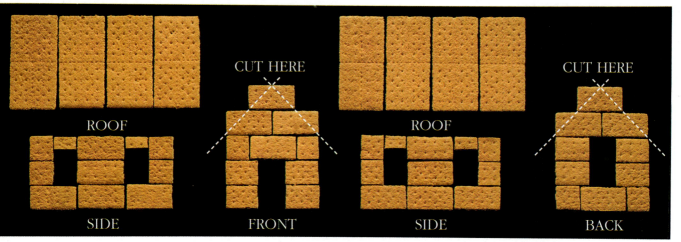

Cottage Pattern. Assemble base, walls and roof panels as directed in Village Basics, pages 172 and 173.

1 Decorating Windows. Fill windows with multicolored hard candies. Pipe mortar around candy pieces to make windowpanes.

2 Pipe mortar over cream-filled wafer cookies in cross-hatch design. Sprinkle with multicolored shot. Use mortar to attach shutters, and attach pieces of licorice for flower boxes.

1 Door. Use 1 brick for door. Use mortar to attach hard round candy to door for wreath. Tie shoestring licorice into bow, and use mortar to attach below wreath. Pipe dot of mortar for handle, and attach silver ball. Let stand until set.

2 Pipe mortar down one long side of door; attach to door frame. Hold in place until mortar begins to set. Let stand until set.

Sidewalks. Pipe mortar in 2" (5 cm) wide strip from front of door to edge of base. Place hard round peppermint candies in mortar for stones. Use red cinnamon candies to fill in between stones.

Icicles. Pipe mortar heavily along edge of roof. Touch with thumb and pull down slightly to form icicles. Let stand until set.

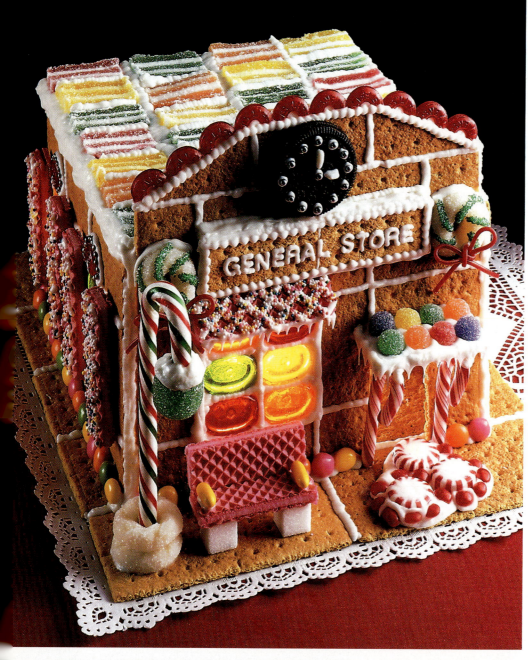

GRAHAM CRACKER GENERAL STORE

What you will need:

- 28 whole graham crackers
- About 1½ lbs. (750 g) white candy coating
- Several 1-qt. (1 L) sealable freezer bags
- Multicolored candy-coated licorice pieces
- Cream-filled wafer cookies (2½"/6 cm)
- Multicolored hard candies
- Red hard candies with hole in center
- Small candy canes
- Large candy cane
- Round peppermint candies
- Sugar cubes
- Red and green gumdrop wreaths
- Small multicolored gumdrops
- Large multicolored gumdrops
- Red shoestring licorice
- Silver balls
- Red cinnamon candies
- Chocolate sandwich cookie
- Multicolored fruit-flavored gumdrop slices

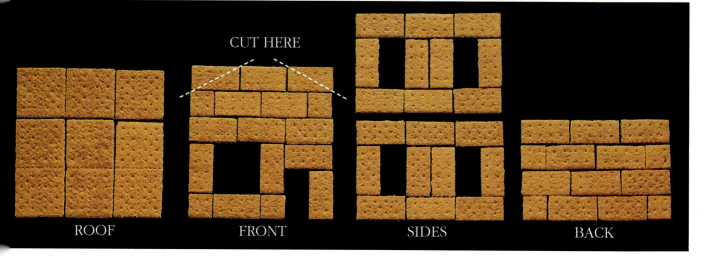

ROOF   FRONT   SIDES   BACK

CUT HERE

Store Pattern. Assemble base, walls and roof panels as directed in Village Basics, pages 172 and 173.

176

Decorating Roof.
Spread mortar in even layer over top of assembled roof. Place multicolored fruit-flavored gumdrop slices evenly on top of roof. Let stand until set. Attach roof as directed, page 173.

1 Awning. Coat the top of 1 brick with mortar. Attach small gumdrop halves, or sprinkle with multicolored sugar. Let stand until set.

2 Pipe mortar heavily along one edge of awning. Position awning in place above door, piped edge against wall. Support with heavy object, or hold until set. Use mortar to attach 1 candy cane support on each side of awning.

1 Lamppost. Cut small hole in top of large gumdrop. Pipe small amount of mortar in hole. Insert curved end of large candy cane in hole. Lay on side until set.

2 Stack 2 or 3 gumdrop wreaths for lamppost base. Insert straight end of candy cane. Attach lamppost to graham cracker base, using mortar. Hold in place until mortar begins to set.

Bench. Use 2 cream-filled wafer cookies for bench. Attach back to seat, using mortar. Attach 2 sugar cubes for legs, and candy-coated licorice pieces for arms. Let stand until set. Place on base in front of store.

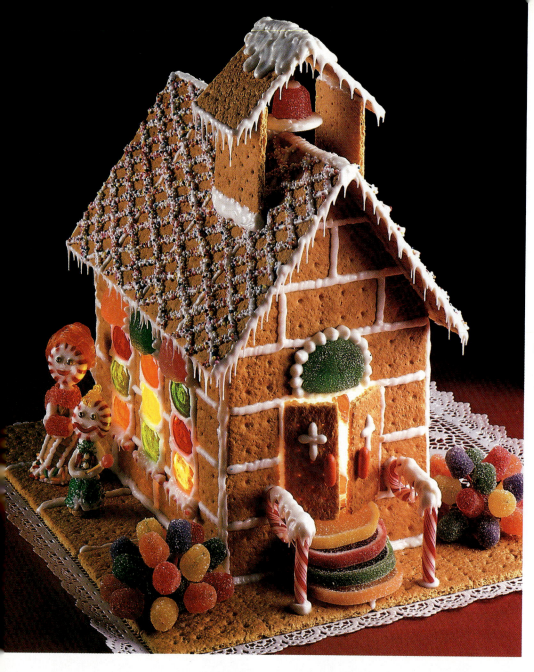

GRAHAM CRACKER CHURCH

- 33 whole graham crackers
- About 1 lb. (500 g) white candy coating
- Several 1-qt. (1 L) sealable freezer bags
- Multicolored candy-coated licorice pieces
- Multicolored hard candies
- Large multicolored gumdrops
- Red shoestring licorice
- Multicolored fruit-flavored gumdrop slices
- Small candy canes
- Round peppermint candies
- Multicolored shot
- Round flat gumdrops

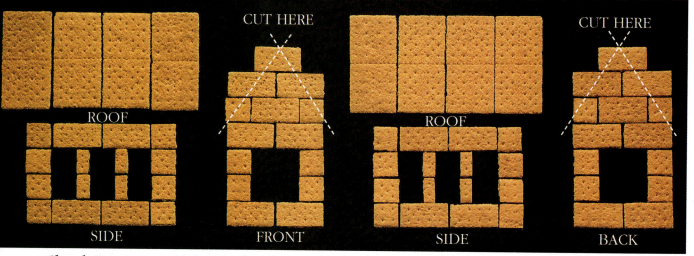

Church Pattern. Assemble base, walls and roof panels as directed in Village Basics, pages 172 and 173.

Stained Glass Windows. Fill windows with multicolored hard candies. Using mortar, fill in spaces around candies. Cut round flat gumdrops in half, and attach one half above each window to make arch. Pipe additional mortar around windows. Use mortar to attach candy cane ledges.

Steps. Overlap 4 multicolored fruit-flavored gumdrop slices slightly. Attach, using small amounts of mortar. Place round peppermint candies under steps for support. Break candy canes to desired lengths for railings. Attach with mortar. Hold in place until set. Attach doors as directed, page 175.

Bell. Cut small hole in top of 1 large gumdrop. Pipe small amount of mortar into hole. Insert one end of a 1½" (4 cm) piece of shoestring licorice for rope. Let stand until set. Pipe mortar around bottom of gumdrop to make bell. Let stand until set.

1 Steeple. Cut 2 whole graham crackers in half crosswise for steeple roof and walls. For steeple roof, hold 2 graham cracker halves at right angle.

2 Pipe mortar along edge where crackers join. While mortar is still wet, insert rope end of bell in roof seam. Support with heavy object, or hold in place until set.

3 Attach walls with mortar; hold in place until set. Attach steeple with mortar to roof. Hold in place until set. Pipe mortar around roof edges and pull to make icicles.

179

TURKEY DINNER

For a large gathering, roast a whole bone-in turkey conventionally and microwave the side dishes. Much of the preparation can be done ahead to reduce last-minute fuss.

To serve a smaller group, microwave a boneless turkey. Although it is possible to microwave a bone-in turkey weighing under 11 pounds (5 kg), the boneless turkey requires less attention, is easier to carve and has no waste.

If you are serving wild turkey as your entrée, omit the turkey and dressing recipes below and follow the recipe for Roast Wild Turkey on pages 202-203.

Turkey
page 184
or
***Boneless Herb-roasted
Turkey***
page 184

Dressing
pages 234-235

Cranberry Waldorf Salad
page 247

***Mashed Potatoes
with Turkey Gravy***
pages 218, 185

***Creamy Tarragon Peas &
Onions in Crispy Toast Cups***
page 215

Rolls, Butter, Relishes

Orange Pumpkin Pie
page 257

TURKEY

- 16 to 20-lb. (7 to 9 kg) whole turkey, defrosted
- Salt and pepper

- 2 tablespoons to ¼ cup (25 to 50 mL) butter or margarine

16 to 20 servings

1 Heat conventional oven to 325°F/160°C. Rinse turkey and pat dry with paper towel. Sprinkle cavity lightly with salt and pepper. Secure legs together with string. Tuck wing tips under. Place turkey in large roasting pan.

2 Place butter in 1-cup (250 mL) measure. Microwave at High for 45 seconds to 1½ minutes, or until melted. Brush turkey with butter. Sprinkle outside of turkey with salt and pepper. Insert meat thermometer in thigh; cover with foil.

3 Estimate total cooking time at 20 to 30 minutes per pound (45 to 65 minutes per kilogram). Bake until internal temperature in inner thigh registers 185°F/85°C. During last 30 minutes, remove foil. Let stand, tented with foil, for 15 to 20 minutes before carving. Reserve drippings for gravy (opposite).

BONELESS HERB-ROASTED TURKEY

- 5 to 6-lb. (2.5 to 3 kg) boneless whole turkey
- 3 cloves garlic, each cut into quarters

- ¾ teaspoon (4 mL) dried marjoram leaves
- ¾ teaspoon (4 mL) dried rosemary leaves

- ¾ teaspoon (4 mL) dried sage leaves
- ¼ teaspoon (1 mL) pepper

8 to 10 servings

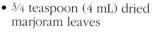

1 Cut twelve 1" (2.5 cm) slits in turkey. Insert 1 garlic piece in each slit. In small bowl, combine remaining ingredients. Sprinkle evenly over turkey.

2 Place turkey in oven cooking bag. Secure bag loosely with nylon tie or string. Place bag in 10" (3 L) square casserole. Insert microwave meat thermometer. Microwave at High for 10 minutes.

3 Microwave at 70% (Medium High) for 45 minutes to 1¼ hours longer, or until internal temperature registers 185°F/85°C in several places, turning turkey over every 30 minutes. Let stand in bag for 15 to 20 minutes before carving. Reserve drippings for gravy (opposite).

TURKEY GRAVY

- 2 cups (500 mL) reserved drippings
- ¼ cup (50 mL) all-purpose flour
- ¼ teaspoon (1 mL) salt
- Pinch of pepper

2 cups (500 mL)

1 Strain drippings into 4-cup (1 L) measure. Add water or chicken broth, if necessary, to equal 2 cups (500 mL).

2 Place remaining ingredients in small mixing bowl. Add small amount of drippings to flour mixture. Stir until mixture is smooth. Add back to remaining drippings, stirring with whisk until smooth.

3 Microwave at High for 6 to 8 minutes, or until mixture thickens and bubbles, stirring 2 or 3 times.

Roast the traditional Christmas goose. While the goose roasts, microwave the Crunchy-topped Twice-baked Potatoes. Whole Wheat Fruit Dressing complements the rich taste of goose, and Hot Cabbage-Apple Slaw garnishes the platter.

If you are serving wild goose as your entrée, omit the goose recipe below and follow the recipe for Roast Goose with Baked Apples on page 207.

ROAST GOOSE

- 6 to 8-lb. (3 to 4 kg) whole goose   • Salt and pepper

6 to 8 servings

1 Heat conventional oven to 325°F/160°C. Rinse goose and pat dry with paper towel. Sprinkle cavity lightly with salt and pepper. Secure legs together with string. Tuck wing tips under. Place breast-side-up on rack in large roasting pan.

2 Sprinkle outside of goose with salt and pepper. Estimate total cooking time at 20 to 25 minutes per pound (45 to 55 minutes per kilogram). Roast until legs move freely and juices run clear, basting frequently with drippings. Drain and discard excess fat during roasting.

CORNISH HEN DINNER

The festive Cornish game hen is ideal for small holiday dinners that serve two to four people. Microwave or bake game hens conventionally. Serve them on a bed of Cranberry Wild Rice for a distinctive presentation of the traditional holiday accompaniments.

189

RED CURRANT-GLAZED CORNISH GAME HENS

- ¼ cup (50 mL) red currant jelly
- 1 tablespoon (15 mL) dry sherry
- Pinch of ground cinnamon
- 2 Cornish game hens (18 oz./500 g each)
- ¼ teaspoon (1 mL) salt
- Pinch of pepper

2 servings

Cornish Game Hens for Four:
Follow recipe above, except double all ingredients. Bake conventionally (opposite), or microwave as directed (opposite), except microwave at High for 22 to 32 minutes, rearranging hens twice.

1 Red Currant Glaze. Combine jelly, sherry and cinnamon in 1-cup (250 mL) measure. Mix well.

2 Microwave at High for 45 seconds to 1½ minutes, or until jelly melts, stirring once. Set aside.

1 Preparing Cornish Game Hens. Remove giblets. Rinse hen cavities with cold water. Pat dry with paper towel.

2 Sprinkle cavities with salt and pepper. Secure legs together with string.

1 **Baking Glazed Cornish Game Hens Conventionally.** Heat conventional oven to 350°F/180°C. Place hens breast-side-up on rack in large roasting pan.

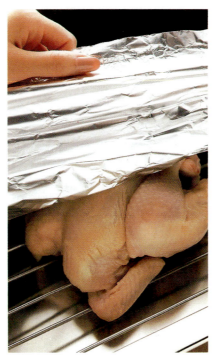

2 Cover loosely with foil. Bake for 1 hour. Prepare glaze (opposite).

3 Brush hens with glaze. Roast, uncovered, for 30 minutes, or until golden brown.

1 **Microwaving Glazed Cornish Game Hens.** Arrange hens breast-side-up on roasting rack. Set aside. Prepare glaze (opposite). Brush hens with one-half of the glaze.

2 Cover hens with wax paper or microwave-safe plastic wrap. Microwave at High for 12 to 17 minutes, or until legs move freely and juices run clear, rearranging hens once and brushing with remaining glaze once.

3 Let hens stand, tented with foil, for 5 minutes.

Use the microwave oven to prepare ham for eight to ten people. When microwaved, a small boneless ham will be juicy. It is easier to roast a large ham conventionally when serving more than ten people.

Tangy Mustard-glazed Ham
page 193

Festive Melon Ball Mold
page 249

Candied Sweet Potatoes
page 221

Holiday Potato Scallop
page 218

Rolls, Butter, Relishes

Mincemeat Parfaits
page 263

TANGY MUSTARD-GLAZED HAM

Conventionally Roasted:

- 1 cup (250 mL) packed brown sugar
- ¼ cup (50 mL) dry mustard
- ¼ cup (50 mL) apple or orange juice
- 8 to 10-lb. (4 to 5 kg) fully cooked boneless whole ham
- Whole cloves

16 to 20 servings

Microwaved:

- ½ cup (125 mL) packed brown sugar
- 2 tablespoons (25 mL) dry mustard
- 2 tablespoons (25 mL) apple or orange juice
- 4 to 5-lb. (2 to 2.5 kg) fully cooked boneless whole ham
- Whole cloves

8 to 10 servings

Scoring & Spicing Ham. Score top of ham in 1" (2.5 cm) diamond pattern, cutting ¼" (5 mm) deep. Insert 1 clove in center of each diamond.

In small mixing bowl, combine all ingredients, except ham and cloves. Mix well. Set aside. Score and spice ham (right). Follow instructions for appropriate cooking method.

1 **Roasting Glazed Ham Conventionally.** Prepare glaze (above). Set aside. Heat conventional oven to 325°F/160°C. Insert meat thermometer. Estimate total cooking time at 10 to 15 minutes per pound (25 to 35 minutes per kilogram). Place ham scored-side-up on rack in large roasting pan.

2 Brush with glaze during last 30 minutes of roasting time. Roast for remaining time, or until internal temperature registers 140°F/60°C, basting with drippings once.

3 Decorate ham with quartered orange slices during last 10 minutes, if desired. Secure orange pieces with cloves in diagonal lines. Baste ham with drippings and return to oven. Let stand for 10 minutes.

1 Microwaving Glazed Ham.
Place ham scored-side-up in 10" (3 L) square casserole. Cover cut surface with microwave-safe plastic wrap. Insert microwave meat thermometer. Microwave at 50% (Medium) for 30 minutes.

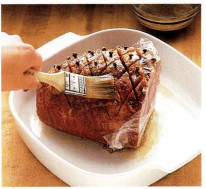

2 Prepare glaze (above). Brush ham with glaze. Microwave at 50% (Medium) for 10 to 15 minutes, or until internal temperature registers 130°F/55°C.

3 Decorate ham with quartered orange slices (left) during last 5 minutes, if desired. Let stand, tented with foil, for 10 minutes before carving. (Internal temperature will rise 5° to 10°F/2° to 5°C during standing time.)

PORK CROWN
ROAST DINNER

Because it requires a lot of attention, a pork crown roast is more suitable for conventional cooking. Roast it conventionally, then fill with a microwaved dressing. Serve with Broccoli & Cauliflower Ball decorated with lemon slices.

Pork Crown Roast with Fruit Glacé
page 195   page 229

Rice & Sausage Dressing
page 234

Sherried Sweet Potatoes
page 220

Broccoli & Cauliflower Ball
page 216

Strawberry-Avocado Salad
page 246

Rolls, Butter, Relishes

Pistachio-Cherry Cheesecake
page 265

PORK CROWN ROAST

- 1½ teaspoons (7 mL) fennel seed, crushed
- 1½ teaspoons (7 mL) onion powder
- 1 teaspoon (5 mL) salt
- 1 teaspoon (5 mL) pepper

- 8-lb. (4 kg) pork crown roast (about 16 ribs)
- Vegetable oil

8 to 10 servings

1 Combine all ingredients, except roast and oil, in small bowl. Rub mixture on all sides of roast. Cover and refrigerate overnight. Heat conventional oven to 325°F/160°C. Place roast on rack in roasting pan. Cover exposed bone ends with foil.

2 Brush roast lightly with oil. Insert meat thermometer. Estimate total cooking time at 20 minutes per pound (45 minutes per kilogram). Roast until internal temperature registers 165°F/72°C. Let stand for 10 minutes before carving.

A boneless pork loin roast can be either cooked conventionally or microwaved. Microwave Hoppin' John, a Southern favorite, up to two days in advance. Garnish serving platter with Apples with Coriander & Orange.

Lightly Seasoned Pork Loin Roast with Cream Gravy
page 197   page 197

Lemony Freezer Slaw
page 247

Apples with Coriander & Orange
page 229

Hoppin' John
page 214

Rolls, Butter, Relishes

Tipsy Cake
page 261

LIGHTLY SEASONED PORK LOIN ROAST

- 1 teaspoon (5 mL) seasoned salt
- ¼ teaspoon (1 mL) paprika

- 3 to 5-lb. (1.5 to 2.5 kg) boneless pork loin roast

6 to 10 servings

1 **Roasting Pork Loin Roast Conventionally.** Heat conventional oven to 325°F/160°C. In small bowl, combine salt and paprika. Rub mixture on all sides of roast. Place roast fattiest-side-up on rack in large roasting pan.

2 Insert meat thermometer. Estimate total cooking time at 30 to 35 minutes per pound (65 to 75 minutes per kilogram). Roast until internal temperature registers 165°F/72°C.

3 Let roast stand for 10 minutes before carving. Strain and reserve drippings for gravy (below).

1 **Microwaving Pork Loin Roast.** Combine salt and paprika in small bowl. Rub mixture on all sides of roast. Place roast fattiest-side-down on roasting rack. Estimate total cooking time at 20 minutes per pound (45 minutes per kilogram).

2 Divide time in half. Microwave at 50% (Medium) for first half of total cooking time. Turn roast fattiest-side-up. Insert microwave meat thermometer in roast.

3 Microwave at 50% (Medium) for second half of cooking time, or until internal temperature registers 160°F/70°C in several places. Let stand, tented with foil, for 10 minutes. Strain and reserve drippings for gravy (below).

CREAM GRAVY

- ⅔ cup (150 mL) reserved drippings
- ⅓ cup (75 mL) half-and-half or milk
- 2 tablespoons (25 mL) all-purpose flour
- Pinch of salt
- Pinch of pepper

1 cup (250 mL)

1 Strain drippings into 2-cup (500 mL) measure. Add water, if necessary, to equal ⅔ cup (150 mL). Add half-and-half. Place remaining ingredients in small mixing bowl. Add small amount of drippings to flour mixture. Stir until mixture is smooth.

2 Add back to remaining drippings, stirring with whisk until smooth. Microwave at High for 3 to 5 minutes, or until mixture thickens and bubbles, stirring twice.

Depending on your timetable or your preference, you may microwave the rolled rib roast or roast it in a conventional oven. The Yorkshire Pudding, which requires conventional baking to develop a crust, can be baked while you microwave the meat, or while a conventionally prepared roast stands.

Peppered Rib Roast
page 199

Holiday Yorkshire Pudding
pages 226-227

Rolls, Butter, Relishes

Date & Cherry Molds
page 248

Brussels Sprouts with Two Mustards
page 214

Strawberry-Amaretto Trifle
page 261

PEPPERED RIB ROAST

- 2 teaspoons (10 mL) coarsely ground black pepper
- ¾ teaspoon (4 mL) garlic powder
- ½ teaspoon (2 mL) salt (optional)
- 4 to 6-lb. (2 to 3 kg) boneless beef rolled rib roast

8 to 12 servings

Conventional Doneness	Internal Temperature
Very rare	120°F/50°C
Medium rare	125°F/52°C
Medium	135°F/57°C
Well	150°F/65°C

1 Roasting Peppered Rib Roast Conventionally. Heat conventional oven to 325°F/160°C. In small bowl, combine all ingredients, except roast. Rub mixture on all sides of roast.

2 Place roast fattiest-side-up on rack in large roasting pan; insert meat thermometer. Estimate total cooking time at 25 to 35 minutes per pound (55 to 75 minutes per kilogram).

3 Roast until internal temperature registers desired doneness (chart above). Let roast stand for 15 to 20 minutes before carving.

1 Microwaving Peppered Rib Roast. Combine all ingredients, except roast, in small bowl. Rub mixture on all sides of roast. Place roast fattiest-side-down on roasting rack. Estimate total cooking time at 12 to 15 minutes per pound (30 to 35 minutes per kilogram). Divide cooking time in half.

2 Microwave at High for 5 minutes. Microwave at 50% (Medium) for remaining part of first half of total cooking time. Turn roast fattiest-side-up. Insert microwave meat thermometer.

3 Microwave at 50% (Medium) for second half of cooking time, or until internal temperature registers 125°F/52°C. Let stand, tented with foil, for 10 minutes before carving. (Internal temperature will rise 5° to 10°F/2° to 5°C during standing time.)

RACK OF LAMB DINNER

For an elegant dinner for two, divide a single rack of lamb, lace it together and microwave. Gingered Acorn Squash can be microwaved in advance and reheated while the roast stands. To serve four, make your roast from two racks and bake it conventionally.

Wine-marinated Rack of Lamb
pages 200-201

Lemon-Vegetable Wreath
page 248

Dijon Potatoes & Chestnuts
page 221

Gingered Acorn Squash
page 213

Rolls, Butter, Relishes

Pecan Tarts
page 258

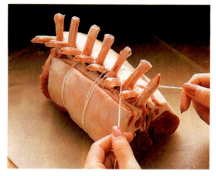

Lacing a Rack of Lamb. Stand racks on backbone edges, with concave sides facing. Press together, interlacing bone ends. Tie racks together with string, weaving around crossed ribs.

WINE-MARINATED RACK OF LAMB

Conventionally Baked:

- 2 single racks of lamb (1¼ lbs./625 g, about 7 to 8 ribs each), rib ends exposed
- 1 cup (250 mL) rosé wine
- 2 cloves garlic, minced
- 1 teaspoon (5 mL) dried rosemary leaves

4 servings

Microwaved:

- 1 single rack of lamb (1¼ lbs./625 g, about 7 to 8 ribs), rib ends exposed, cut in half
- ½ cup (125 mL) rosé wine
- 1 clove garlic, minced
- ½ teaspoon (2 mL) dried rosemary leaves

2 servings

Place tied racks of lamb (above) in oven cooking bag. Add remaining ingredients. Secure bag with nylon tie or string. Refrigerate overnight, turning bag several times.

1 Roasting Rack of Lamb Conventionally. Heat conventional oven to 325°F/160°C. Place lamb on rack in large roasting pan. Insert meat thermometer. Estimate total cooking time at 20 minutes per pound (45 minutes per kilogram).

2 Roast until internal temperature registers desired doneness (chart opposite).

3 Let lamb stand for 10 minutes before carving.

1 Microwaving Rack of Lamb.
Place lamb on roasting rack. Insert microwave meat thermometer. Microwave at 50% (Medium) for 11 to 20 minutes, or until internal temperature registers desired doneness (chart right), rotating lamb ¼ turn 2 or 3 times.

2 Let stand, tented with foil, for 10 minutes before carving. (Internal temperature will rise 5° to 10°F/2° to 5°C during standing time.) Not recommended for ovens with less than 600 cooking watts.

Conventional Doneness	Internal Temperature
Rare	130°F/55°C
Medium	145°F/62°C
Well	160°F/70°C

Microwave Doneness	Internal Temperature
Rare	120°F/50°C
Medium	135°F/57°C
Well	150°F/65°C

ROASTING GAME BIRDS

Birds with the skin on can be roasted in an open pan in a slow (325°F/160°C) oven. Frequent basting helps keep the meat moist and makes the skin crisp and brown. Some cooks prefer roasting in oven cooking bags; the birds baste themselves, the skin browns well, and cleanup is easy.

Skinned birds should be handled differently. Moist cooking methods such as braising or steaming work better than open-pan roasting. If you choose to roast a skinned bird, cover the meat with strips of bacon, or rub it with softened butter and baste it frequently. Small birds like doves, quail, and woodcock can be wrapped in cabbage or grape leaves to retain moisture.

Only young birds should be roasted. Older, tougher ones should be cooked with moist heat.

Insert a standard meat thermometer into the thigh of a turkey or pheasant before roasting, or check near the end of the roasting time with an instant-reading meat thermometer. Birds are done when the thigh temperature reaches 185°F/85°C. If roasting smaller birds, test for doneness by wiggling the leg. When it moves freely, the bird is done. You can also prick the thigh; the juices should run clear. Don't prick too often or it will lose too much juice.

ROAST WILD TURKEY

- 1 tablespoon (15 mL) all-purpose flour
- 1 medium onion, sliced
- 3 stalks celery with leaves, chopped
- 1 wild turkey, skin on, thawed completely
- Salt and pepper
- 1 recipe Apricot Stuffing (page 237) or other dressing (optional)
- Melted butter or margarine
- 2 tablespoons (25 mL) all-purpose flour
- 3 tablespoons (50 mL) cold water

Turkey	Weight Before Stuffing	Approximate Cooking Time*
Stuffed	4-8 lbs. (2 to 4 kg)	2-2¾ hrs.
	8-12 lbs. (4 to 5.5 kg)	2½-3 hrs.
	12-15 lbs. (5.5 to 7 kg)	3-3½ hrs.
	15-20 lbs. (7 to 9 kg)	3½-4 hrs.
	20-25 lbs. (9 to 11.5 kg)	4½-5 hrs.
Unstuffed	4-8 lbs. (2 to 4 kg)	1¾-2¼ hrs.
	8-12 lbs. (4 to 5.5 kg)	2-2½ hrs.
	12-15 lbs. (5.5 to 7 kg)	2½-3 hrs.
	15-20 lbs. (7 to 9 kg)	3-3½ hrs.
	20-25 lbs. (9 to 11.5 kg)	4-4½ hrs.

* Roast at 350°F/180°C to an internal temperature of 185°F/85°C

1 Add 1 tablespoon (15 mL) flour to turkey-size (19 x 23½"/48 x 58 cm) oven cooking bag. Shake to distribute. Place cooking bag in 13 x 9" (3.5 L) roasting pan. Add onion and celery. Heat oven to 350°F/180°C.

2 Season cavity of bird with salt and pepper. Stuff lightly with dressing. Place any extra dressing in buttered casserole. Cover and refrigerate. You can also roast turkey unstuffed.

3 Truss the turkey by tying its legs together over the body cavity with kitchen string. To prevent the wings from drying out during roasting, tuck the tips under the turkey's back.

4 Brush entire turkey with melted butter; season with salt and pepper. Place turkey in oven cooking bag with onion and celery. Close bag with provided nylon tie.

5 Insert meat thermometer into thigh through top of oven cooking bag. Make six ½" (1 cm) slits in top of bag. Roast according to chart. Bake extra dressing during the last 30 minutes.

6 Remove turkey from bag; wait 20 minutes before carving. For gravy: Blend 2 tablespoons (25 mL) flour into water. In saucepan, blend into drippings; cook over medium heat until thickened.

BASQUE PHEASANT ↑

- 2 pheasants, cut up
- ⅓ cup (75 mL) packed brown sugar
- ¾ cup (175 mL) white wine
- ½ cup (125 mL) olive oil
- ½ cup (125 mL) vinegar
- 1 cup (250 mL) pitted medium prunes
- 1 cup (250 mL) pitted medium Spanish green olives
- ¼ cup (50 mL) capers, with liquid
- 3 cloves garlic, minced
- 2 bay leaves
- 2 tablespoons (25 mL) snipped fresh parsley
- 2 tablespoons (25 mL) dried basil leaves

4 to 6 servings

1 In 13 x 9" (3.5 L) baking dish, arrange pheasant pieces in single layer. In medium bowl, combine brown sugar, wine, oil and vinegar. Stir to mix. Add remaining ingredients. Stir to combine.

2 Pour mixture over pheasant pieces. Cover baking dish with plastic wrap. Refrigerate at least 6 hours or overnight, turning pheasant pieces twice.

3 Heat oven to 350°F/180°C. Remove plastic wrap from pan. Bake until pheasant is tender, about 1 hour, turning once. Transfer pheasant, olives and prunes to platter with slotted spoon, if desired.

PHEASANT IN CREAMY MUSHROOM SAUCE

- 1 can (10¾ oz./284 mL) condensed cream of mushroom soup
- ½ cup (125 mL) dairy sour cream
- ¼ cup (50 mL) milk
- 2 tablespoons (25 mL) sherry (optional)
- ½ cup (125 mL) all-purpose flour
- 1 teaspoon (5 mL) salt
- ¼ teaspoon (1 mL) pepper
- 2 pheasants, cut up
- ¼ cup (50 mL) vegetable oil
- 8 oz. (250 g) fresh whole mushrooms
- 1 medium onion, cut into 8 chunks
- ¼ teaspoon (1 mL) dried thyme leaves (optional)

4 to 6 servings

1 Heat oven to 300°F/150°C. In small mixing bowl, blend soup, sour cream, milk and sherry. Set aside. In large plastic food-storage bag, combine flour, salt and pepper. Shake to mix. Add pheasant pieces. Shake to coat.

2 In Dutch oven, heat oil over medium-high heat. Add pheasant pieces. Brown on all sides. Brown pieces in two batches, if necessary. Return all pheasant to Dutch oven. Add mushrooms, onion, thyme and reserved soup mixture. Cover. Bake until pheasant is tender, 1½ to 2 hours.

Variation: *Follow recipe above, omitting the soup, sour cream, milk and sherry. Reserve 3 tablespoons (50 mL) of seasoned flour after coating pheasant. After browning pheasant pieces, remove from Dutch oven. Remove Dutch oven from heat. Stir in reserved flour. Add 2 cups (500 mL) half-and-half. Cook over medium-low heat, stirring constantly, just until mixture bubbles. Return pheasant pieces to pan. Add mushrooms, onion and thyme. Cover. Bake as directed above.*

PHEASANT WITH APPLES

- 3 tablespoons (50 mL) butter or margarine
- 2 pheasants, cut up
- 2 medium green apples, cored and cut into ½" (1 cm) slices
- 1 cup (250 mL) sliced celery, ½" (1 cm) thick
- 1 medium onion, finely chopped
- 1 medium shallot, finely chopped
- ¾ cup (175 mL) dry white wine
- 1½ cups (375 mL) pheasant stock or chicken broth
- 2 tablespoons (25 mL) cornstarch
- 2 tablespoons (25 mL) cold water
- ½ cup (125 mL) heavy cream
- 1 tablespoon (15 mL) snipped fresh parsley
- Pinch of salt
- Pinch of pepper
- 2 medium red apples
- Sugar
- 3 tablespoons (50 mL) butter or margarine

4 to 6 servings

1 Heat oven to 350°F/180°C. In Dutch oven, melt 3 tablespoons (50 mL) butter over medium heat. Add pheasant pieces. Brown on all sides. Remove pheasant pieces with slotted spoon. Set aside.

2 Add green apples, celery, onion and shallot. Cook over medium-low heat until tender. Add wine and stock. Cook over medium heat 5 minutes. Add pheasant pieces. Remove from heat. Cover and bake until tender, about 40 minutes. Transfer pheasant to warm platter with tongs. Set aside and keep warm.

3 Into small bowl, strain liquid from Dutch oven. Return strained liquid to Dutch oven. Discard vegetables and apples in strainer. In small bowl, blend cornstarch and water. Add to liquid in Dutch oven. Cook over medium heat, stirring constantly, until thickened and bubbly. Reduce heat to low. Add cream, parsley, salt and pepper. Cook until hot. Set aside and keep warm.

4 Core red apples and cut into ½" (1 cm) slices. On wax paper, sprinkle apples lightly with sugar. In medium skillet, melt 3 tablespoons (50 mL) butter over medium-low heat. Add apple slices. Brown on both sides. Serve apples with pheasant. Top with sauce.

205

BLUE GOOSE WITH CHERRIES

- 2 to 3-lb. (1 to 1.5 kg) blue goose, skin on or skinned
- 1 can (16 oz./454 mL) pitted dark sweet cherries
- 1 tablespoon (15 mL) butter or margarine
- 1 tablespoon (15 mL) vegetable oil
- 1 small onion, chopped
- 1 tablespoon (15 mL) all-purpose flour
- ½ cup (125 mL) water
- 2 tablespoons (25 mL) cream sherry
- 1 tablespoon (15 mL) packed brown sugar
- 1 teaspoon (5 mL) instant beef bouillon granules
- ½ teaspoon (2 mL) ground cinnamon
- ¼ teaspoon (1 mL) salt
- 2 tablespoons (25 mL) cold water (optional)
- 1 to 2 tablespoons (15 to 25 mL) cornstarch (optional)

2 or 3 servings

1 Split goose into halves, removing backbone. Cut each half into two pieces, cutting at a right angle to the first cuts. Set aside. Drain cherries, reserving ½ cup (125 mL) juice. Set aside.

2 In Dutch oven, melt butter in oil over medium heat. Add onion. Cook and stir until tender. Add goose pieces. Brown lightly on all sides. Remove goose pieces. Set aside.

3 Stir flour into onion mixture. Stir in reserved cherry juice, ½ cup (125 mL) water, sherry, brown sugar, bouillon granules, cinnamon and salt. Add goose pieces and cherries. Heat to boiling. Reduce heat. Cover. Simmer until goose pieces are tender, 1½ to 2 hours, turning pieces once.

4 Transfer goose to heated serving platter. Set aside and keep warm. Skim sauce. If sauce is thinner than desired, blend 2 tablespoons (25 mL) water with the cornstarch. Stir into sauce. Cook over medium heat, stirring constantly, until thickened and translucent. Serve sauce over goose pieces.

BLUE GOOSE WITH CHERRIES FOR ELECTRIC COOKING POT

1 Follow recipe above, except transfer browned goose pieces to electric cooking pot. Stir flour into onion mixture. Omit ½ cup (125 mL) water. Stir in reserved cherry juice, sherry, brown sugar, bouillon granules, cinnamon and salt. Cook, stirring constantly, until thickened. Stir in cherries. Pour over goose pieces in pot. Cover. Cook on low heat until tender, 6 to 7 hours.

2 Transfer goose pieces to heated serving platter. Set aside and keep warm. Skim sauce. If sauce is thinner than desired, blend 2 tablespoons (25 mL) water with cornstarch. Stir into sauce. Increase heat setting to high. Cook, stirring constantly, until thickened and translucent. Serve sauce over goose pieces.

ROAST GOOSE
WITH BAKED APPLES

- 1 whole wild goose, 6 to 8 lbs. (3 to 4 kg), skin on
- Seasoned salt
- Salt and pepper
- 1 carrot, cut into 1" (2.5 cm) pieces
- 1 stalk celery, cut into 1" (2.5 cm) pieces
- 1 medium onion, cut into 8 pieces
- Apple brandy or Calvados, optional

Baked Apples:

- 6 to 8 medium apples, cored
- 1 cup (250 mL) mashed cooked sweet potatoes
- ¼ cup (50 mL) packed brown sugar
- 2 tablespoons (25 mL) butter or margarine, melted
- ¼ teaspoon (1 mL) salt
- Pinch of pepper

6 to 8 servings

1 Remove a thin strip of peel from the top of each apple. In medium mixing bowl, combine remaining apple ingredients. Mix well.

2 Stuff apples with sweet potato mixture, mounding on top. Place in shallow baking dish. Set apples aside. Heat oven to 325°F/160°C.

3 Pat goose dry with paper towels. Sprinkle cavity lightly with seasoned salt, salt and pepper. Place carrot, celery and onion in cavity.

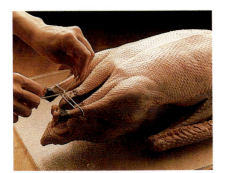

4 Tie drumsticks across cavity. Tuck wing tips behind back. Place breast-side-up on rack in roasting pan. Sprinkle outside of goose with seasoned salt, salt and pepper.

5 Roast, basting frequently with pan juices and sprinkling occasionally with brandy, until desired doneness, 20 to 25 minutes per pound (45 to 55 minutes per kilogram). Drain and discard excess fat during roasting.

6 Place stuffed apples in oven during last 30 to 45 minutes of roasting. Baste apples frequently with goose drippings. Remove apples when fork-tender. Serve with goose.

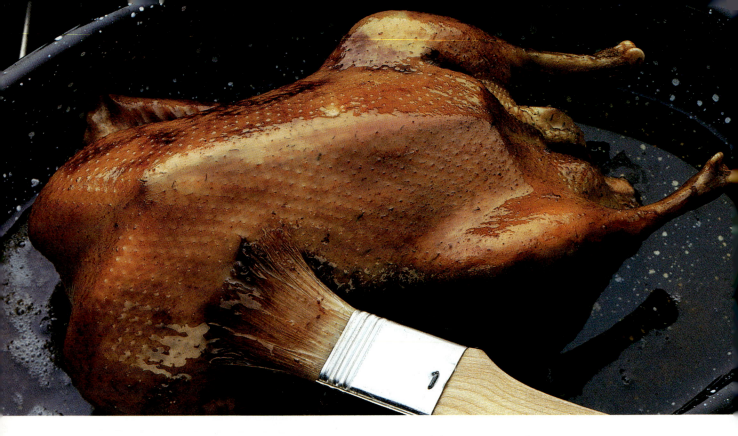

ROAST LEMON-MINT DUCK ↑

- 1 whole mallard or other large wild duck, skin on
- 1 tablespoon (15 mL) finely chopped fresh mint
- Grated rind and juice from 1 small lemon
- 3 tablespoons (50 mL) softened butter
- ¼ teaspoon (1 mL) pepper
- Pinch of salt
- 1 cup (250 mL) duck stock or chicken broth
- 1½ teaspoons (7 mL) finely chopped fresh mint
- 1 medium lemon, cut into 6 slices

2 servings

1 Heat oven to 400°F/200°C. Pat inside and outside of duck dry with paper towels. In small bowl, combine 1 tablespoon (15 mL) mint, the lemon rind, juice and 1 tablespoon (15 mL) butter; mix well. Rub butter mixture inside cavity.

2 Place duck in 9" (2.5 L) square baking pan. In small saucepan, combine remaining 2 tablespoons (25 mL) butter, the pepper and salt. Heat over low heat until butter melts. Brush over outside of duck.

3 Roast duck until skin is brown and crisp and duck is desired doneness, 40 to 60 minutes, basting frequently with pan juices. Transfer duck to heated serving platter. Set aside and keep warm. Pour pan juices into medium saucepan. Add stock. Cook over medium heat until reduced by one-half. Remove from heat. Add 1½ teaspoons (7 mL) mint and the lemon slices. Let stand for about 2 minutes. Arrange lemon slices on duck. Pour sauce over lemon slices and duck.

GRILLED TEAL

- 4 whole teal, skin on
- 1 whole lemon, quartered
- Olive oil
- Salt and pepper
- 8 whole juniper berries
- 4 celery tops with leaves
- 4 small potatoes
- 4 small white onions
- Dried oregano leaves (optional)

4 servings

1 Start charcoal briquets in grill. Pat cavities and outsides of ducks dry with paper towels. Rub each duck cavity with 1 lemon quarter, then with olive oil. Set aside lemon quarters. Sprinkle cavity with salt and pepper. Inside each cavity, place 2 juniper berries, 1 celery top, 1 potato and 1 onion. Tie drumsticks across cavity with wet kitchen string. Tuck wing tips behind back. Rub outside of each duck with lemon quarter, then with olive oil. Sprinkle with salt, pepper and oregano.

2 When charcoal briquets are covered with ash, spread them evenly in grill Place above hot coals. Grill ducks until desired doneness, 15 to 35 minutes, turning once or twice and brushing with olive oil. Remove and discard stuffing.

TIP: *This recipe also works well on a rotisserie.*

WINE-BRAISED DUCK

- ¼ cup (50 mL) all-purpose flour
- ¼ teaspoon (1 mL) salt
- ¼ teaspoon (1 mL) pepper
- 2 mallards or other large wild ducks, cut up
- 2 tablespoons (25 mL) butter or margarine
- 2 tablespoons (25 mL) vegetable oil
- 1 medium onion, chopped
- 2 medium shallots, minced
- 1 cup (250 mL) red wine
- 1 cup (250 mL) duck stock or chicken broth
- 8 oz. (250 g) fresh mushrooms, sliced
- 1 small bay leaf
- 1 teaspoon (5 mL) dried thyme leaves
- 1 teaspoon (5 mL) dried rosemary leaves
- 1 tablespoon (15 mL) snipped fresh parsley
- 3 tablespoons (50 mL) cold water
- 2 tablespoons (25 mL) all-purpose flour
- Salt and pepper

4 or 5 servings

1 On a sheet of wax paper, mix ¼ cup (50 mL) flour, the salt and pepper. Dip duck pieces in flour, turning to coat. In Dutch oven, melt butter in oil over medium heat. Add duck pieces. Brown on all sides. Remove duck pieces with slotted spoon. Set aside.

2 Add onion and shallots to Dutch oven. Cook and stir over medium heat until tender. Return duck pieces to Dutch oven. Add wine, stock, mushrooms, bay leaf, thyme, rosemary and parsley. Heat to boiling. Reduce heat. Cover. Simmer until duck pieces are tender, 1 to 1¾ hours.

3 With slotted spoon, transfer duck pieces to heated serving platter. Set aside and keep warm. Remove and discard bay leaf. Skim excess fat from cooking liquid. In small bowl, blend water and 2 tablespoons (25 mL) flour. Blend into cooking liquid. Cook over medium heat, stirring constantly, until thickened and bubbly. Season with salt and pepper to taste. Serve sauce over duck pieces.

DUCK WITH ORANGE SAUCE ↑

- ½ cup (125 mL) chopped onion
- ½ cup (125 mL) chopped apple
- ¼ cup (50 mL) chopped celery
- 2 whole canvasbacks or other large wild ducks, or 3 to 4 smaller wild ducks, skin on

Orange Sauce:
- 2 tablespoons (25 mL) butter or margarine
- 2 tablespoons (25 mL) all-purpose flour
- 2 teaspoons (10 mL) sugar
- 2 teaspoons (10 mL) grated orange peel
- ¾ teaspoon (4 mL) salt
- ⅛ teaspoon (0.5 mL) dry mustard
- ⅔ cup (150 mL) fresh orange juice
- ⅓ cup (75 mL) duck stock or chicken broth
- ¼ cup (50 mL) orange marmalade
- 2 tablespoons (25 mL) orange liqueur (optional)
- Orange slices for garnish (optional)

4 servings

1 Heat oven to 350°F/180°C. In small mixing bowl, combine onion, apple and celery. Mix well. Divide mixture. Stuff into duck cavities. Place ducks on rack in roasting pan. Bake for 45 minutes.

2 While ducks are baking, prepare orange sauce. In small saucepan, melt butter over medium heat. Remove from heat. Blend in flour. Stir in sugar, orange peel, salt and dry mustard. Blend in orange juice and stock. Cook over medium heat, stirring constantly, until thickened and bubbly. Add marmalade. Cook and stir until marmalade melts. Remove from heat. Blend in orange liqueur. Cover and keep warm.

3 When ducks have baked for 45 minutes, brush lightly with orange sauce. Continue baking until ducks are tender, about 45 minutes longer, brushing with sauce once or twice. Discard vegetable stuffing. Garnish ducks with orange slices. Serve with extra sauce.

Holiday Dinner Trimmings

CREAMY DILLED VEGETABLE MEDLEY

- 1 tablespoon (15 mL) butter or margarine
- 1 tablespoon (15 mL) all-purpose flour
- ½ teaspoon (2 mL) instant chicken bouillon granules
- ⅛ teaspoon (0.5 mL) dried dill weed
- ½ cup (125 mL) milk
- ¼ cup (50 mL) sour cream
- 2 cups (500 mL) julienne carrots (1½ x ¼"/4 cm x 5 mm strips)
- 1 medium zucchini, cut in half lengthwise and thinly sliced
- 2 tablespoons (25 mL) water

6 to 8 servings

1 In 2-cup (500 mL) measure, microwave butter at High for 45 seconds to 1 minute, or until melted. Stir in flour, bouillon and dill weed. Blend in milk. Microwave at High for 2 to 2½ minutes, or until mixture thickens and bubbles, stirring after every minute. Add sour cream. Mix well. * Set aside.

2 In 2-quart (2 L) casserole, combine remaining ingredients. Cover. Microwave at High for 8 to 10 minutes, or until vegetables are tender, stirring once. Drain. Add sauce. Toss to coat. Re-cover. Microwave at High for 2 to 3 minutes, or until hot, stirring once.

Advance preparation: *Up to 2 days in advance, cut vegetables. Sprinkle with 1 to 2 teaspoons (5 to 10 mL) cold water and store in covered container. Prepare recipe to * above. Cover with plastic wrap and refrigerate. To serve, continue as directed.*

- ¼ cup (50 mL) flaked coconut
- 2 acorn squash (1½ lbs./750 g each)
- ¼ cup (50 mL) butter or margarine, cut up
- 2 tablespoons (25 mL) maple syrup
- 1 teaspoon (5 mL) finely chopped fresh gingerroot

8 servings

Advance preparation: *Up to 3 days in advance, toast coconut. Store in airtight container. Up to 1 day in advance, prepare squash halves to * below. Refrigerate after standing time. To serve, quarter squash and continue as directed, except after pouring butter mixture over squash, microwave at High for 8 to 13 minutes, or until hot.*

1 Sprinkle coconut in 9" (23 cm) pie plate. Microwave at High for 3 to 4 minutes, or until lightly browned, tossing with fork after the first minute and then every 30 seconds. Set aside.

2 Pierce each squash twice with fork and place in microwave oven. Microwave at High for 3 to 4 minutes, or until warm. (This makes it easier to cut squash.) Cut in half lengthwise. Remove seeds from each half.

3 Wrap each half in microwave-safe plastic wrap and arrange cut-side-up in microwave oven. Microwave at High for 8 to 12 minutes, or until tender, rotating and rearranging once. Let stand, covered, for 5 minutes. *

4 Remove plastic wrap and cut each half lengthwise into quarters. Arrange quarters cut-side-up on 12" (30 cm) platter or in 10" (3 L) square casserole. Set aside.

5 Combine remaining ingredients in 2-cup (500 mL) measure. Microwave at High for 1¼ to 1½ minutes, or until butter melts. Stir to combine. Pour butter mixture over squash. Microwave at High for 4 to 6 minutes, or until hot. Sprinkle with toasted coconut.

BRUSSELS SPROUTS WITH TWO MUSTARDS ↑

- 1 tablespoon (15 mL) butter or margarine
- 1 tablespoon (15 mL) Dijon mustard
- 2 teaspoons (10 mL) stone-ground mustard
- 2 teaspoons (10 mL) honey
- ¼ teaspoon (1 mL) salt
- 2 pkgs. (10 oz./300 g each) frozen Brussels sprouts

8 servings

1 In 1½-quart (1.5 L) casserole, microwave butter at High for 45 seconds to 1 minute, or until melted.

2 Stir in mustards, honey and salt. Add Brussels sprouts and toss to coat. Cover. Microwave at High for 10 to 14 minutes, or until Brussels sprouts are tender-crisp, stirring once or twice.

HOPPIN' JOHN

- 4 slices bacon, cut into 1" (2.5 cm) pieces
- ½ cup (125 mL) chopped green pepper
- ¼ cup (50 mL) sliced green onions
- 1½ cups (375 mL) uncooked instant rice
- 1 pkg. (10 oz./300 g) frozen black-eyed peas
- 1½ cups (375 mL) hot water
- ½ teaspoon (2 mL) salt
- ¼ teaspoon (1 mL) dried thyme leaves
- Pinch of pepper
- Pinch of cayenne

8 servings

1 Place bacon in 2-quart (2 L) casserole. Cover. Microwave at High for 4 to 5 minutes, or until brown and crisp. Do not drain. Add green pepper and onions. Re-cover. Microwave at High for 1½ to 3 minutes, or until vegetables are tender-crisp.

2 Stir in remaining ingredients. Re-cover. Microwave at High for 10 to 13 minutes, or until rice and peas are tender and water is absorbed.

HONEYED SWEET POTATOES & PEAS

- 3 cups (750 mL) peeled, cubed sweet potatoes (½"/1 cm cubes), about 1½ lbs. (750 g)
- 2 tablespoons (25 mL) butter or margarine
- 1 tablespoon (15 mL) honey
- ½ teaspoon (2 mL) dry mustard
- ¼ teaspoon (1 mL) salt
- 1 cup (250 mL) frozen peas

6 to 8 servings

1 In 1½-quart (1.5 L) casserole, combine all ingredients, except peas. Cover. Microwave at High for 8 to 9 minutes, or until sweet potatoes are tender, stirring once.

2 Add peas. Re-cover. Microwave at High for 3 to 5 minutes, or until hot, stirring once.

CRISPY TOAST CUPS →

- 8 slices soft white bread, crusts trimmed
- 2 tablespoons (25 mL) butter or margarine

8 servings

1 Heat oven to 350°F/180°C. Press each bread slice into ungreased muffin cup. In 1-cup (250 mL) measure, microwave butter at High for 45 seconds to 1 minute, or until melted. Brush bread with butter.

2 Bake for 20 to 25 minutes, or until light golden brown. Fill with creamed vegetables.

Advance preparation: *Up to 2 days in advance, prepare as directed above. Store in airtight container.*

CREAMY TARRAGON PEAS & ONIONS ↑

- 1 tablespoon (15 mL) butter or margarine
- 1½ cups (375 mL) pearl onions, peeled
- 1½ cups (375 mL) frozen peas

Sauce:

- 2 tablespoons (25 mL) butter or margarine
- 1 tablespoon plus 1 teaspoon all-purpose flour (20 mL)

- ¼ teaspoon (1 mL) salt
- ¼ teaspoon (1 mL) grated lemon peel
- ⅛ teaspoon (0.5 mL) dried tarragon leaves
- Pinch of white pepper
- 1 cup (250 mL) half-and-half

8 servings

Advance preparation: *Up to 2 days in advance, prepare onions and peas to * below. Cover and refrigerate. To serve, continue as directed.*

1 Place 1 tablespoon (15 mL) butter in 1½-quart (1.5 L) casserole. Microwave at High for 45 seconds to 1 minute, or until melted. Add onions. Cover. Microwave at High for 3 to 5 minutes, or until tender, stirring once. Stir in peas. * Set aside.

2 Place 2 tablespoons (25 mL) butter in 4-cup (1 L) measure. Microwave at High for 45 seconds to 1 minute, or until melted. Stir in remaining sauce ingredients, except half-and-half. Blend in half-and-half. Microwave at High for 3 to 4 minutes, or until mixture thickens and bubbles, stirring twice.

3 Pour sauce over peas and onions. Stir to blend. Microwave at High for 1 to 2 minutes, or until hot. Spoon evenly into Crispy Toast Cups (above), if desired.

215

BROCCOLI & CAULIFLOWER BALL →

- 4 cups (1 L) fresh broccoli flowerets
- 4 cups (1 L) fresh cauliflowerets
- 2 tablespoons (25 mL) water
- 6 thin strips red pepper
- 3 tablespoons (50 mL) butter or margarine
- 2 teaspoons (10 mL) lemon juice
- ¼ teaspoon (1 mL) salt
- Zest of 1 lemon
- Lemon slices

6 to 8 servings

Advance Preparation: *Up to 1 day in advance, prepare to * below. Refrigerate. To serve, continue as directed.*

1 Combine broccoli, cauliflower and water in 2-quart (2 L) casserole. Cover. Microwave at High for 5 to 9 minutes, or until vegetables are very hot and color brightens, stirring once. Rinse with cold water. Drain.

2 Arrange red pepper in 1½-quart (1.5 L) deep mixing bowl. Arrange broccoli and cauliflower over red pepper, pressing floweret ends toward outside of bowl. (Alternate rows of broccoli and cauliflower, if desired.) Set aside.

3 Place butter, lemon juice and onion salt in 1-cup (250 mL) measure. Microwave at High for 1 to 1¼ minutes, or until butter melts. Pour evenly over broccoli and cauliflower. Cover with microwave-safe plastic wrap.*

4 Microwave vegetables at High for 4 to 11 minutes, or until hot, rotating bowl once. Remove plastic wrap. Place serving plate over top of bowl and invert. Sprinkle with lemon zest, and garnish with lemon slices.

HOT CABBAGE-APPLE SLAW ↑

- 4 slices bacon, cut into 1" (2.5 cm) pieces
- 2 tablespoons (25 mL) sugar
- 2 tablespoons (25 mL) white vinegar
- ½ teaspoon (2 mL) salt
- ½ teaspoon (2 mL) dried marjoram leaves
- 6 cups (1.5 L) shredded red cabbage
- 2 cups (500 mL) sliced Granny Smith apples (about ⅛"/3 mm slices)
- ⅓ cup (75 mL) hazelnuts

8 servings

1 Place bacon in 2-quart (2 L) casserole. Cover. Microwave at High for 4 to 6 minutes, or until brown and crisp. Do not drain. Stir in sugar, vinegar, salt and marjoram. Microwave at High for 1 minute.

2 Stir in cabbage and apples. Cover. Microwave at High for 5 to 6 minutes, or until cabbage and apples are tender-crisp, stirring once. Stir in hazelnuts.

CRANBERRY WILD RICE

- 2 cups (500 mL) water
- 1 cup (250 mL) uncooked wild rice
- 1 cup (250 mL) whole-berry cranberry sauce
- 3 tablespoons (50 mL) dry sherry
- ¼ teaspoon (1 mL) salt
- ½ cup (125 mL) chopped walnuts

6 to 8 servings

1 In 2-quart (2 L) saucepan, combine all ingredients, except walnuts. Bring to a boil over high heat. Reduce heat to low. Cover. Simmer for 35 to 45 minutes, or until rice kernels are open and almost all water is absorbed.

2 Let stand, covered, for 15 minutes. * Stir in walnuts.

Advance Preparation: *Up to 2 days in advance, cook rice mixture to * above. Cover and refrigerate. To serve, place in 1-quart (1 L) casserole. Stir in walnuts. Cover. Microwave at High for 6 to 7 minutes, or until hot, stirring once.*

217

HOLIDAY POTATO SCALLOP ↑

- 6 cups (1.5 L) peeled, sliced potatoes (⅛"/3 mm slices)
- ¼ cup (50 mL) sliced green onions
- 3 tablespoons (50 mL) all-purpose flour
- ½ teaspoon (2 mL) salt
- ¼ teaspoon (1 mL) dried thyme leaves
- Pinch of white pepper
- 2 cups (500 mL) half-and-half
- ⅓ cup (75 mL) snipped fresh parsley
- Sliced pimiento

6 to 8 servings

1 In 3-quart (3 L) casserole, combine all ingredients, except half-and-half, parsley and pimiento. Pour half-and-half over potato mixture. Toss gently to coat. Cover. Microwave at High for 6 minutes. Microwave at 50% (Medium) for 25 to 40 minutes longer, or until potatoes are tender and sauce is thickened, stirring twice.

2 Spoon potatoes into serving dish. Sprinkle parsley in wreath shape over potatoes. Arrange pimiento to form bow on wreath.

Holiday Au Gratin Potatoes: *Follow recipe above, except stir in 1 cup (250 mL) shredded Swiss cheese at end of cooking time. Cover. Let stand for 1 to 2 minutes, or until cheese melts.*

MASHED POTATOES

- 2 lbs. (1 kg) potatoes, peeled and quartered
- ¼ cup (50 mL) water
- ¼ to ⅓ cup (50 to 75 mL) milk
- ¼ cup (50 mL) butter or margarine
- ½ teaspoon (2 mL) salt
- Pinch of pepper

6 to 8 servings

1 In 2-quart (2 L) casserole, combine potatoes and water. Cover. Microwave at High for 12 to 18 minutes, or until tender, stirring once. Let potatoes stand, covered, for 5 minutes. Drain.

2 In medium mixing bowl, place potatoes and remaining ingredients. Mash with a potato masher, or beat at medium speed of electric mixer, until mixture is smooth.

BAKED POTATOES & BAKED SWEET POTATOES

Potatoes	Time (High)
2 (8 oz./250 g each)	5-10 min.
4 (8 oz./250 g each)	10-16 min.
6 (8 oz./250 g each)	18-25 min.

Sweet Potatoes	Time (High)
2 (8 oz./250 g each)	8-10 min.
4 (8 oz./250 g each)	12-18 min.
6 (8 oz./250 g each)	20-30 min.

1 Pierce potatoes with fork. Place on roasting rack or paper towel and arrange in a circle in microwave oven.

2 Microwave at High as directed in chart above, or just until tender, turning over and rearranging once. Let stand for 5 minutes.

Advance preparation: *Up to 45 minutes in advance, microwave potatoes. Wrap each in foil to keep hot.*

CRUNCHY-TOPPED TWICE-BAKED POTATOES ↑

- 4 medium baking potatoes (8 oz./250 g each)
- 2 tablespoons (25 mL) butter or margarine
- ¼ cup (50 mL) half-and-half
- 1 egg
- 1 tablespoon (15 mL) chopped pimiento
- ¼ teaspoon (1 mL) salt
- Pinch of cayenne
- 1 pkg. (3 oz./85 g) cream cheese

Topping:
- ½ cup (125 mL) seasoned dry bread crumbs
- ⅓ cup (75 mL) chopped pecans
- 1 teaspoon (5 mL) dried parsley flakes
- 3 tablespoons (50 mL) butter or margarine

8 servings

1 Pierce potatoes with fork. Arrange in a circle on paper towel in microwave oven. Microwave at High for 10 to 16 minutes, or just until tender, turning over and rearranging once. Let cool slightly. Cut potatoes in half lengthwise. Scoop out and reserve pulp, leaving ¼" (5 mm) shells. Set shells aside.

2 In medium mixing bowl, combine pulp and remaining ingredients, except cream cheese and topping. In small bowl, microwave cream cheese at High for 15 to 30 seconds, or until softened. Add to potato mixture. Beat at medium speed of electric mixer until smooth. Pipe or spoon mixture evenly into shells. * Set aside.

3 In small mixing bowl, combine bread crumbs, pecans and parsley. In small bowl, microwave 3 tablespoons (50 mL) butter at High for 1 to 1¼ minutes, or until melted. Add to bread crumb mixture. Toss to coat. Top each potato with about 1 tablespoon (15 mL) mixture, pressing so crumbs adhere. Arrange potatoes in 10" (3 L) square casserole. Microwave at High for 9 to 11 minutes, or until hot, rotating dish and rearranging potatoes once.

Advance preparation: *Up to 1 month in advance, prepare potatoes to * above. Wrap in foil and freeze. To serve, continue as directed, except cover and microwave potatoes at High for 10 minutes, rotating dish once. Top with bread crumb mixture. Microwave at High, uncovered, for 5 to 7 minutes, or until hot.*

CREAMY STUFFED SWEET POTATOES ↑

- 3 sweet potatoes (12 to 16 oz./375 to 500 g each)
- 2 tablespoons (25 mL) butter or margarine
- ¾ cup (175 mL) half-and-half
- ¼ cup (50 mL) orange marmalade
- ¼ teaspoon (1 mL) salt
- 2 tablespoons (25 mL) sliced almonds

6 servings

1 Pierce sweet potatoes with fork. Arrange in circle on paper towel in microwave oven. Microwave at High for 10 to 13 minutes, or just until tender, turning over and rearranging once. Let cool slightly. Cut potatoes in half lengthwise. Scoop out and reserve pulp, leaving about ¼" (5 mm) shells. Set shells aside.

2 In medium mixing bowl, combine pulp and remaining ingredients, except almonds. Beat at medium speed of electric mixer until smooth. Pipe or spoon mixture evenly into shells. * Sprinkle each potato with 1 teaspoon (5 mL) almonds. Arrange potatoes in 10" (3 L) square casserole. Cover. Microwave at High for 10 to 12 minutes, or until hot, rotating dish and rearranging potatoes once.

Advance preparation: Up to 1 month in advance, prepare potatoes to * above. Wrap in foil and freeze. To serve, continue as directed, except microwave at High for 10 minutes. Sprinkle with almonds. Microwave at High for 5 to 7 minutes, or until hot, rotating dish and rearranging potatoes once.

SHERRIED SWEET POTATOES

- 2 cans (18 oz./511 mL each) sweet potatoes, drained
- ½ cup (125 mL) apricot nectar
- 2 eggs
- 2 tablespoons (25 mL) honey
- 2 tablespoons (25 mL) dry sherry
- ½ teaspoon (2 mL) salt
- ¼ teaspoon (1 mL) ground nutmeg
- ¼ cup (50 mL) chopped pecans

6 to 8 servings

1 In large mixing bowl, combine all ingredients, except pecans. Beat at medium speed of electric mixer until light and fluffy. Spread mixture in 10" (25 cm) pie plate. * Sprinkle evenly with pecans.

2 Cover with wax paper. Microwave at High for 4 minutes. Microwave at 50% (Medium) for 9 to 15 minutes longer, or until center is set, rotating dish once or twice.

Advance preparation: Up to 2 days in advance, prepare sweet potato mixture to * above. Cover with plastic wrap and refrigerate. To serve, continue as directed, except microwave at 50% (Medium) for 12 to 20 minutes, or until center is set, rotating dish once or twice.

DIJON POTATOES & CHESTNUTS →

- 1½ cups (375 mL) fresh chestnuts (about 7 oz./200 g)
- 1 cup (250 mL) water
- ¼ cup (50 mL) butter or margarine
- 2 tablespoons (25 mL) Dijon mustard
- ½ teaspoon (2 mL) sugar
- ⅛ teaspoon (0.5 mL) dried dill weed
- 4 cups (1 L) quartered new potatoes (about 2 lbs./1 kg)
- ½ cup (125 mL) julienne red pepper (1½ x ¼"/4 cm x 5 mm strips)
- ½ cup (125 mL) snipped fresh parsley

8 servings

1 Make a horizontal cut through rounded part of shell of each chestnut without cutting into nutmeat. Place chestnuts and water in 1½-quart (1.5 L) casserole. Cover. Microwave at High for 3 to 4 minutes, or until water boils. Microwave at High for 1 minute longer. Let stand for 10 minutes. Rinse with cold water. Peel shell and inner skin from each chestnut. Cut each chestnut in half. * Set aside.

2 Place butter in 2-quart (2 L) casserole. Microwave at High for 1¼ to 1½ minutes, or until melted. Stir in mustard, sugar and dill weed. Add chestnuts, potatoes and red pepper. Toss to coat. Cover. Microwave at High for 15 to 20 minutes, or until potatoes are tender, stirring twice. Stir in parsley.

Advance preparation: *Up to 1 day in advance, prepare chestnuts to * above. Place in covered container and refrigerate. To serve, continue as directed.*

CANDIED SWEET POTATOES

- 2 sweet potatoes (12 to 16 oz./375 to 500 g each), peeled and sliced
- 2 tablespoons (25 mL) butter or margarine
- ½ cup (125 mL) packed brown sugar
- 2 tablespoons (25 mL) light corn syrup
- 1 tablespoon (15 mL) unsweetened pineapple juice
- ⅛ teaspoon (0.5 mL) ground allspice
- 2 cups (500 mL) miniature marshmallows

6 to 8 servings

1 Arrange sweet potato slices, slightly overlapping, in 10" (25 cm) pie plate. Set aside. In 1-cup (250 mL) measure, microwave butter at High for 45 seconds to 1 minute, or until melted. Stir in remaining ingredients, except marshmallows. Pour evenly over potatoes. Cover with microwave-safe plastic wrap.

2 Microwave at High for 8 to 11 minutes, or until tender, rotating dish once. Remove plastic wrap. Sprinkle potatoes with marshmallows. Place under broiler, 8" (20 cm) from heat. Broil just until marshmallows are light golden brown, about 1 minute.

ORIENTAL SESAME ← BROCCOLI

- 1 tablespoon (15 mL) butter or margarine
- 2 tablespoons (25 mL) sesame seed
- 1 medium onion, cut into ½" (1 cm) wedges
- 3 tablespoons (50 mL) teriyaki sauce
- 1 tablespoon (15 mL) sesame oil
- ½ teaspoon (2 mL) sugar
- ¼ teaspoon (1 mL) crushed red pepper flakes
- 1 pkg. (16 oz./500 g) frozen broccoli cuts

4 servings

1 In 1-cup (250 mL) measure, microwave butter at High for 30 to 45 seconds, or until melted. Stir in sesame seed. Microwave at High for 2 to 3 minutes, or until light golden brown, stirring after every minute. Let stand for 2 to 3 minutes (seeds will continue to toast during standing time). Drain seeds on paper-towel-lined plate. Set aside.

2 Place onion in 2-quart (2 L) casserole. Cover. Microwave at High for 1½ to 2 minutes, or until tender.

3 In small bowl, combine teriyaki sauce, sesame oil, sugar and red pepper flakes. Add teriyaki mixture and broccoli to onion. Toss to coat.

4 Re-cover. Microwave at High for 7 to 8 minutes, or until broccoli is hot, stirring once. Sprinkle with sesame seed.

COUNTRY VEGETABLE MEDLEY

- 1 tablespoon (15 mL) butter or margarine
- 2 teaspoons (10 mL) lemon juice
- 2 teaspoons (10 mL) stone-ground mustard
- ¼ teaspoon (1 mL) salt
- 1 pkg. (16 oz./500 g) frozen broccoli, cauliflower and carrots
- ⅓ cup (75 mL) water

6 servings

1 In small bowl, microwave butter at High for 45 seconds to 1 minute, or until melted. Add lemon juice, mustard and salt. Mix well. Set aside.

2 In 2-quart (2 L) casserole, combine vegetables and water. Cover. Microwave at High for 8 to 11 minutes, or until hot, stirring once. Drain. Add butter mixture. Toss to coat.

WARM FRUITED SLAW ↑

- 3 cups (750 mL) shredded cabbage
- 1 pkg. (6 oz./170 g) dried fruit bits
- 1 can (11 oz./312 mL) mandarin orange segments, drained (reserve ¼ cup/50 mL liquid)
- Pinch of salt
- ½ cup (125 mL) orange-flavored low-fat yogurt
- ¼ teaspoon (1 mL) ground cinnamon

6 servings

1 In 2-quart (2 L) casserole, combine cabbage, fruit bits, reserved mandarin orange liquid and the salt. Cover. Microwave at High for 3 to 4 minutes, or until cabbage is tender-crisp, stirring once.

2 Add oranges, yogurt and cinnamon. Toss gently to combine. Serve immediately.

BLUE CHEESE CAULIFLOWER & PEAS

- 1 pkg. (16 oz./500 g) frozen cauliflowerets
- 1 cup (250 mL) frozen peas
- ⅓ cup (75 mL) water
- 1 jar (5 oz./142 mL) blue cheese-flavored cream cheese spread

6 servings

1 In 2-quart (2 L) casserole, combine cauliflower, peas and water. Cover. Microwave at High for 10 to 13 minutes, or until hot, stirring once or twice. Drain.

2 Add cream cheese spread. Re-cover. Microwave at High for 2 to 4 minutes, or until melted, stirring once to coat vegetables.

GREEK BEANS & TOMATOES

- 1 pkg. (16 oz./500 g) frozen whole green beans
- 2 tablespoons (25 mL) olive oil
- 1 clove garlic, minced
- ½ teaspoon (2 mL) dried basil leaves
- ¼ teaspoon (1 mL) salt
- 1 medium tomato, cut into 8 wedges
- 2 tablespoons (25 mL) crumbled feta cheese

6 servings

1 In 2-quart (2 L) casserole, combine all ingredients, except tomato and cheese. Cover. Microwave at High for 8 to 10 minutes, or until beans are hot, stirring once.

2 Add tomato. Toss gently to combine. Sprinkle with cheese.

CORN & SPINACH MEDLEY

- 1 pkg. (3 oz./85 g) cream cheese
- 1 tablespoon (15 mL) milk
- ¼ teaspoon (1 mL) salt
- Pinch of garlic powder
- 1 can (11 oz./312 mL) corn with red and green peppers, drained
- 1 can (4 oz./114 mL) chopped green chilies, drained
- 2 cups (500 mL) torn fresh spinach leaves

4 servings

1 In 2-quart (2 L) casserole, combine cream cheese, milk, salt and garlic powder. Microwave at High for 30 to 45 seconds, or until cheese is softened. Stir mixture until smooth.

2 Stir in corn and chilies. Microwave at High for 2 to 3 minutes, or until hot, stirring once.

3 Stir in spinach. Microwave at High for 1 to 1½ minutes, or until mixture is hot and spinach is wilted.

HOT PEPPER SUMMER SQUASH ↑

- 1 tablespoon (15 mL) butter or margarine
- 1½ cups (375 mL) sliced yellow summer squash
- 1½ cups (375 mL) sliced zucchini squash
- ½ teaspoon (2 mL) dried oregano leaves
- ¼ teaspoon (1 mL) salt
- ½ cup (125 mL) shredded hot pepper Monterey Jack cheese

4 servings

1 In 2-quart (2 L) casserole, microwave butter at High for 45 seconds to 1 minute, or until melted. Stir in squashes, oregano and salt. Cover. Microwave at High for 4 to 6 minutes, or until squashes are tender-crisp, stirring once.

2 Stir in cheese. Re-cover. Let stand for 1 minute, or until cheese is melted. Before serving, toss gently.

CREAM-STYLE PEPPERS & CORN

- 1 tablespoon (15 mL) butter or margarine
- ½ teaspoon (2 mL) fennel seed, crushed
- Pinch of garlic powder
- Pinch of salt
- 1 medium green pepper, cut into ¼" (5 mm) strips
- 1 medium red pepper, cut into ¼" (5 mm) strips
- 1 cup (250 mL) frozen corn
- ¼ cup (50 mL) sour cream

4 servings

1 In 2-quart (2 L) casserole, combine butter, fennel seed, garlic powder and salt. Microwave at High for 45 seconds to 1 minute, or until butter is melted.

2 Add peppers and corn. Toss to coat. Cover. Microwave at High for 4 to 6 minutes, or until peppers are tender-crisp, stirring once. Add sour cream. Toss to coat.

JULIENNE CARROTS & BEETS →

- 2 tablespoons (25 mL) horseradish
- 2 teaspoons (10 mL) packed brown sugar
- 1 teaspoon (5 mL) grated orange peel
- 1 can (16 oz./454 mL) julienne beets, rinsed and drained
- 1 can (16 oz./454 mL) julienne carrots, rinsed and drained

6 servings

1 In small bowl, combine horseradish, sugar and peel. Mix well. Set aside.

2 In 2-quart (2 L) casserole, combine beets and carrots. Cover. Microwave at High for 3 to 6 minutes, or until hot, stirring once. Add horseradish mixture. Toss to coat.

SPICY GLAZED CARROTS →

- 1 pkg. (16 oz./500 g) frozen crinkle-cut carrots
- ¼ cup (50 mL) apricot preserves
- 1 tablespoon (15 mL) water
- ¼ teaspoon (1 mL) chili powder
- ¼ teaspoon (1 mL) salt
- ⅛ teaspoon (0.5 mL) ground ginger
- Pinch of cayenne

6 servings

1 In 2-quart (2 L) casserole, combine all ingredients. Cover.

2 Microwave at High for 7 to 10 minutes, or until carrots are hot, stirring once.

HOLIDAY YORKSHIRE PUDDING →

- 1¾ cups (425 mL) all-purpose flour
- 1 teaspoon (5 mL) seasoned salt
- 1 cup (250 mL) milk
- 4 eggs
- 1 cup (250 mL) cold water
- 2 cups (500 mL) fresh broccoli flowerets
- 2 tablespoons (25 mL) water
- ⅓ cup (75 mL) reserved beef drippings or butter
- ½ cup (125 mL) thin strips carrot or carrot curls

8 to 10 servings

Advance preparation: *Up to 1½ hours in advance, prepare batter to * below. If serving pudding with Peppered Rib Roast (page 199); bake while roast is standing.*

1 Combine flour and salt in medium mixing bowl. Make a well in flour. Pour milk into well and stir to combine. In medium mixing bowl, beat eggs at medium speed of electric mixer until light and fluffy.

2 Add eggs to flour and milk mixture and continue to beat just until smooth. Add water and beat just until large bubbles rise to the surface, about 30 seconds. Cover with plastic wrap and refrigerate batter for 1 hour. *

3 Combine broccoli and 2 tablespoons (25 mL) water in 2-quart (2 L) casserole. Cover and microwave at High for 2 to 3 minutes, or until broccoli is very hot and color brightens. Rinse with cold water. Drain. Set aside.

226

4 Heat oven to 400°F/200°C. Place beef drippings in bottom of 9 x 13" (3.5 L) or 3-quart (3 L) glass baking dish. Place in oven for about 3 minutes, or until drippings are hot and melted.

5 Remove batter from refrigerator. Beat at medium speed of electric mixer until large bubbles rise to the surface, about 30 seconds.

6 Pour batter into heated baking dish. Sprinkle with broccoli and carrots. Bake for 20 minutes. Reduce oven temperature to 350°F/180°C. Bake for 10 to 20 minutes longer, or until edges are deep golden brown. Serve immediately.

FRUIT GARNISHES

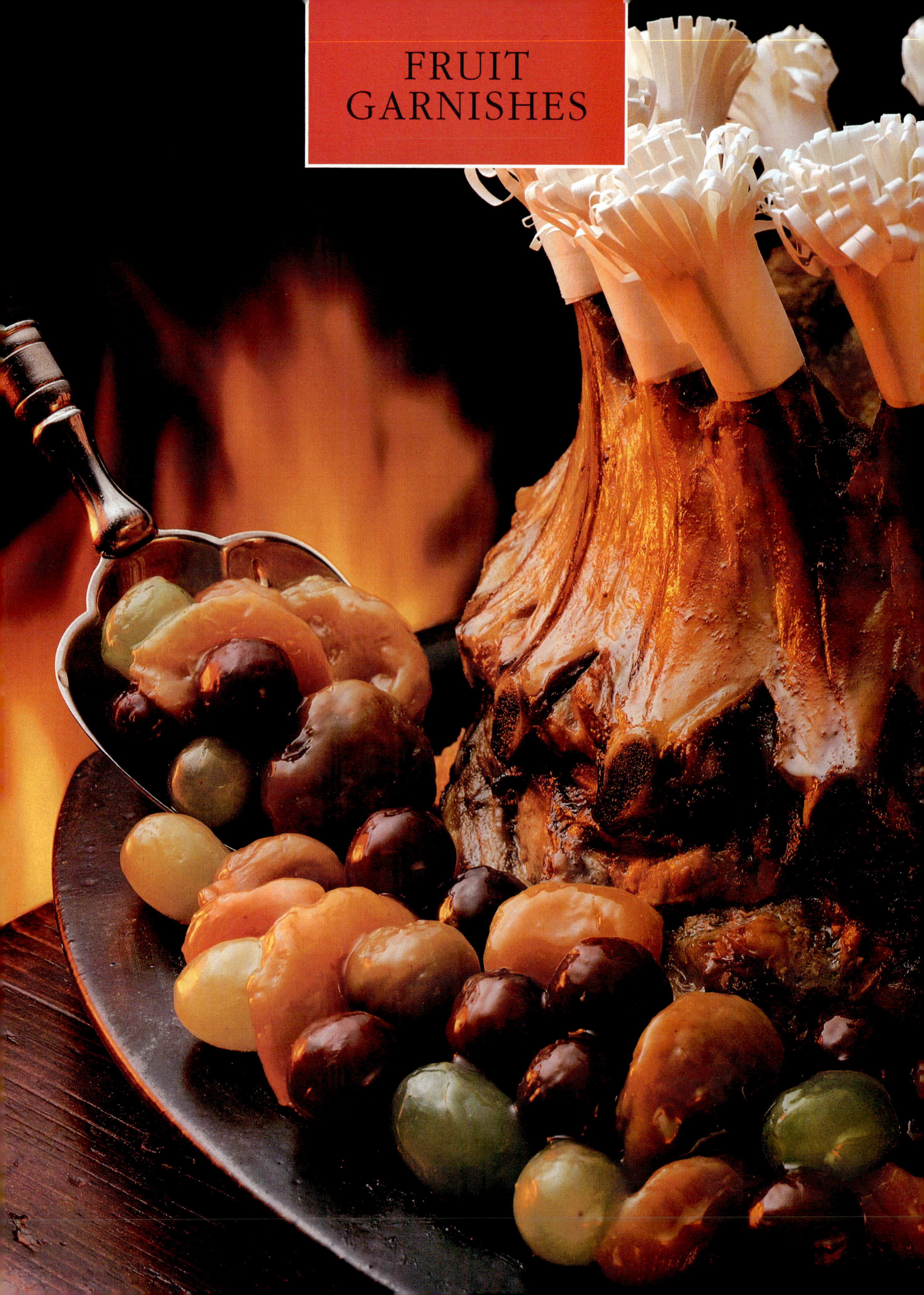

← FRUIT GLACÉ

- ½ cup (125 mL) dried apricot halves
- ½ cup (125 mL) dried calimyrna figs
- ½ cup (125 mL) dried peach halves
- ¾ cup (175 mL) apple juice, divided
- ¼ teaspoon (1 mL) ground cardamom
- 2 teaspoons (10 mL) cornstarch
- 1 cup (250 mL) seedless green grapes
- 1 cup (250 mL) seedless red grapes

6 to 8 servings

1 In 1½-quart (1.5 L) casserole, combine apricots, figs and peaches. Add ½ cup (125 mL) apple juice and the cardamom. Cover. Microwave at High for 5 to 8 minutes, or until fruits are plumped, stirring once.

2 In small bowl, combine cornstarch and remaining ¼ cup (50 mL) apple juice. Stir until smooth. Add to fruit mixture. Mix well. Microwave at High, uncovered, for 1½ to 2½ minutes, or until mixture is thickened and translucent, stirring once. Add grapes. Stir gently to coat. Spoon as garnish around Pork Crown Roast (page 195) or Glazed Ham (page 192), if desired.

Advance preparation: *Up to 2 days in advance, prepare as directed above and serve cold, if desired. To reheat, microwave at High, covered, for 1½ to 2½ minutes, or until hot, stirring once.*

APPLES WITH CORIANDER & ORANGE ↑

- 2 tablespoons (25 mL) butter or margarine
- 2 medium Rome apples, cored and cut into ½" (1 cm) cubes (about 3 cups/750 mL)
- 2 tablespoons (25 mL) packed brown sugar
- ½ teaspoon (2 mL) grated orange peel
- ¼ teaspoon (1 mL) ground coriander

6 to 8 servings

1 In 1-quart (1 L) casserole, microwave butter at High for 45 seconds to 1 minute. Add remaining ingredients. Toss gently to coat. Cover. Microwave at High for 3 to 4 minutes, or until apples are tender, stirring once.

2 Spoon as garnish around Lightly Seasoned Pork Loin Roast (page 197), if desired.

SPICED APPLE RELISH ↑

- 6 cups (1.5 L) chopped apples
- ⅓ cup (75 mL) chopped onion
- ¼ cup (50 mL) sugar
- ¼ cup (50 mL) chopped spiced peaches or raisins, optional
- ¼ cup (50 mL) water
- ¼ teaspoon (1 mL) ground cloves
- Pinch of salt

Makes 2½ to 3 cups
(625 to 750 mL)

1 Combine all ingredients in 2-quart (2 L) casserole; cover. Microwave at High 10 to 15 minutes, or until apples are soft, stirring once or twice.

2 Mash apples. Serve with pork or poultry.

Advance preparation: *Prepare relish the day before; refrigerate. Let stand at room temperature while preparing meal. Serve at room temperature.*

CRANBERRY-ORANGE RELISH ↑

- 2 oranges
- 8 cups (2 L) fresh cranberries
- 1⅓ cups (325 mL) sugar
- ¼ cup (50 mL) chopped crystallized ginger
- ½ cup (125 mL) chopped pecans, optional

12 to 14 servings

1 Squeeze juice from oranges; refrigerate in covered container for other use. Remove pulp from orange peels; discard pulp. Cut peels in quarters; grind finely in food processor. Add half the cranberries and continue processing until ground. Repeat with remaining cranberries.

2 In 3-quart (3 L) bowl mix cranberries, sugar and ginger. Stir in pecans. Refrigerate.

NOTE: *A blender or grinder can be substituted for food processor.*

FRESH FRUIT CHUTNEY ↑

- 3 large apples, peeled and chopped
- 1 mango, peeled and chopped
- 1 medium onion, chopped
- 1½ cups (375 mL) sugar
- 1 cup (250 mL) raisins
- ½ cup (125 mL) cider vinegar
- 1 teaspoon (5 mL) salt
- ½ teaspoon (2 mL) dry mustard

Makes 4 cups (1 L)

1 Combine all ingredients in 3-quart (3 L) casserole. Microwave, uncovered, at High 20 to 30 minutes, or until fruit is very soft and liquid is slightly thickened, stirring 2 or 3 times during cooking time.

2 Remove fruit from liquid and coarsely mash. Return fruit to liquid. Cover and refrigerate. Store no longer than 2 weeks.

POACHED
ORANGES →

- 7 large oranges
- ½ cup (125 mL) sangria
- ½ teaspoon (2 mL) grated lemon peel

6 to 8 servings

Advance preparation: *Prepare early in day; refrigerate.*

1 Slice off ends of fruit. Using a sawing motion, peel in spiral. Remove membrane, leaving as much fruit as possible.

2 Hold fruit over bowl to catch juice. Cut to center between fruit segment and dividing membrane with sharp knife.

3 Place orange sections in 1- to 1½-quart (1 to 1.5 L) casserole. Combine sangria and lemon peel. Pour over orange sections; cover.

4 Microwave at High 2 to 5 minutes, or until heated, stirring once or twice during cooking time. Serve warm or cold.

DRESSING RECIPES

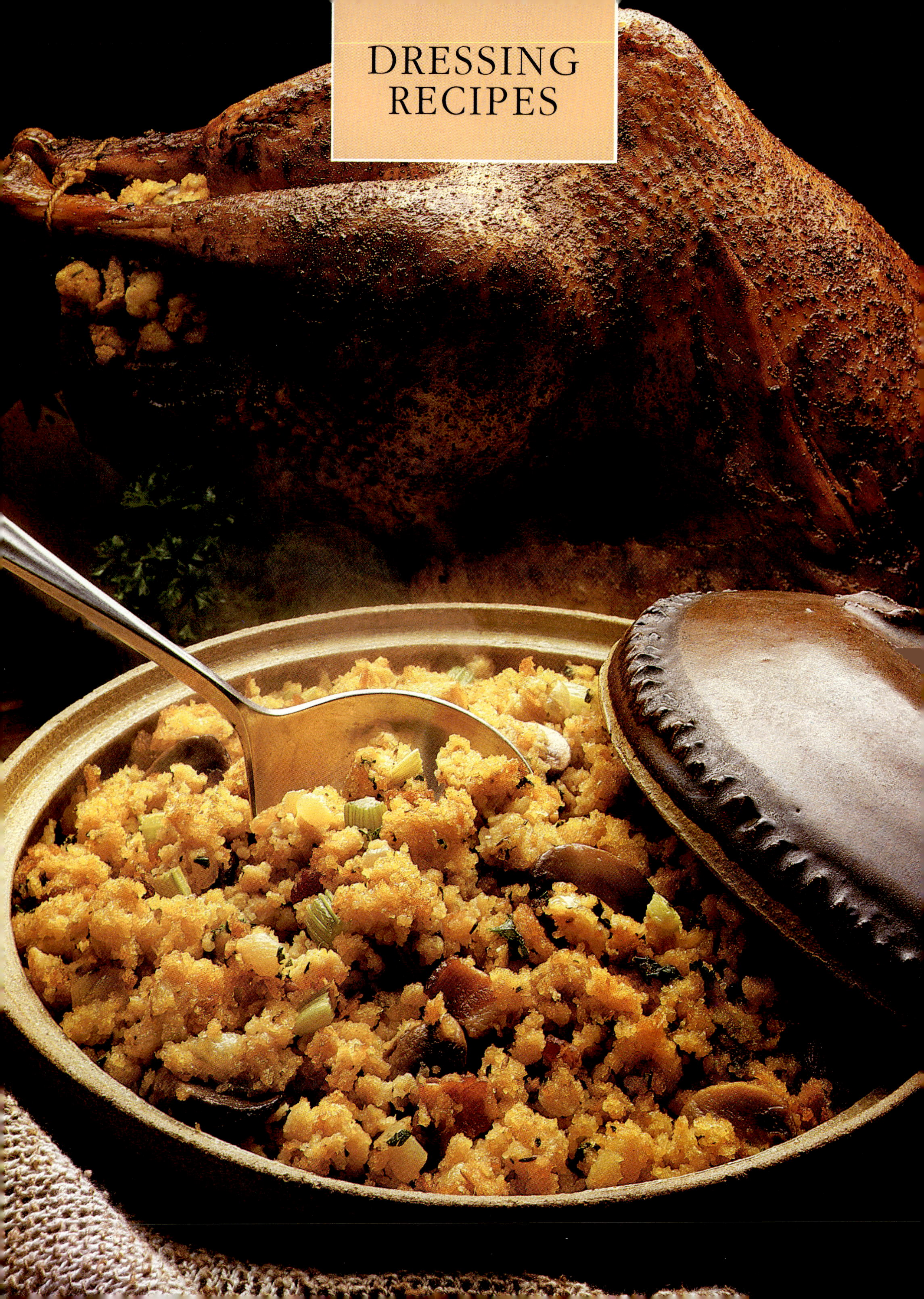

Dressing and stuffing can be spooned into the bird just before roasting or can be baked separately in a casserole. When baked in the bird, the stuffing should be packed lightly, to allow room for expansion. If baked separately as a side dish to accompany roasts, grilled meats or other main courses, the stuffing may be basted with pan juices for added flavor.

GINGERED RICE STUFFING →

- 2 cups (500 mL) chopped celery
- 1 medium onion, chopped
- 2 teaspoons (10 mL) grated fresh gingerroot
- ½ cup (125 mL) butter or margarine
- 2 cups (500 mL) cooked rice
- 1 can (8 oz./227 mL) sliced water chestnuts, drained
- ⅓ cup (75 mL) unseasoned dry bread crumbs

Makes about 5 cups (1.25 L)

1 In medium skillet, cook and stir celery, onion and gingerroot in butter over medium heat until tender.

2 In medium mixing bowl, combine vegetable mixture and remaining ingredients; mix well.

3 In greased 1½-quart (1.5 L) casserole, bake stuffing, covered, at 350°F/180°C for 30 minutes. Uncover, and continue baking until hot, 15 to 25 minutes.

← CORNBREAD STUFFING

- 5 slices bacon
- 3 tablespoons (50 mL) butter or margarine
- 1 small onion, chopped
- ⅓ cup (75 mL) chopped celery
- 1½ cups (375 mL) sliced fresh mushrooms
- 4 cups (1 L) cornbread stuffing mix
- ⅓ cup (75 mL) snipped fresh parsley
- 1 cup (250 mL) game bird stock or chicken broth
- 1 egg, beaten

Makes about 5 cups (1.25 L)

1 In medium skillet, fry bacon over medium-low heat until crisp. Remove bacon to paper towels to drain. Crumble bacon; set aside.

2 Over medium heat, melt butter in bacon drippings. Add onion and celery. Cook and stir for 3 minutes. Add mushrooms. Cook and stir until vegetables are just tender, about 2 minutes longer. Remove from heat.

3 In medium mixing bowl, combine cornbread stuffing mix, parsley, reserved crumbled bacon and vegetable mixture. Mix well. Add broth and egg. Mix well.

4 In greased 1½-quart (1.5 L) casserole, bake stuffing, covered, at 350°F/180°C for 30 minutes. Uncover, and continue baking until hot, 15 to 25 minutes.

CABBAGE DRESSING

- 3 cups (750 mL) unseasoned croutons
- ½ cup (125 mL) thinly sliced onion
- ½ cup (125 mL) shredded cabbage
- ½ cup (125 mL) finely chopped celery
- 1 cup (250 mL) game bird stock or chicken broth
- 1 egg
- ½ to 1 teaspoon (2 to 5 mL) dried crushed sage leaves
- 1 teaspoon (5 mL) lemon-pepper seasoning
- ½ teaspoon (2 mL) salt

Makes about 5 cups (1.25 L)

1 In large mixing bowl, combine croutons, onion, cabbage, and celery. Mix well.

2 In small mixing bowl, blend stock, egg, sage, lemon-pepper seasoning and salt. Add to crouton mixture. Mix well.

3 In greased 1½-quart (1.5 L) casserole, bake dressing, covered, at 350°F/180°C for 30 minutes. Uncover, and continue baking until hot, 15 to 25 minutes.

WHOLE WHEAT FRUIT DRESSING

- ½ cup (125 mL) butter or margarine
- ¼ cup (50 mL) sliced green onions
- 6 cups (1.5 L) soft whole wheat bread cubes
- 1 cup (250 mL) chopped dried fruit
- ½ cup (125 mL) chopped pecans
- ½ teaspoon (2 mL) grated orange peel
- 1 medium orange, peeled and chopped (about ½ cup/125 mL)
- ½ teaspoon (2 mL) salt
- ¼ teaspoon (1 mL) ground allspice
- 1 cup (250 mL) water

8 servings

1 In large mixing bowl, microwave butter at High for 1½ to 1¾ minutes, or until melted. Add onions. Microwave at High for 1 minute.

2 Stir in remaining ingredients. Spoon into 9" (2.5 L) square baking dish. * Cover with wax paper. Microwave at High for 5 to 7 minutes, or until hot, stirring once.

Advance preparation: *Up to 2 days in advance, prepare as directed to * above. Cover with plastic wrap and refrigerate. To serve, cover with wax paper. Microwave at High for 7 to 9 minutes, or until hot, stirring once.*

RICE & SAUSAGE DRESSING ↑

- ½ cup (125 mL) butter or margarine
- ½ cup (125 mL) chopped onion
- ½ cup (125 mL) chopped green pepper
- ½ cup (125 mL) chopped carrot
- 4 cups (1 L) cooked long-grain white or brown rice
- 1 pkg. (8 oz./250 g) frozen, fully cooked pork sausage links, cut into ½" (1 cm) pieces
- ½ teaspoon (2 mL) salt
- ½ teaspoon (2 mL) dried thyme leaves
- ¼ teaspoon (1 mL) garlic powder
- Pinch of pepper

8 servings

1 In large mixing bowl, microwave butter at High for 1½ to 1¾ minutes, or until melted. Add onion, green pepper and carrot. Cover with microwave-safe plastic wrap. Microwave at High for 3 to 4 minutes, or until vegetables are tender, stirring once.

2 Stir in remaining ingredients. Spoon into 2-quart (2 L) casserole. Re-cover. * Microwave at High for 7 to 9 minutes, or until hot, stirring once.

Advance preparation: *Up to 2 days in advance, prepare as directed to * above. Refrigerate. To serve, microwave at High for 10 to 12 minutes, or until hot, stirring once.*

LEMON SAGE DRESSING →

- ½ cup (125 mL) butter or margarine
- 1 cup (250 mL) sliced celery
- ½ cup (125 mL) sliced green onions
- ½ cup (125 mL) shredded carrot
- 8 cups (2 L) unseasoned stuffing cubes
- ½ teaspoon (2 mL) grated lemon peel
- ½ teaspoon (2 mL) dried sage leaves
- ½ teaspoon (2 mL) salt
- ½ teaspoon (2 mL) pepper
- 1½ cups (375 mL) ready-to-serve chicken broth

8 servings

1 In large mixing bowl, microwave butter at High for 1½ to 1¾ minutes, or until melted. Add celery, onions and carrot. Cover with microwave-safe plastic wrap. Microwave at High for 3 to 4 minutes, or until vegetables are tender, stirring once.

2 Stir in remaining ingredients. Re-cover. * Microwave at High for 5 to 8 minutes, or until hot, stirring once or twice.

Advance preparation: *Up to 2 days in advance, prepare as directed to * above. Refrigerate. To serve, microwave at High, covered, for 9 to 12 minutes, or until hot, stirring once.*

SPICY COUSCOUS DRESSING

- 1 cup (250 mL) ready-to-serve chicken broth
- 1 cup (250 mL) water
- 1 cup (250 mL) uncooked couscous
- ¼ cup (50 mL) chopped red pepper
- ¼ cup (50 mL) chopped green pepper
- 1 tablespoon (15 mL) butter or margarine
- 1 can (5 oz./142 mL) corn, drained
- 2 tablespoons (25 mL) snipped fresh parsley
- ½ teaspoon (2 mL) salt
- ¼ to ½ teaspoon (1 to 2 mL) cayenne
- ¼ teaspoon (1 mL) ground cumin

8 servings

1 In 2-quart (2 L) casserole, place chicken broth and water. Cover. Microwave at High for 4 to 5 minutes, or until mixture boils. Add couscous. Microwave, uncovered, at High for 2 minutes. Let stand for 15 minutes, covered, or until couscous is tender and liquid is absorbed.

2 In small mixing bowl, combine peppers and butter. Cover with microwave-safe plastic wrap. Microwave at High for 2 to 3 minutes, or until peppers are tender-crisp. Add peppers and remaining ingredients to couscous. Mix well. Microwave at High for 3 to 5 minutes, or until hot, stirring once.

Advance preparation: *Up to 2 days in advance, prepare as directed above. Cover and refrigerate. To serve, microwave at High, covered, for 4 to 6 minutes, or until hot, stirring once.*

235

ONION-BREAD DRESSING

- 1 medium onion, cut in half lengthwise and thinly sliced
- ¼ cup (50 mL) butter or margarine
- 4½ cups (1.125 L) herb-seasoned croutons
- 2 teaspoons (10 mL) dried parsley flakes
- ½ teaspoon (2 mL) salt
- ½ teaspoon (2 mL) dried crushed sage leaves, optional
- ½ teaspoon (2 mL) dried basil leaves
- ¼ teaspoon (1 mL) dried marjoram leaves
- 1 cup (250 mL) game bird stock or chicken broth
- 1 egg

Makes about 5 cups (1.25 L)

1 In medium skillet, cook and stir onion in butter over medium heat until tender. Remove from heat; set aside.

2 In medium mixing bowl, combine croutons, parsley, salt, sage, basil and marjoram. Mix well. Stir in onions and butter.

3 In small mixing bowl, blend stock and egg. Add to crouton mixture. Mix well.

4 In greased 1½-quart (1.5 L) casserole, bake dressing, covered, at 350°F/180°C for 30 minutes. Uncover, and continue baking until hot, 15 to 25 minutes.

CHESTNUT DRESSING

- 1 pound (500 g) whole chestnuts (about 3 cups/750 mL)
- 1 medium onion, chopped
- 1 tablespoon (15 mL) butter or margarine
- 2 large apples, cored and chopped
- ¾ cup (175 mL) unseasoned dry bread crumbs
- 1 tablespoon (15 mL) snipped fresh parsley
- ½ teaspoon (2 mL) dried thyme leaves
- ½ teaspoon (2 mL) salt
- ¼ teaspoon (1 mL) pepper
- ¼ cup (50 mL) brandy or chicken stock

Makes about 5 cups (1.25 mL)

1 To prepare chestnuts, make two crosscut gashes on the flat side of each chestnut, using the point of a knife. In Dutch oven, boil 2 quarts (2 L) water. Add chestnuts. Boil for 15 to 25 minutes. Drain. Allow chestnuts to cool enough to handle. Peel chestnuts, and cut each into 4 pieces. Place into medium mixing bowl; set aside.

2 In medium skillet, cook and stir onion in butter over medium heat until tender. Add to reserved chestnuts. Add remaining ingredients; mix well.

3 In greased 1½-quart (1.5 L) casserole, bake dressing, covered, at 350°F/180°C for 30 minutes. Uncover, and continue baking until hot, 15 to 25 minutes.

APRICOT STUFFING

- 7 to 8 slices whole wheat or white bread (or half whole wheat, half white bread)
- ½ cup (125 mL) cut-up dried apricots
- ½ cup (125 mL) chopped pecans or walnuts
- 1 teaspoon (5 mL) dried crushed sage leaves
- 1 teaspoon (5 mL) dried parsley flakes
- ½ teaspoon (2 mL) salt
- ¼ teaspoon (1 mL) pepper
- 1 medium onion, chopped
- 1 cup (250 mL) chopped celery
- ¼ cup (50 mL) butter or margarine
- 1 cup (250 mL) game bird stock or chicken broth

Makes about 5 cups (1.25 L)

1 Heat oven to 325°F/160°C. Place bread directly on oven rack. Bake until bread is dry, 5 to 10 minutes. Cool. Cut into ½" (1 cm) cubes. There should be about 5 cups (1.25 L) bread cubes. Place bread cubes in medium mixing bowl. Add apricots, pecans, sage, parsley, salt and pepper. Mix well; set aside.

2 In medium skillet, cook and stir onion and celery in butter over medium heat until tender. Stir into bread-cube mixture. Add stock; mix well.

3 In greased 1½-quart (1.5 L) casserole, bake stuffing, covered, at 350°F/180°C for 30 minutes. Uncover, and continue baking until hot, 15 to 25 minutes.

SPICY SAUSAGE DRESSING

- ¼ cup (50 mL) butter or margarine
- 5 cups (1.25 L) cubed French bread, ¾" (2 cm) cubes
- ½ pound (250 g) spicy pork sausage
- 1 small onion, chopped
- ⅓ cup (75 mL) thinly sliced celery
- 1 medium apple, cored and chopped
- ½ cup (125 mL) chopped pecans or walnuts
- ⅓ cup (75 mL) game bird stock or chicken broth

Makes about 5 cups (1.25 L)

1 In large skillet, melt butter over medium-low heat. Add bread cubes, stirring to coat. Cook and stir over medium heat until bread cubes are lightly toasted. Transfer bread cubes to large mixing bowl. Set aside.

2 In same skillet, cook sausage over medium heat until meat loses pink color, stirring to break up pieces. Add onion and celery. Cook and stir until vegetables are tender and pork sausage is cooked through. Add sausage mixture to bread cubes. Add apple and pecans. Mix well. Add stock. Mix well.

3 In greased 1½-quart (1.5 L) casserole, bake dressing, covered, at 350°F/180°C for 30 minutes. Uncover, and continue baking until hot, 15 to 25 minutes.

SOUPS

PEPPER & CHEESE BISQUE

- 3 cups (750 mL) chopped red, green and yellow peppers
- 1 cup (250 mL) sliced celery
- 1 red chili pepper or jalapeño pepper, sliced and seeded
- 2 tablespoons (25 mL) butter or margarine
- ¼ cup (50 mL) all-purpose flour
- 1 teaspoon (5 mL) instant chicken bouillon granules
- ½ teaspoon (2 mL) celery salt
- 3 cups (750 mL) milk
- 1 cup (250 mL) shredded Cheddar cheese or pasteurized process American cheese loaf

6 servings

1 In 3-quart (3 L) casserole, combine peppers, celery, chili pepper and butter. Cover. Microwave at High for 10 to 12 minutes, or until vegetables are tender, stirring once.

2 Stir in flour, bouillon and salt. Blend in milk. Microwave at High, uncovered, for 6 to 8 minutes, or until bisque is slightly thickened, stirring every 2 minutes. Stir in cheese until melted.

SPINACH BISQUE

- 1 cup (250 mL) sliced celery
- ⅓ to ½ cup (75 to 125 mL) sliced green onions
- 1 tablespoon (15 mL) olive oil
- 1 clove garlic, minced
- 3 tablespoons (50 mL) all-purpose flour
- 3 cups (750 mL) milk
- 3 tablespoons (50 mL) tomato paste
- ¼ teaspoon (1 mL) salt
- ⅛ teaspoon (0.5 mL) cayenne
- 3 cups (750 mL) shredded spinach leaves

4 servings

1 In 2-quart (2 L) casserole, combine celery, onions, oil and garlic. Cover. Microwave at High for 4 to 6 minutes, or until celery is tender, stirring once. Stir in flour. Blend in milk. Microwave at High, uncovered, for 8 to 13 minutes, or until mixture is slightly thickened, stirring every 2 minutes.

2 Using wire whisk, blend in tomato paste, salt and cayenne. Add spinach. Cover. Microwave at High for 1 to 2 minutes, or until spinach is wilted.

NOTE: *If desired, add 1 can (6 oz./170 g) crabmeat, rinsed and drained, with spinach.*

VEGETABLE GUMBO →

- ¼ cup (50 mL) all-purpose flour
- 1 can (14½ oz./412 mL) ready-to-serve chicken broth, divided
- 1 medium zucchini squash, sliced (1 cup/250 mL)
- 1 medium yellow squash, sliced (1 cup/250 mL)
- 1 ear corn on the cob (8 oz./250 g), kernels sliced off (¾ cup/175 mL) and cob discarded
- ½ cup (125 mL) chopped peeled kohlrabi
- ½ cup (125 mL) chopped peeled carrot
- ½ cup (125 mL) sliced leek
- 2 medium tomatoes, chopped (2 cups/500 mL)
- 1 cup (250 mL) sliced okra (½"/1 cm slices)
- ¼ teaspoon (1 mL) freshly ground pepper
- Hot cooked rice

4 to 5 servings

1 Heat oven to 400°F/200°C. Sprinkle flour evenly into 8" (2 L) square baking pan. Bake 10 to 15 minutes, or until flour is deep golden brown, stirring every 5 minutes. Set aside.

2 In 3-quart (3 L) casserole, combine ¼ cup (50 mL) broth, the squashes, corn, kohlrabi, carrot and leek. Cover. Microwave at High for 11 to 15 minutes, or until zucchini is tender, stirring once.

3 Stir in flour. Blend in remaining broth. Add tomatoes, okra and pepper. Mix well. Re-cover. Microwave at High for 15 to 20 minutes, or until gumbo is slightly thickened and vegetables are tender, stirring 3 times. Serve over hot cooked rice.

CREAM OF THREE-ONION SOUP

- 1 cup (250 mL) sliced leek
- 1 cup (250 mL) halved peeled white pearl onions
- ½ cup (125 mL) sliced green onions
- 2 tablespoons (25 mL) butter or margarine
- ¼ cup plus 2 tablespoons (75 mL) all-purpose flour
- 1 tablespoon (15 mL) Dijon mustard
- ¼ teaspoon (1 mL) garlic powder
- ⅛ teaspoon (0.5 mL) white pepper
- 1 can (14½ oz./412 mL) ready-to-serve chicken broth
- 1½ cups (375 mL) half-and-half

4 to 6 servings

1 In 3-quart (3 L) casserole, combine leek, onions and butter. Cover. Microwave at High for 6 to 8 minutes, or until vegetables are tender, stirring once. Stir in flour, mustard, garlic powder and pepper. Blend in broth and half-and-half.

2 Microwave at 70% (Medium High), uncovered, for 10 to 13 minutes, or until soup thickens slightly and bubbles, stirring twice. (Do not boil.) Garnish with snipped fresh chives or green onion, if desired.

CREAM OF CARROT SOUP ↑

- 1 lb. (500 g) carrots, peeled and sliced (3 cups/750 mL)
- 1 cup (250 mL) ready-to-serve chicken broth, divided
- ½ cup (125 mL) chopped onion
- 2 tablespoons (25 mL) all-purpose flour
- ⅛ teaspoon (0.5 mL) white pepper
- 1 cup (250 mL) milk

4 servings

1 In 2-quart (2 L) casserole, combine carrots, ¼ cup (50 mL) broth and the onion. Cover. Microwave at High for 11 to 15 minutes, or until carrots are tender, stirring twice. In food processor or blender, process carrot mixture until smooth. Return purée to casserole.

2 In 2-cup (500 mL) measure, combine flour and pepper. Blend in remaining ¾ cup (175 mL) broth. Add broth mixture to casserole. Microwave at High, uncovered, for 3 to 4 minutes, or until mixture is slightly thickened, stirring every minute. Stir in milk. Microwave at 70% (Medium High) for 3 to 4 minutes, or until soup is hot, stirring once. Garnish with croutons, if desired.

CREAM OF TOMATO-BASIL SOUP

- 1/3 cup (75 mL) chopped shallots
- 1 tablespoon (15 mL) olive oil
- 1 clove garlic, minced
- 1 can (28 oz./796 mL) Roma tomatoes, undrained and cut up
- 1/2 cup (125 mL) ready-to-serve chicken broth
- 1/4 cup (50 mL) snipped fresh basil leaves
- 1/2 teaspoon (2 mL) sugar
- 1/2 teaspoon (2 mL) freshly ground pepper
- 1/4 teaspoon (1 mL) salt
- 4 Roma tomatoes, chopped (2 cups/500 mL), divided
- 1 cup (250 mL) half-and-half, divided

6 servings

1 In 2-quart (2 L) casserole, combine shallots, oil and garlic. Cover. Microwave at High for 2 to 3 minutes, or until tender. Add canned broth, basil, sugar, pepper and salt. Microwave at High, uncovered, for 4 to 6 minutes, or until mixture is hot and flavors are blended, stirring once.

2 In food processor or blender, combine half of tomato mixture, 2 Roma tomatoes and 1/2 cup (125 mL) half-and-half. Process until smooth. Set purée aside. Repeat with remaining ingredients. Return purée to casserole. Cover. Microwave at 70% (Medium High) for 13 to 15 minutes, or until soup is hot, stirring twice. Spoon into serving dishes. Top each serving with 1 crostini*, if desired.

To make crostini, arrange 6 thin slices Italian bread on baking sheet. Brush slices evenly with 1 tablespoon (15 mL) olive oil. Top each with 2 thin slices Roma tomato, 1 small fresh basil leaf and 1 teaspoon (5 mL) shredded fresh Parmesan cheese. Broil 5" (12 cm) from heat for 4 to 5 minutes, or until golden brown.

SPICED TOMATO & ← ZUCCHINI SOUP

- 1 can (28 oz./796 mL) Roma tomatoes, undrained and cut up
- 2 medium tomatoes, chopped (2 cups/500 mL)
- 1 medium zucchini, thinly sliced (1 cup/250 mL)
- 2 ears corn on the cob (8 oz./250 g each), kernels sliced off (1½ cups/375 mL) and cobs discarded
- 1 cup (250 mL) ready-to-serve chicken broth
- 1 tablespoon (15 mL) olive oil
- 1 tablespoon (15 mL) chili powder
- ½ teaspoon (2 mL) sugar
- ¼ teaspoon (1 mL) ground cinnamon

6 to 8 servings

1 In 3-quart (3 L) casserole, combine all ingredients. Cover.

2 Microwave at High for 25 to 30 minutes, or until vegetables are tender and flavors are blended, stirring every 5 minutes.

SWEET POTATO VICHYSSOISE

- 2 medium sweet potatoes, peeled and cut into ½" (1 cm) cubes (2 cups/500 mL)
- 1 cup (250 mL) sliced leek
- ¼ cup (50 mL) dry white wine
- 2 tablespoons (25 mL) butter or margarine
- 1 teaspoon (5 mL) grated fresh gingerroot
- 1 cup (250 mL) ready-to-serve chicken broth
- 1 cup (250 mL) milk

4 servings

1 In 2-quart (2 L) casserole, combine all ingredients, except broth and milk. Cover. Microwave at High for 8 to 13 minutes, or until potatoes are very tender, stirring once.

2 In food processor or blender, process potato mixture until smooth. Return purée to casserole. Stir in broth and milk. Microwave at 70% (Medium High), uncovered, for 8 to 10 minutes, or until soup is hot and flavors are blended, stirring once. Serve hot or cold. Garnish with snipped fresh chives, if desired.

SPICY TORTELLINI SOUP ↑

- 8 oz. (250 g) mushrooms, sliced (2 cups/500 mL)
- 1 cup (250 mL) chopped onions
- 1 tablespoon (15 mL) olive oil
- 1 clove garlic, minced
- 2 medium tomatoes, chopped (2 cups/500 mL)
- 1 can (14½ oz./412 mL) ready-to-serve beef broth
- 1 can (8 oz./227 mL) tomato sauce
- ½ cup (125 mL) thick and chunky salsa
- 2 tablespoons (25 mL) snipped fresh basil leaves
- 1 pkg. (9 oz./255 g) uncooked fresh cheese tortellini

6 servings

1 In 3-quart (3 L) casserole, combine mushrooms, onions, oil and garlic. Cover. Microwave at High for 8 to 10 minutes, or just until mushrooms are tender, stirring once.

2 Add remaining ingredients, except tortellini. Mix well. Re-cover. Microwave at High for 10 to 12 minutes, or until mixture is hot and flavors are blended, stirring once. Add tortellini. Re-cover. Microwave at High for 10 to 15 minutes, or until tortellini are tender, stirring once. Sprinkle with shredded fresh Parmesan cheese, if desired.

RATATOUILLE SOUP

- 1 medium eggplant (1 lb./500 g), peeled and cut into cubes
- 1 cup (250 mL) chopped onions
- 2 tablespoons (25 mL) olive oil
- 1 tablespoon (15 mL) snipped fresh rosemary
- 1 tablespoon (15 mL) lemon juice
- 1 to 2 cloves garlic, minced
- 1 can (28 oz./796 mL) Roma tomatoes, undrained and cut up
- 1 medium zucchini, sliced (1 cup/250 mL)
- 1 cup (250 mL) chopped green peppers
- 4 oz. (125 g) mushrooms, sliced (1 cup/250 mL)
- 1 cup (250 mL) ready-to-serve chicken broth
- ¼ to ½ teaspoon (1 to 2 mL) freshly ground pepper

8 servings

1 In 3-quart (3 L) casserole, combine eggplant, onions, oil, rosemary, juice and garlic. Cover. Microwave at High for 10 to 15 minutes, or until eggplant is tender, stirring twice.

2 Add remaining ingredients. Mix well. Re-cover. Microwave at High for 18 to 21 minutes, or until vegetables are tender, stirring twice.

EASY CHEESY CLAM CHOWDER

- 1 pkg. (10 oz./300 g) frozen broccoli, cauliflower and carrots in cheese-flavored sauce
- 2 cans (10¾ oz./284 mL each) condensed cream of potato soup
- 1 can (6½ oz./185 g) minced clams, undrained
- ½ cup (125 mL) milk
- ½ cup (125 mL) water
- 1 tablespoon (15 mL) dried parsley flakes
- 3 drops red pepper sauce

4 to 6 servings

Advance preparation: *Up to 1 day in advance, prepare as directed below. Cover and refrigerate. To serve, microwave at High for 10 to 15 minutes, or until hot, stirring twice.*

1 Cut a small slit in center of vegetable pouch using scissors. Microwave slit-side-up at High for 4 to 6 minutes, or until defrosted, rotating once. Set aside.

2 Combine remaining ingredients in 3-quart (3 L) casserole. Cover. Microwave at High for 6 to 8 minutes, or until mixture is hot, stirring once.

3 Stir in vegetables and cheese sauce. Mix well. Re-cover. Microwave at High for 5 to 8 minutes, or until chowder is hot, stirring once.

PUMPKIN SOUP

- 1 small pumpkin (2 lbs./1 kg), peeled, seeded and cut into cubes
- 1 can (5½ oz./156 mL) apricot nectar
- ½ cup (125 mL) sliced green onions
- 1 tablespoon (15 mL) butter or margarine
- ½ teaspoon (2 mL) grated fresh orange peel
- ¼ to ½ teaspoon (1 to 2 mL) grated fresh gingerroot
- ¼ teaspoon (1 mL) ground nutmeg
- ¼ teaspoon (1 mL) salt
- ¼ teaspoon (1 mL) freshly ground pepper
- 1 cup (250 mL) milk

4 servings

1 In 3-quart (3 L) casserole, combine pumpkin and nectar. Cover. Microwave at High for 13 to 15 minutes, or until pumpkin is tender, stirring twice. In food processor or blender, process pumpkin mixture until smooth. Set aside.

2 In same casserole, combine onions and butter. Cover. Microwave at High for 2 to 3 minutes, or until onions are tender-crisp, stirring once. Add pumpkin purée and remaining ingredients, except milk, to casserole. Re-cover.

3 Microwave at High for 4 to 5 minutes, or until mixture is hot and bubbly, stirring once. Stir in milk. Re-cover. Microwave at High for 2 to 3 minutes, or until soup is hot. Garnish with toasted pumpkin seeds*, if desired.

* To make toasted pumpkin seeds, save ½ cup (125 mL) seeds from pumpkin. Heat oven to 300°F/150°C. Rinse, drain and pat seeds dry. In small mixing bowl, combine seeds, 1 teaspoon (5 mL) vegetable oil and ½ teaspoon (2 mL) seasoned salt. Spread seeds in single layer on baking sheet. Bake for 25 to 28 minutes, or until golden brown, stirring every 10 minutes.

FALL FRUIT GAZPACHO ↓

- 2 cups (500 mL) apple juice
- ½ cup (125 mL) orange juice
- ½ cup (125 mL) golden raisins
- ½ cup (125 mL) snipped dried apricots
- 2 tablespoons (25 mL) packed brown sugar
- 2 tablespoons (25 mL) lemon juice
- 1 small stick cinnamon
- 4 cups (1 L) chopped mixed fruits (apple, pear, peach, grapes, figs)

5 to 6 servings

1 In 2-quart (2 L) casserole, combine all ingredients, except chopped fruits. Microwave at High, uncovered, for 7 to 9 minutes, or until mixture is hot and raisins are plumped.

2 Discard cinnamon stick. Add fruits. Mix well. Cool slightly. Cover and chill.

SALADS

STRAWBERRY-AVOCADO SALAD ↑

- 6 cups (1.5 L) trimmed and torn curly endive
- 2 cups (500 mL) fresh strawberries, hulled and sliced
- 1 avocado, sliced

Dressing:

- ⅓ cup (75 mL) honey
- ⅓ cup (75 mL) orange juice
- ⅓ cup (75 mL) vegetable oil
- 1 tablespoon (15 mL) poppy seed

6 to 8 servings

1 In large mixing bowl, toss endive, strawberries and avocado. Set aside. In 2-cup (500 mL) measure, combine dressing ingredients. Microwave at High for 45 seconds to 1 minute, or until hot. Pour over endive mixture and toss to coat. Serve immediately.

Advance preparation: Up to 1 day in advance, combine dressing ingredients and refrigerate. To serve, toss endive, strawberries and avocado in large mixing bowl. Microwave dressing for 1½ to 2 minutes, or until hot. Pour over endive mixture and toss to coat.

MARINATED GREEN BEAN SALAD

- 1 lb. (500 g) fresh green beans, cut into 1" (2.5 cm) lengths
- ½ cup (125 mL) sugar
- ½ cup (125 mL) white vinegar
- 1 teaspoon (5 mL) celery seed
- ¼ teaspoon (1 mL) dry mustard
- 1 cup (250 mL) fresh mushrooms, cut into quarters
- 1 cup (250 mL) cherry tomatoes, cut in half

8 servings

1 Place green beans in 2-quart (2 L) casserole. In 2-cup (500 mL) measure, combine remaining ingredients, except mushrooms and tomatoes. Pour vinegar mixture over green beans. Toss to coat.

2 Microwave at High for 6 to 10 minutes, or until green beans are tender-crisp, stirring twice. Stir in mushrooms and tomatoes. Cover and refrigerate 4 to 6 hours, or overnight. Use slotted spoon to serve.

ENDIVE-BROCCOLI SALAD

- 4 cups (1 L) fresh broccoli flowerets
- 1 cup (250 mL) julienne red pepper (1½ x ¼"/4 cm x 5 mm strips)
- 2 tablespoons (25 mL) water
- 4 cups (1 L) trimmed and torn curly endive
- ½ cup (125 mL) olive oil
- ¼ cup (50 mL) white wine vinegar
- ½ teaspoon (2 mL) sugar
- ½ teaspoon (2 mL) salt
- ¼ teaspoon (1 mL) dried basil leaves
- ¼ teaspoon (1 mL) garlic powder
- Pinch of white pepper
- ½ cup (125 mL) pitted black olives

8 servings

1 In 2-quart (2 L) casserole, combine broccoli, red pepper and water. Cover. Microwave at High for 5 to 6 minutes, or until vegetables are very hot and color brightens, stirring once or twice. Rinse with cold water. Drain. In large mixing bowl, combine broccoli mixture and endive.

2 In 2-cup (500 mL) measure, combine remaining ingredients, except olives. Microwave at High for 2 to 3 minutes, or until mixture boils, beating well with whisk once. Cool 10 minutes. Pour over broccoli mixture. Toss gently. Sprinkle with olives.

LEMONY FREEZER SLAW →

- 3 cups (750 mL) sliced green cabbage
- 3 cups (750 mL) sliced red cabbage
- 1 cup (250 mL) shredded carrot
- 2 teaspoons (10 mL) grated lemon peel
- 1 cup (250 mL) sugar
- 1 cup (250 mL) white vinegar
- 1 teaspoon (5 mL) poppy seed
- ½ teaspoon (2 mL) salt
- ¼ teaspoon (1 mL) onion powder

8 servings

1 In large mixing bowl, combine cabbages, carrot and lemon peel. Set aside. In 4-cup (1 L) measure, combine remaining ingredients. Microwave at High for 4 to 5½ minutes, or until boiling. Cool slightly. Pour over cabbage mixture. Stir gently. Transfer to plastic freezer container. Label and freeze no longer than 1 month.

2 To serve, remove cover. Microwave at High for 2 minutes. Stir to break apart. Microwave at 50% (Medium) for 4 to 5 minutes, or until defrosted, stirring once. Mixture should still be very cold.

CRANBERRY WALDORF SALAD

Dressing:

- 2 eggs
- ⅓ cup (75 mL) sugar
- ¼ cup (50 mL) orange juice
- 2 tablespoons (25 mL) water
- 2 tablespoons (25 mL) grated orange peel

Salad:

- 2 cups (500 mL) fresh or frozen cranberries, chopped
- 2 medium oranges, peeled and chopped (about 1 cup/250 mL)
- 1 large apple, chopped (about 1 cup/250 mL)
- 1 cup (250 mL) chopped dates
- ½ cup (125 mL) chopped walnuts
- 2 cups (500 mL) miniature marshmallows

1 In 4-cup (1 L) measure, beat eggs well with whisk. Add remaining dressing ingredients. Beat with whisk until mixture is smooth. Microwave at 50% (Medium) for 4 to 6 minutes, or until mixture thickens, beating with whisk every 2 minutes. Chill about 2 hours, or until cold.

2 In large mixing bowl, combine salad ingredients. * Spoon dressing over salad. Toss gently to coat.

Advance preparation: *Up to 1 day in advance, prepare as directed to * above, except omit marshmallows. Cover and refrigerate dressing and salad in separate containers. To serve, add marshmallows to salad. Spoon dressing over salad. Toss gently to coat.*

8 servings

DATE & CHERRY MOLDS

- 2 cups (500 mL) hot water
- 1 pkg. (6 oz./170 g) cherry gelatin
- 1½ cups (375 mL) cold water
- 1½ cups (375 mL) diced Granny Smith apples
- 1 cup (250 mL) maraschino cherries, cut into quarters
- ¾ cup (175 mL) chopped dates
- ¾ cup (175 mL) blanched almonds, chopped
- 1 pkg. (3 oz./85 g) cream cheese

8 servings

1 Brush the inside of eight (6 to 8-oz./175 to 250 mL each) salad molds or custard cups lightly with vegetable oil. Set aside. Place hot water in medium mixing bowl. Cover with plastic wrap. Microwave at High for 2 to 3 minutes, or until boiling. Stir in gelatin until dissolved. Add cold water. Chill 45 minutes to 1 hour, or until gelatin is soft-set.

2 Stir in remaining ingredients, except cream cheese. Spoon mixture evenly into prepared molds. Chill 2 hours or until set. *

3 Dip each mold into warm water for 30 seconds. Loosen edges and unmold onto serving plates. In small bowl, microwave cream cheese at High for 15 to 30 seconds, or until softened. Pipe or spoon cream cheese evenly onto each salad.

Advance preparation: *Up to 1 day in advance, prepare to * above. Up to 4 hours in advance, unmold onto serving plates and decorate with softened cream cheese. Chill until serving time.*

LEMON-VEGETABLE WREATH ↑

- 2 envelopes (0.25 oz./7 g each) unflavored gelatin
- ½ cup (125 mL) cold water
- 2½ cups (625 mL) hot water
- ⅓ cup (75 mL) sugar
- ¼ cup (50 mL) fresh lemon juice
- 1 pkg. (6 oz./170 g) frozen pea pods
- 1 medium cucumber, quartered lengthwise and thinly sliced (about 1¼ cups/300 mL)

- ½ cups (125 mL) thinly sliced celery
- ½ cup (125 mL) chopped red pepper
- ½ cup (125 mL) fresh parsley sprigs
- 1 teaspoon (5 mL) grated lemon peel
- Leaf lettuce

8 servings

1 Brush the inside of 6-cup (1.5 L) ring mold lightly with vegetable oil. Set aside. In medium mixing bowl, sprinkle gelatin over cold water to soften. Set aside. Place hot water in 4-cup (1 L) measure. Cover with microwave-safe plastic wrap. Microwave at High for 5 to 8 minutes, or until boiling. Add boiling water to gelatin and stir until gelatin is completely dissolved. Stir in sugar and lemon juice. Chill 1¾ to 2 hours, or until very cold.

2 Place pea pods in 1-quart (1 L) casserole. Cover. Microwave at High for 2 to 2½ minutes, or just until defrosted. Rinse with cold water. Drain. Stir pea pods and remaining ingredients, except lettuce, into gelatin mixture. Pour into prepared ring mold. Chill until set, about 2 hours. *

3 Line serving platter with lettuce. Dip mold into warm water for 30 seconds. Loosen edges and unmold onto platter.

Advance preparation: *Up to 1 day in advance, prepare to * above. Up to 4 hours in advance, unmold onto serving platter and chill until serving time.*

FESTIVE MELON BALL MOLD

- 1 cup (250 mL) hot water
- 1 pkg. (3 oz./85 g) lime gelatin
- ¾ cup (175 mL) cold water
- 2 cups (500 mL) cantaloupe balls
- 1 can (8 oz./227 mL) pineapple tidbits, drained
- 1 cup (250 mL) seedless red grapes
- ½ cup (125 mL) sliced celery
- Red-tipped leaf lettuce
- 1 pkg. (3 oz./85 g) cream cheese (optional)

8 servings

1 Brush the inside of 4 or 5-cup (1 L) mold lightly with vegetable oil. Set aside. Place hot water in 4-cup (1 L) measure. Cover with plastic wrap. Microwave at High for 2 to 3 minutes, or until boiling. Stir in gelatin until dissolved. Add cold water. Chill 1½ to 1¾ hours, or until gelatin is soft-set.

2 Add remaining ingredients, except lettuce and cream cheese. Pour into prepared mold. Chill 2 hours, or until set. * Arrange lettuce leaves on serving platter. Dip mold in hot water for 15 to 20 seconds. Loosen edges and unmold onto serving platter. Chill until serving time.

3 In small mixing bowl, microwave cream cheese at High for 15 to 30 seconds, or until softened. Stir until smooth. Spoon or pipe as desired onto salad.

Advance preparation: *Up to 1 day in advance, prepare mold to * above. Up to 4 hours in advance, unmold onto serving platter and decorate with cream cheese. Chill until serving time.*

249

FRUITED ← TABBOULEH

- 1¼ cups (300 mL) hot water
- ¾ cup (175 mL) uncooked bulgur (cracked wheat)
- 2 medium seedless oranges, peeled and sectioned
- ½ cup (125 mL) raspberries
- ¼ cup (50 mL) chopped pecans

Dressing:

- ¼ cup (50 mL) vegetable oil
- 3 tablespoons (50 mL) red wine vinegar
- 2 tablespoons (25 mL) frozen orange juice concentrate, defrosted
- ¼ teaspoon (1 mL) ground cinnamon
- ⅛ teaspoon (0.5 mL) ground allspice
- Leaf lettuce

6 servings

1 Place water in 1½-quart (1.5 L) casserole. Cover. Microwave at High for 4 to 6 minutes, or until boiling. Stir in bulgur. Re-cover. Let stand for 15 to 20 minutes, or until liquid is absorbed. Fluff with fork. Add oranges, raspberries and pecans. Stir to combine. Set aside.

2 In 1-cup (250 mL) measure, combine dressing ingredients. Pour dressing over salad. Toss to coat. Cover with plastic wrap. Chill. Serve on lettuce-lined plates.

ORANGE-SPROUT SALAD

- 1 medium cucumber, cut in half lengthwise and sliced (2 cups/500 mL)
- 1 cup (250 mL) thinly sliced radishes
- 1 cup (250 mL) bean sprouts
- 1 cup (250 mL) alfalfa sprouts

Dressing:

- 2 tablespoons (25 mL) honey
- 1 tablespoon (15 mL) grated orange peel
- 1 tablespoon (15 mL) orange juice
- Sorrel leaves

4 servings

1 In large mixing bowl or salad bowl, combine cucumber, radishes and sprouts. Set aside.

2 In 1-cup (250 mL) measure, combine dressing ingredients. Microwave at High for 30 seconds to 1½ minutes, or until hot, stirring once. Pour over cucumber mixture, tossing to coat. Serve on sorrel-lined plates.

SPICED PEAR
SALAD →

- ½ cup (125 mL) packed brown sugar
- ¼ cup (50 mL) sherry
- 1 can (29 oz./824 mL) pear halves, drained and ¼ cup (50 mL) juice reserved
- 1 tablespoon (15 mL) vinegar
- ¼ teaspoon (1 mL) ground cinnamon
- ¼ teaspoon (1 mL) ground nutmeg
- Pinch of ground cloves
- ½ pkg. (8 oz./250 g) cream cheese
- ¼ cup (50 mL) chopped nuts
- 8 lettuce leaves

8 servings

1 In medium bowl mix brown sugar, sherry, reserved juice, vinegar, cinnamon, nutmeg and cloves. Microwave at High 1 to 3 minutes, or until boiling, stirring after half the time. Add pear halves, stirring to coat. Microwave at High 1 to 3 minutes, or until heated. Refrigerate until chilled.

2 Cut cream cheese into eight pieces. Shape into balls; roll in nuts. For each serving, place 1 pear half on a lettuce leaf. Spoon on sauce. Place cheese ball in hollow of each pear half.

Advance preparation: *Pears and sauce can be made 1 to 2 days in advance. Assemble salad before serving.*

ORANGE-ENDIVE
SALAD →

- 1 small head endive, torn into bite-size pieces
- 1 small head leaf lettuce, torn into bite-size pieces
- 2 oranges, peeled and sectioned
- ½ small red onion, cut into thin slices and separated into rings

4 servings

1 Toss endive and lettuce together. Add orange sections and onion rings. Serve with Italian dressing, if desired.

Advance preparation: *Assemble salad early in the day. Refrigerate until serving.*

SCALLOP, BLACK BEAN & AVOCADO SALAD ↑

- 1 lb. (500 g) fresh bay scallops, rinsed and drained
- 2 medium tomatoes, seeded and chopped (2 cups/500 mL)
- 1 can (15 oz./426 mL) black beans, rinsed and drained
- 1½ cups (375 mL) chopped green pepper
- 1 medium avocado, peeled and chopped (1 cup/250 mL)

Dressing:

- ⅓ cup (75 mL) lemon juice
- ¼ cup (50 mL) olive oil
- ¼ cup (50 mL) sliced green onions
- 2 tablespoons (25 mL) catsup
- ½ teaspoon (2 mL) ground cumin
- ½ teaspoon (2 mL) sugar
- ½ teaspoon (2 mL) seasoned salt
- ¼ teaspoon (1 mL) cayenne

6 to 8 servings

1 In 9" (2.5 L) round cake dish, arrange scallops in single layer. Set aside. In 2-cup (500 mL) measure, combine dressing ingredients. Drizzle 2 tablespoons (25 mL) dressing over scallops. Cover scallops with wax paper or microwave cooking paper. Microwave at 70% (Medium High) for 6 to 7 minutes, or until scallops are firm and opaque, stirring once to rearrange. Drain. Set aside.

2 In medium mixing bowl, combine remaining ingredients and remaining dressing. Add scallops. Toss to combine. Cover with plastic wrap. Chill.

SWEET POTATO SALAD

- 3 medium sweet potatoes, peeled and cut into 2½ x ½"/6 cm x 1 cm chunks (5 cups/1.25 L)
- 4 cups (1 L) hot water, divided
- 2 cups (500 mL) broccoli flowerets
- ½ cup (125 mL) finely chopped fully cooked lean ham
- ⅓ cup (75 mL) sliced green onions

Dressing:

- ⅓ cup (75 mL) French dressing
- ⅓ cup (75 mL) sour cream
- 1 tablespoon (15 mL) snipped fresh chervil leaves

4 to 6 servings

1 In 2-quart (2 L) casserole, combine potatoes and ¼ cup (50 mL) water. Cover. Microwave at High for 9 to 12 minutes, or just until potatoes are tender, stirring once. Drain. Set aside.

2 In 2-quart (2 L) saucepan, bring remaining water to boil over high heat. Plunge broccoli into boiling water for 30 seconds, or until color brightens. Using slotted spoon, remove broccoli and immediately plunge into ice water. Drain.

3 In large mixing bowl or salad bowl, combine potatoes, broccoli, ham and onions. In small mixing bowl, combine dressing ingredients. Add to potato mixture. Toss to coat. Chill.

FENNEL & ORANGE SALAD →

- 1½ teaspoons (7 mL) butter or margarine
- ¼ cup (50 mL) sliced almonds
- 2 medium seedless oranges, peeled and thinly sliced
- 1 bulb fennel (8 oz./250 g), cut into ¼" (5 mm) wedges and separated
- 4 oz. (125 g) cooked smoked turkey breast, cut into 2 x ¼"/5 cm x 5 mm strips (optional)

Dressing:

- 2 tablespoons (25 mL) olive oil
- 2 tablespoons (25 mL) red wine vinegar
- 1 tablespoon (15 mL) snipped fresh tarragon leaves
- 1 teaspoon (5 mL) sugar
- Leaf lettuce

4 servings

1 In 9" (23 cm) pie plate, microwave butter at High for 30 to 45 seconds, or until melted. Stir in almonds, tossing to coat. Microwave at High for 4 to 5 minutes, or until golden brown, stirring every 2 minutes. Set aside.

2 In large mixing bowl or salad bowl, combine oranges, fennel and turkey. In 1-cup (250 mL) measure, combine dressing ingredients. Add to orange mixture. Toss to coat. Serve on lettuce-lined plates. Garnish evenly with toasted almonds.

HOT APPLE & PEAR WALDORF SALAD

- 2 medium d'Anjou pears, cored and cut into ½" (1 cm) cubes
- 1 medium red cooking apple, cored and cut into ½" (1 cm) cubes
- 2 tablespoons (25 mL) lemon juice
- 1 bulb fennel (8 oz./250 g), cut in half lengthwise and sliced
- ½ cup (125 mL) chopped walnuts
- ½ cup (125 mL) raisins

Dressing:

- ⅓ cup (75 mL) mayonnaise
- 2 tablespoons (25 mL) apple cider
- ¼ teaspoon (1 mL) ground cinnamon

6 servings

1 In 2-quart (2 L) casserole, combine pears, apple and juice. Cover. Microwave at High for 5 to 6 minutes, or until fruit is tender-crisp, stirring once. Drain. Stir in fennel, walnuts and raisins.

2 In small mixing bowl, combine dressing ingredients. Add to salad. Toss to coat. Serve warm. Garnish with additional apple and pear slices, if desired.

- 1 cup (250 mL) cranberry cocktail juice
- 1 pkg. (3 oz./85 g) raspberry gelatin mix
- ¼ cup (50 mL) sugar
- ¾ cup (175 mL) sangria
- 1 can (8 oz./227 mL) whole-berry cranberry sauce
- 1 cup (250 mL) chilled whipping cream, whipped
- ½ cup (125 mL) chopped pecans

8 servings

1 Place cranberry juice in medium bowl. Microwave at High 2 to 3 minutes, or until boiling. Add gelatin, stirring to dissolve. Mix in sugar and sangria. Chill 1 hour, or until soft-set.

2 Fold in remaining ingredients. Pour into 6-cup (1.5 L) mold. Chill 3 to 4 hours, or until set. Unmold onto plate.

PINEAPPLE CHEESE SALAD

- 1 cup (250 mL) hot water
- 1 pkg. (3 oz./85 g) lime gelatin mix
- ¾ cup (175 mL) cold water
- 1 can (8 oz./227 mL) crushed pineapple, drained
- 1 carton (4 oz./114 g) frozen whipped dessert topping
- ½ cup (125 mL) ricotta cheese
- ½ cup (125 mL) chopped pecans
- ¼ cup (50 mL) chopped maraschino cherries

6 to 8 servings

1 Pour hot water into medium bowl; cover. Microwave at High 1½ to 2 minutes, or until boiling. Stir in gelatin until dissolved. Mix in cold water. Refrigerate about 1 hour, or until slightly thickened.

2 Stir in remaining ingredients. Pour into 4-cup (1 L) mold. Chill until set. Unmold to serve.

MARINATED VEGETABLE SALAD

- 4 large firm tomatoes, peeled and chopped
- 2 medium cucumbers, peeled and chopped
- 1 cup (250 mL) snipped fresh parsley
- ½ cup (125 mL) chopped green onion
- 1 or 2 cloves garlic, minced

- 2 tablespoons (25 mL) snipped fresh mint or 1 tablespoon (15 mL) dried mint flakes
- ¼ cup (50 mL) fresh lemon juice
- ¼ cup (50 mL) olive oil
- ¼ teaspoon (1 mL) salt
- ¼ teaspoon (1 mL) sugar

6 to 8 servings

1 In medium bowl, combine tomatoes, cucumbers, parsley, green onion, garlic and mint. Blend lemon juice, olive oil, salt and sugar. Pour over vegetables; stir to coat.

Advance preparation: *Can be served immediately but flavors are enhanced by marinating overnight.*

PARMESAN LETTUCE WEDGES

- 1 cup (250 mL) vegetable oil
- ½ cup (125 mL) red wine vinegar
- 3 tablespoons (50 mL) grated Parmesan cheese
- 1 clove garlic, minced
- ½ teaspoon (2 mL) sugar
- ¼ teaspoon (1 mL) dry mustard
- ¼ teaspoon (1 mL) pepper
- 1 large head iceberg lettuce, cut into 6 to 8 wedges

6 to 8 servings

1 In 4-cup (1 L) measure or medium bowl mix all ingredients except lettuce. Serve over lettuce wedges. Garnish with cherry tomatoes, if desired.

TOSSED SALAD

- Iceberg lettuce, torn into bite-size pieces
- Tomato wedges
- Cucumber slices
- Radish slices
- Dried oregano leaves

2 to 12 servings

1 Toss all ingredients in bowl. Serve with oil and red wine vinegar or Italian salad dressing, if desired.

LETTUCE CUPS

Dressing:
- 2 slices bacon, cut into ½" (1 cm) pieces
- Vegetable oil
- ¼ cup (50 mL) red wine vinegar
- 1 teaspoon (5 mL) grated Parmesan cheese
- ½ teaspoon (2 mL) dried parsley flakes
- ½ teaspoon (2 mL) dried basil leaves
- ¼ teaspoon (1 mL) salt
- ⅛ teaspoon (0.5 mL) dry mustard
- Pinch of pepper

Salad:
- 1 head iceberg lettuce
- Chopped tomato
- Chopped hard-cooked egg
- Croutons

2 servings

1 Place bacon in 1-cup (250 mL) measure. Microwave at High 1½ to 2½ minutes, or until crisp, stirring once during cooking. Remove bacon; place on paper towel. Add enough vegetable oil to bacon drippings to measure ⅓ cup (75 mL). Mix in remaining dressing ingredients. Microwave at High 30 to 45 seconds, or until hot. Stir in bacon.

2 Remove outer leaves from head of lettuce; arrange on plate to form cups. Tear enough remaining lettuce into bite-size pieces to fill lettuce cups. Sprinkle with chopped tomato, chopped hard-cooked egg and croutons. Spoon hot dressing over top.

SHREDDED LETTUCE SALAD ↑

- 1 large head iceberg lettuce, shredded
- 2 cups (500 mL) shredded Cheddar cheese
- 2 medium tomatoes, chopped
- ½ cup (125 mL) chopped onion
- ½ cup (125 mL) sliced pitted black olives
- ¼ cup plus 2 tablespoons taco sauce (75 mL)
- ¼ teaspoon (1 mL) cumin
- 1½ cups (375 mL) dairy sour cream

10 to 12 servings

1 On large round platter or in large bowl layer lettuce, cheese, tomatoes, onion and olives.

2 In small bowl mix taco sauce and cumin. Microwave at High 45 seconds to 1½ minutes, or until heated. Stir in sour cream. Serve with lettuce salad.

HOLIDAY DESSERTS

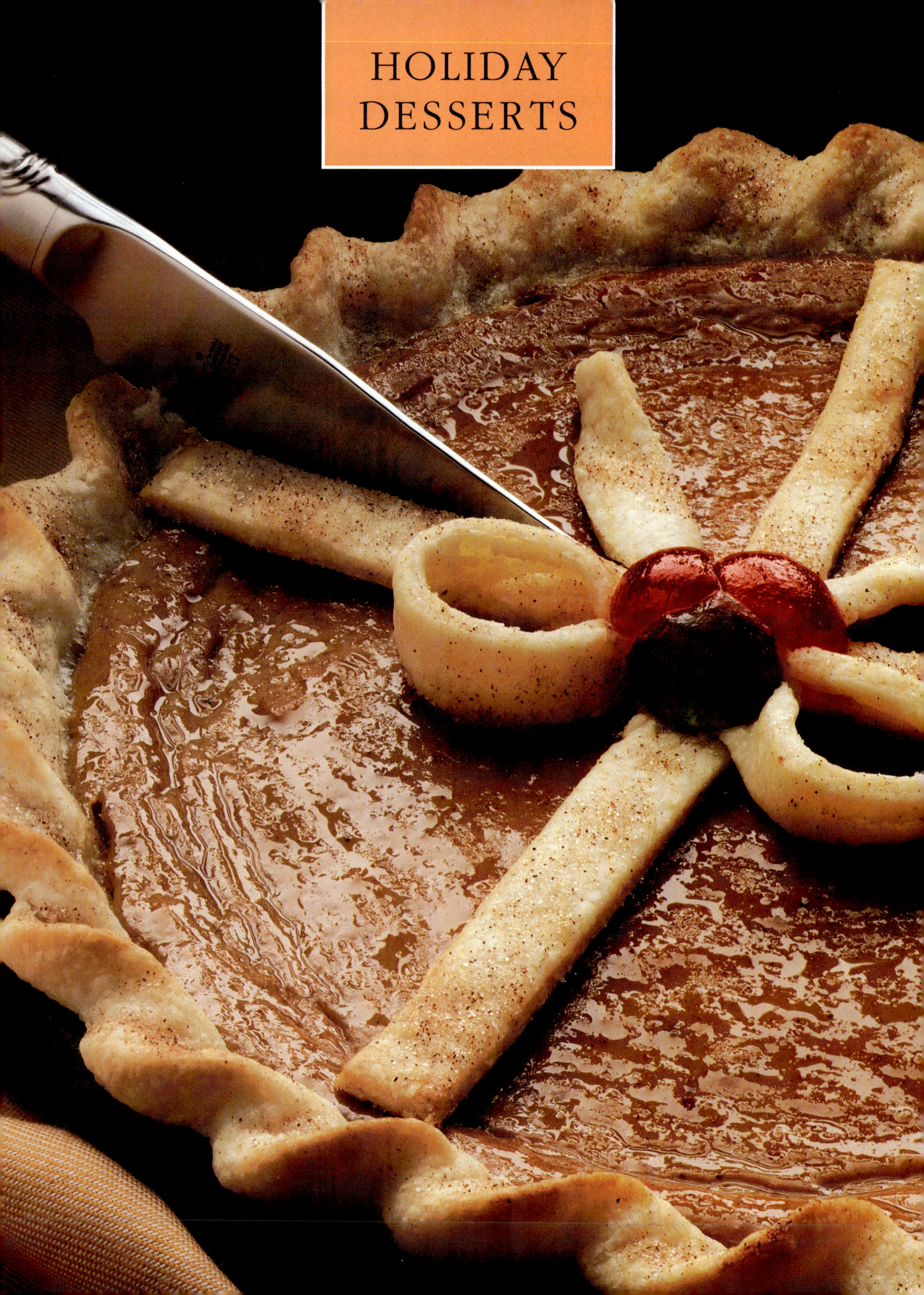

ORANGE PUMPKIN PIE

- 1 pkg. (15 oz./425 g) refrigerated prepared pie crusts
- 2 teaspoons (10 mL) sugar
- 1¼ teaspoons (6 mL) ground cinnamon, divided
- 1 tablespoon (15 mL) milk
- Red and green candied cherries
- 1 can (16 oz./454 mL) pumpkin
- 1 can (14 oz./398 mL) sweetened condensed milk
- 2 eggs
- 1 teaspoon (5 mL) grated orange peel
- ¼ teaspoon (1 mL) ground nutmeg

8 servings

Advance preparation: *Up to 1 day in advance prepare pie to * below and refrigerate. To serve, decorate with pastry bow.*

1 Heat oven to 425°F/220°C. Let pie crusts stand at room temperature for 15 to 20 minutes. Unfold 1 crust, ease into 9" (23 cm) pie plate and flute edges.

2 Combine sugar and ¼ teaspoon (1 mL) cinnamon in small bowl. Brush edges of crust lightly with milk. Sprinkle with about ½ teaspoon (2 mL) sugar mixture. Bake for 8 to 10 minutes, or until lightly browned. Cool.

3 Use remaining crust to form pastry bow and ribbon. Cut 4 strips each 8" by ¾" (20 x 2 cm). Place 1 strip on baking sheet. Cross at center with another strip. Secure strips together, using a small amount of cold water.

4 Form bow over center of crossed strips, squeezing gently in center. Brush bow and ribbon lightly with milk. Sprinkle with remaining sugar mixture. Decorate center with red and green cherries. Bake at 425°F/220°C for 6 to 8 minutes, or until lightly browned. Cool.

5 Combine remaining 1 teaspoon (5 mL) cinnamon and the remaining ingredients in medium mixing bowl. Beat at low speed of electric mixer until mixture is smooth. Microwave at High for 4 to 5 minutes, or until mixture is very hot and starts to set, stirring once or twice.

6 Pour into prepared pie crust. Place pie plate on saucer in microwave oven. Microwave at 50% (Medium) for 15 to 21 minutes, or until center is set, rotating 3 or 4 times. * Using spatula, carefully loosen bow and ribbon from baking sheet. Place on top of filling. Cool.

PECAN TARTS →

- 1 pkg. (15 oz./425 g) refrigerated prepared pie crusts
- ½ cup (125 mL) chopped pecans
- ½ cup (125 mL) dark corn syrup
- ¼ cup (50 mL) packed brown sugar
- 1 egg
- 1 tablespoon (15 mL) butter or margarine
- ¼ teaspoon (1 mL) salt
- 1 tablespoon (15 mL) grated orange peel

10 tarts

Advance preparation: Up to 2 days in advance, prepare tart shells to * below. Cool and store in airtight containers. Up to 2 hours in advance, prepare filling and spoon into tart shells. Cool and cover loosely with wax paper until serving time. Sprinkle with grated orange peel.

1 Heat oven to 425°F/220°C. Let pie crusts stand at room temperature for 15 to 20 minutes. Unfold crusts and place each crust over five 3½" (9 cm) individual tart pans.

2 Press top of dough over each pan lightly with fingers until dough lines pans. Press rolling pin lightly over top of pans to cut off excess dough. Using fork, prick bottom of crusts several times.

3 Bake for 10 to 12 minutes or until light golden brown. Cool and remove tart shells from pans. Arrange shells on serving platter. * Set aside. Combine remaining ingredients, except orange peel, in large mixing bowl.

4 Microwave at 50% (Medium) for 8 to 11 minutes, or until mixture thickens and boils slightly, stirring every 2 minutes. Spoon mixture evenly into prepared tart shells. Let cool. (Mixture sets as it cools.) Before serving, sprinkle with grated orange peel.

GOLDEN RUM FRUITCAKE

- 2 to 3 tablespoons (25 to 50 mL) graham cracker crumbs
- 3 eggs
- ¾ cup (175 mL) packed brown sugar
- ¾ cup (175 mL) all-purpose flour
- ½ teaspoon (2 mL) baking powder
- ¼ teaspoon (1 mL) salt
- ¼ teaspoon (1 mL) ground allspice

- ½ teaspoon (2 mL) vanilla
- 1 cup (250 mL) candied red and green cherries
- 1 cup (250 mL) candied chopped pineapple
- 1 cup (250 mL) walnut halves
- ½ cup (125 mL) golden raisins
- Rum

8 to 12 servings

1 Generously grease 9" (23 cm) ring mold. Sprinkle bottom and sides with graham cracker crumbs. Set aside. In medium mixing bowl, beat eggs and brown sugar until light and fluffy. Beat in flour, baking powder, salt, allspice and vanilla until smooth. Stir in remaining ingredients, except rum. Spoon into prepared ring mold.

2 Microwave at 50% (Medium) for 10 minutes. Rotate dish one-half turn. Microwave at High for 3 to 6 minutes longer, or until wooden pick inserted in center comes out clean. (Top may still appear moist.) Let stand on counter for 10 minutes.

3 Invert fruitcake onto plate. Cool 30 minutes. Moisten cheesecloth with rum and wrap fruitcake tightly in cheesecloth. Place in large plastic food-storage bag. Chill at least 24 hours, or up to 2 weeks, before slicing.

← STRAWBERRY-AMARETTO TRIFLE

- 2 eggs
- ½ cup (125 mL) sugar
- 2 tablespoons (25 mL) quick-cooking tapioca
- 2 cups (500 mL) milk
- ¼ cup (50 mL) plus 1 tablespoon (15 mL) amaretto liqueur
- 2 cups (500 mL) whipping cream
- 1 pint (500 mL) fresh strawberries, hulled and cut in half, reserving 1 whole strawberry for garnish
- 1 un-iced strawberry-filled jelly roll (16-oz./454 g), cut into 1" (2.5 cm) slices

8 servings

1 In 4-cup (1 L) measure, beat eggs with whisk until frothy. Beat in sugar, tapioca and milk. Microwave at 50% (Medium) for 15 to 20 minutes, or until mixture thickens and bubbles, beating well twice. Stir in 1 tablespoon (15 mL) liqueur. Place plastic wrap directly on surface of pudding. * Refrigerate 4 to 6 hours, or until very cold. (Mixture thickens as it cools.)

2 In medium mixing bowl, beat whipping cream until soft peaks form. Reserve ½ cup (125 mL) whipped cream for topping. Fold remaining whipped cream into chilled pudding.

3 Arrange 1 cup (250 mL) of the strawberries in bottom of 3-quart (3 L) trifle dish or clear, straight-sided glass bowl. Spoon 1 cup (250 mL) of the pudding mixture over strawberries. Place jelly roll slices upright around inside of bowl, pressing lightly into pudding. Place any remaining jelly roll slices in center. Drizzle remaining ¼ cup (50 mL) liqueur evenly over jelly roll slices. Spoon remaining pudding mixture in center of bowl.

4 Arrange remaining strawberries around top edge. Spoon reserved ½ cup (125 mL) whipped cream in center. Garnish top with reserved whole strawberry.

Advance preparation: *Up to 1 day in advance, prepare pudding to * above and refrigerate. Up to 6 hours in advance, continue recipe as directed, except for garnish. To serve, garnish top with whole strawberry.*

TIPSY CAKE

- 1 pkg. (3⅛ oz./92 g) vanilla pudding and pie filling
- 2 cups (500 mL) milk
- 1 tablespoon (15 mL) bourbon
- 2 cups (500 mL) whipping cream
- 2 tablespoons (25 mL) powdered sugar
- 1 tablespoon (15 mL) grated orange peel
- 1 pkg. (3 oz./85 g) ladyfingers (about 12 split)
- ½ cup (125 mL) orange marmalade
- ½ cup (125 mL) plus 2 tablespoons (25 mL) raisins, divided
- ½ cup (125 mL) plus 2 tablespoons (25 mL) sliced almonds, divided

8 to 10 servings

1 Place pudding mix in 4-cup (1 L) measure. Blend in milk. Microwave at High for 6 to 9 minutes, or until mixture thickens and bubbles, stirring after first 3 minutes and then every minute. Stir in bourbon. Place plastic wrap directly on surface of pudding. Refrigerate until completely cool, about 4 hours or overnight. *

2 Place whipping cream in medium mixing bowl. Beat, gradually adding sugar, until soft peaks form. Fold in orange peel. Set aside.

3 Spread cut sides of ladyfinger halves with marmalade. Arrange 16 ladyfinger halves marmalade-side-up over bottom and along sides of 3-quart (3 L) clear glass serving bowl. Sprinkle with ¼ cup (50 mL) raisins and ¼ cup (50 mL) almonds. Spread ½ cup (125 mL) pudding over raisins and almonds. Spread ½ cup (125 mL) whipped cream over pudding. Arrange remaining 8 ladyfingers, marmalade-side-up, on whipped cream. Sprinkle ¼ cup (50 mL) raisins and ¼ cup (50 mL) almonds over ladyfingers. Spread remaining pudding over raisins and almonds. Spread remaining whipped cream over pudding.

4 Sprinkle top with remaining 2 tablespoons (25 mL) raisins and 2 tablespoons (25mL) almonds. Garnish with orange slices or thin piece of orange peel, if desired.

Advance preparation: *Up to 2 days in advance, prepare recipe as directed to * above. To serve, continue as directed.*

PUMPKIN PARFAIT ↑

- 1 cup (250 mL) granulated sugar
- ¼ cup (50 mL) cornstarch
- 2 tablespoons (25 mL) all-purpose flour
- ½ teaspoon (2 mL) ground cinnamon
- ½ teaspoon (2 mL) ground nutmeg
- ½ teaspoon (2 mL) salt
- 1 can (16 oz./454 mL) pumpkin
- 2 cups (500 mL) milk
- 1½ cups (375 mL) whipping cream
- 2 tablespoons (25 mL) powdered sugar
- ½ teaspoon (2 mL) vanilla
- 1 cup (250 mL) finely crushed gingersnap cookie crumbs (about 15 gingersnaps)

8 servings

1 In 3-quart (3 L) casserole, combine granulated sugar, cornstarch, flour, cinnamon, nutmeg and salt. Add pumpkin and milk. Mix well. Microwave at High for 11 to 18 minutes, or until mixture thickens and bubbles, stirring after the first 3 minutes and then every 2 minutes. Place plastic wrap directly on surface of pudding. * Refrigerate about 4 hours, or until cool.

2 In small mixing bowl, beat whipping cream, gradually adding powdered sugar, until soft peaks form. Fold in vanilla. In each of eight 8-oz. (250 mL) parfait or wine glasses, layer scant 1 tablespoon (15 mL) cookie crumbs, 2 tablespoons (25 mL) pudding, 2 tablespoons (25 mL) whipped cream, scant 1 tablespoon (15 mL) cookie crumbs, 2 tablespoons (25 mL) pudding. Top each parfait with dollop of whipped cream and a sprinkle of cookie crumbs.

Advance preparation: *Up to 1 day in advance, prepare pudding to * above and refrigerate. Up to 2 hours in advance, assemble parfaits.*

- 1 pkg. (3⅛ oz./92 g) vanilla pudding and pie filling
- 2 cups (500 mL) milk
- 2 cups (500 mL) prepared mincemeat
- ½ teaspoon (2 mL) imitation rum extract
- 2 jars (6 oz./170 mL each) maraschino cherries, drained
- 2½ cups (625 mL) prepared whipped topping, divided

8 servings

Advance preparation: *Up to 1 day in advance, prepare pudding, mincemeat mixture and cherries to * below. Cover and refrigerate in separate containers. Up to 2 hours in advance, assemble parfaits as directed below.*

1 Place pudding mix in 4-cup (1 L) measure. Blend in milk. Microwave at High for 6 to 9 minutes, or until mixture thickens and bubbles, stirring after the first 3 minutes and then every minute.

2 Place plastic wrap directly on surface of pudding. Refrigerate about 4 hours, or until completely cool.

3 Combine mincemeat and rum extract in small mixing bowl. Set aside. Reserve 8 whole cherries for garnish. Set aside. Coarsely chop remaining cherries. * Fold 2 cups (500 mL) whipped topping into cold pudding.

4 Layer ¼ cup (50 mL) pudding mixture, ¼ cup (50 mL) mincemeat mixture, scant 1 tablespoon (15 mL) chopped cherries and ¼ cup (50 mL) pudding mixture in each of eight 8-oz. (250 mL) parfait or wine glasses.

5 Garnish each parfait with a dollop of remaining whipped topping and a whole cherry before serving.

PUMPKIN CHEESECAKE

Crust:

- ¼ cup (50 mL) butter or margarine
- 1 cup (250 mL) graham cracker crumbs
- 2 tablespoons (25 mL) sugar

Filling:

- 2 pkgs. (8 oz./250 g each) cream cheese
- 1 cup (250 mL) canned pumpkin
- 4 eggs
- ⅔ cup (150 mL) sugar
- 1 teaspoon (5 mL) imitation brandy extract
- ¼ teaspoon (1 mL) ground cinnamon
- ¼ teaspoon (1 mL) ground ginger
- ¼ teaspoon (1 mL) ground nutmeg

Topping:

- ½ cup (125 mL) sour cream
- 2 tablespoons (25 mL) powdered sugar
- ¼ teaspoon (1 mL) imitation brandy extract

8 to 10 servings

1 In 9" (23 cm) round baking dish, microwave butter at High for 1¼ to 1½ minutes, or until melted. Stir in graham cracker crumbs and sugar. Mix well. Press mixture firmly against bottom of dish. Microwave at High for 1½ to 2 minutes, or until set, rotating dish once. Set aside.

2 In 8-cup (2 L) measure, microwave cream cheese at 50% (Medium) for 2¼ to 4 minutes, or until softened. Add remaining filling ingredients. Beat at medium speed of electric mixture until well blended. Microwave at High for 4 to 5 minutes, or until mixture is very hot and starts to set, beating with whisk every 2 minutes.

3 Pour filling over prepared crust. Place dish on saucer in microwave oven. Microwave at 50% (Medium) for 7 to 15 minutes, or until center is almost set, rotating dish twice. (Filling becomes firm as it cools.) Chill 1 hour.

4 In small mixing bowl, combine topping ingredients. Stir until smooth. Spread topping over cheesecake. Refrigerate at least 8 hours, or overnight.

PISTACHIO-CHERRY CHEESECAKE

Crust:

- ¼ cup (50 mL) butter or margarine
- 1 cup (250 mL) finely crushed chocolate wafer crumbs (about 20 wafers)

Filling:

- 1 pkg. (6 oz./170 g) white baking bar
- 2 pkgs. (8 oz./250 g each) cream cheese
- ⅔ cup (150 mL) sugar
- 2 egg whites
- 1 tablespoon (15 mL) all-purpose flour
- 1 teaspoon (5 mL) vanilla
- ½ cup (125 mL) chopped pistachio nuts
- ½ cup (125 mL) chopped candied cherries

8 to 10 servings

1 In 9" (23 cm) round baking dish, microwave butter at High for 1¼ to 1½ minutes, or until melted. Stir in wafer crumbs. Mix well. Press mixture firmly against bottom of dish. Microwave at High for 1½ to 2 minutes, or until set, rotating dish once. Set aside.

2 In small mixing bowl, microwave baking bar at 50% (Medium) for 4 to 5 minutes, or until bar melts and can be stirred smooth, stirring after the first 2 minutes and then every minute. Set aside.

3 In 2-quart (2 L) measure, microwave cream cheese at 50% (Medium) for 2¼ to 4 minutes, or until softened. Blend in melted baking bar. Add remaining filling ingredients, except pistachios and cherries. Beat at medium speed of electric mixer until well blended. Microwave at High for 2 minutes, or until mixture starts to set, beating with whisk every minute. Stir in pistachios and cherries.

4 Pour filling over prepared crust. Place dish on saucer in microwave oven. Microwave at 50% (Medium) for 7 to 10 minutes, or until cheesecake is set in center, rotating dish twice. (Filling becomes firm as it cools.) Refrigerate at least 8 hours, or overnight. Garnish with whole candied cherries, if desired.

Advance preparation: *Up to 2 days in advance, prepare as directed above. Cover with plastic wrap and refrigerate.*

MINT-STRAWBERRY CHEESECAKE

- 1 frozen plain cheesecake (17 to 23 oz./500 to 650 g), defrosted (below)
- 1 square (1 oz./30 g) semisweet chocolate
- 1 teaspoon (5 mL) shortening
- ¼ cup (50 mL) mint jelly
- 2 drops green food coloring
- 2 teaspoons (10 mL) light corn syrup, divided
- ¼ cup (50 mL) strawberry jelly
- 2 drops red food coloring

8 servings

Advance preparation: Up to 1 hour in advance, prepare as directed below.

Defrosting Cheesecake. Unwrap cheesecake. Remove from foil pan and place on serving plate or platter. Microwave at 30% (Medium Low) for 2½ to 4 minutes, or until wooden pick inserted in center meets no resistance, rotating plate once or twice. Let cheesecake stand for 10 minutes to complete defrosting.

1 **Making Mint-Strawberry Cheesecake.** Place chocolate and shortening in small bowl. Microwave at 50% (Medium) for 2½ to 4½ minutes, or until chocolate is glossy and can be stirred smooth. Place melted chocolate in 1-quart (1 L) sealable freezer bag. Using scissors, snip corner to form writing tip. Use melted chocolate to pipe outline of design on cheesecake.

2 Place mint jelly, green food coloring and 1 teaspoon (5 mL) corn syrup in small bowl. Microwave at High for 45 seconds to 1 minute, or until melted. Repeat with strawberry jelly, red food coloring and remaining 1 teaspoon (5 mL) corn syrup. Fill center of chocolate design with melted jellies.

SNOWFLAKE
CHEESECAKE →

- 1 frozen plain cheesecake (17 to 23 oz./500 to 650 g), defrosted (opposite)
- 1 doily (6"/15 cm)
- Red and green colored sugar
- 1 pkg. (3 oz./85 g) cream cheese (optional)
- 2 to 3 drops green food coloring (optional)

8 servings

1 Place doily on top of cheesecake. Sprinkle with sugars. Remove doily.

2 In small bowl, microwave cream cheese at High for 15 to 30 seconds, or until softened. Stir in food coloring.

3 Place cream cheese mixture in pastry bag and pipe around edges of cheesecake to decorate.

Advance preparation: *Up to 1 hour in advance, prepare as directed above.*

PEPPERMINT
CHEESECAKE →

- 1 frozen plain cheesecake (17 to 23 oz./500 to 650 g), defrosted (opposite)
- 3 tablespoons (50 mL) crushed peppermint candies
- 1 square (1 oz./30 g) semisweet chocolate
- 1 teaspoon (5 mL) shortening

8 servings

1 Sprinkle peppermint candies over top of cheesecake.

2 In small bowl, microwave chocolate and shortening at 50% (Medium) for 2 to 3 minutes, or until chocolate is glossy and can be stirred smooth.

3 Using spoon, drizzle chocolate over top of candies and cheesecake. Chill until chocolate is set.

Advance preparation: *Up to 1 hour in advance, prepare as directed above.*

267

EASY YULE LOG CAKE

- 2 frozen chocolate layer cakes (11½ oz./327 g each)
- ⅓ cup (75 mL) butter or margarine
- 1¾ to 2 cups (425 to 500 mL) powdered sugar
- ⅔ cup (150 mL) cocoa
- ⅓ cup (75 mL) half-and-half
- 1 teaspoon (5 mL) vanilla
- 1 pkg. (3 oz./85 g) cream cheese
- 2 teaspoons (10 mL) granulated sugar
- 4 drops yellow food coloring
- 3 drops red food coloring
- 1 drop green food coloring
- Spearmint gumdrop leaves
- Red cinnamon candies

8 to 10 servings

1 Unwrap cakes and place end to end on serving platter. Set aside. In large mixing bowl, microwave butter at 30% (Medium Low) for 45 seconds to 1 minute, or until softened, checking every 15 to 30 seconds.

2 Beat butter at medium speed of electric mixer until creamed. Add powdered sugar and cocoa alternately with half-and-half while beating at medium speed of electric mixer, until of desired spreading consistency. Blend in vanilla. Reserve 2 tablespoons (25 mL) frosting. Set aside.

268

3 Spread top and sides of cake with remaining frosting. Draw tines of fork through frosting for barklike appearance of log. Set log aside.

4 Place cream cheese in small bowl. Microwave at High for 15 to 30 seconds, or until softened. Add granulated sugar and food colorings. Mix well.

5 Spread ends of log with cream cheese mixture. Use wooden pick to apply reserved frosting in concentric circles on each end of log. Garnish log with gumdrop leaves and red cinnamon candies.

RASPBERRY ICE CREAM CAKE

- 1 frozen pound cake (16 oz./454 g)
- 1 pint (500 mL) raspberry sherbet
- 1 pint (500 mL) chocolate ice cream
- 1 square (1 oz./30 g) semisweet chocolate
- ½ teaspoon (2 mL) shortening
- ½ cup (125 mL) raspberry preserves
- 2 teaspoons (10 mL) light corn syrup
- Fresh raspberries (optional)

8 servings

Advance preparation: *Up to 1 week in advance, prepare cake to * below. To serve, prepare raspberry sauce and continue as directed.*

1 Cut pound cake lengthwise into thirds. Place bottom cake layer on serving platter. Set aside. Remove covers from sherbet and ice cream. Microwave sherbet at 50% (Medium) for 30 seconds to 1 minute, or until softened. Repeat with ice cream.

2 Spread bottom cake layer with about 1 cup (250 mL) of the raspberry sherbet. Top with next cake layer. Spread second layer with about ½ cup (125 mL) of the chocolate ice cream. Place remaining cake layer on top.

3 Spread top with remaining raspberry sherbet. Spread sides with remaining chocolate ice cream. (If sherbet or ice cream becomes too soft, freeze 10 to 15 minutes.) Freeze cake 15 to 30 minutes, or until very firm.

4 Combine chocolate and shortening in 1-cup (250 mL) measure. Microwave at 50% (Medium) for 1½ to 3 minutes, or until chocolate is glossy and can be stirred smooth, stirring once. Cool slightly.

5 Drizzle chocolate over top of raspberry sherbet. Freeze uncovered until firm. * To serve, combine raspberry preserves and corn syrup in 1-cup (250 mL) measure. Microwave at 50% (Medium) for 1 minute, or until mixture is melted and can be stirred smooth. Drizzle raspberry sauce over servings of cake. Garnish each serving with fresh raspberries.

Give your brunch an Indian touch with Curried Eggs, or choose the Tex-Mex flavor of Picante Potato Pie. Fruit Salad, muffins and assorted butters complete either menu.

CURRIED EGGS & MUFFINS

- 4 English muffins, split and toasted
- 8 hard-cooked eggs, peeled
- ¼ cup (50 mL) butter or margarine
- ¼ cup (50 mL) all-purpose flour
- 2 teaspoons (10 mL) curry powder
- ½ teaspoon (2 mL) salt
- Pinch of white pepper
- 2 cups (500 mL) milk

Toppings:
- Crumbled cooked bacon
- Sliced green onions
- Shredded carrot
- Chopped nuts
- Shredded coconut
- Chopped fully cooked ham
- Chopped red and green pepper

8 servings

1 Heat oven to 200°F/95°C. Arrange muffin halves on large oven-proof platter. Slice each egg lengthwise into 4 slices. Place 4 egg slices on each toasted muffin half. Cover platter with foil. Place in oven for 15 to 20 minutes.

2 In 4-cup (1 L) measure, microwave butter at High for 1¼ to 1½ minutes, or until melted. Stir in flour, curry powder, salt and pepper. Blend in milk. Microwave at High for 7 to 9 minutes, or until sauce thickens and bubbles, stirring twice.

3 Remove platter from oven. Remove foil. Spoon curry sauce over eggs and muffins. Sprinkle with desired toppings.

Advance preparation: *Up to 1 day in advance, cook eggs, but do not peel. Refrigerate. To serve, peel eggs and prepare recipe as directed above.*

BUTTER SPREADS & WARM QUICK BREADS →

Tangy Lime Butter:
- ½ cup (125 mL) butter or margarine
- 1 teaspoon (5 mL) grated lime peel
- 1 tablespoon (15 mL) fresh lime juice

Rum-Walnut Butter:
- ½ cup (125 mL) butter or margarine
- 2 tablespoons (25 mL) chopped walnuts
- ¼ teaspoon (1 mL) imitation rum extract

Spiced Butter:
- ½ cup (125 mL) butter or margarine
- ¼ teaspoon (1 mL) ground allspice

Cherry Butter:
- ½ cup (125 mL) butter or margarine
- 1 tablespoon (15 mL) cherry preserves

Quick Breads:
- 1 pkg. (10 oz./284 g) frozen muffins (4 muffins)
- 1 pkg. (12 oz./340 g) frozen snack loaves (6 loaves)

10 servings

1 In small mixing bowl, microwave butter at 30% (Medium Low) for 15 seconds to 1 minute, or until softened, checking every 15 seconds. Blend in remaining ingredients for desired flavor. *

2 To warm muffins and loaves, arrange in napkin-lined nonmetallic basket. Cover with another napkin. Microwave at High for 2 to 2½ minutes, or until muffins and loaves are warm, rearranging once.

Advance preparation: *Up to 2 weeks in advance, prepare as directed to * above. Cover and refrigerate.*

PICANTE POTATO PIE

- 4 cups (1 L) frozen hash brown potato cubes
- 4 eggs
- 2 tablespoons (25 mL) all-purpose flour
- 1 cup (250 mL) finely chopped fully cooked ham
- 1 cup (250 mL) shredded Monterey Jack cheese
- ¾ cup (175 mL) picante sauce
- 1 can (4 oz./114 mL) chopped green chilies
- ¼ cup (50 mL) sliced green onions
- ¼ teaspoon (1 mL) salt
- Pinch of pepper
- ½ cup (125 mL) shredded Cheddar cheese
- 1 large tomato, chopped (about 1 cup/250 mL)

8 servings

1 In 10" (25 cm) deep-dish pie plate, microwave potatoes at High for 4 to 6 minutes, or until defrosted, stirring once. Set aside.

2 In medium mixing bowl, combine remaining ingredients, except Cheddar cheese and tomato. Stir in potatoes. Spoon back into pie plate. Cover with wax paper.

3 Place pie plate on saucer in microwave oven. Microwave at High for 5 minutes. Stir. Microwave at 50% (Medium) for 10 to 15 minutes longer, or until knife inserted in center comes out clean, stirring once.

4 Sprinkle Cheddar cheese around edge of pie. Microwave at High for 30 to 45 seconds, or until cheese melts. Sprinkle tomato in center of pie. Sprinkle with sliced green onions, if desired.

HOT STRAWBERRY TEA

- 6 cups (1.5 L) hot water
- 4 tea bags
- 1 pkg. (16 oz./454 g) frozen strawberries without syrup
- ½ cup (125 mL) orange juice
- ¼ cup (50 mL) sugar
- ½ teaspoon (2 mL) grated orange peel
- Pinch of ground nutmeg
- 8 orange slices

8 servings

1 Place water in 8-cup (2 L) measure. Cover with plastic wrap. Microwave at High for 10 to 14 minutes, or until boiling. Add tea bags. Let stand, covered, for 5 minutes. Remove tea bags. Re-cover.

2 Reserve 4 frozen strawberries. In 2-quart (2 L) casserole, combine remaining strawberries and remaining ingredients, except orange slices. Cover. Microwave at High for 10 to 14 minutes, or until boiling, stirring once.

3 Place strawberry mixture in strainer. Press liquid through strainer into medium mixing bowl. Discard pulp. Add strained mixture to tea. Stir gently.

4 Cut each reserved strawberry into 4 slices. Garnish each serving with 2 strawberry slices and 1 orange slice. To serve cold, chill at least 2 hours and serve over ice.

Hot Raspberry Tea: *Follow recipe above, except substitute 1 pkg. (12 oz./340 g) frozen raspberries for strawberries, and decrease sugar to 2 tablespoons (25 mL). Reserve 16 frozen raspberries. Garnish each serving with 2 raspberries and 1 orange slice.*

WINTER SALAD WITH TART CINNAMON DRESSING ↑

Salad:

- 4 cups (1 L) leaf lettuce, torn into bite-size pieces
- 3 medium oranges, peeled and sectioned
- 2 medium pears, sliced
- 1 avocado, peeled and sliced
- Pomegranate seeds (optional)

Dressing:

- ½ cup (125 mL) olive oil
- 3 tablespoons (50 mL) apple juice
- 2 tablespoons (25 mL) sugar
- 1 tablespoon (15 mL) vinegar
- 1 teaspoon (5 mL) ground cinnamon
- ½ teaspoon (2 mL) dry mustard

8 servings

1 In large mixing bowl, combine all salad ingredients, except pomegranate seeds. * Set aside.

2 In blender, combine all dressing ingredients. Blend for about 30 to 45 seconds, or until smooth. Pour dressing over salad. Toss gently to coat. Sprinkle with pomegranate seeds. Serve immediately.

Advance preparation: *Up to 2 hours in advance, dip pear and avocado slices in lemon juice to prevent browning. Prepare salad mixture to * above. Cover and refrigerate. To serve, continue as directed.*

BOWL GAMES

Holiday-season bowl games have become important occasions for casual entertaining. Offer foods for nibbling — like the Cheese & Garlic-flavored Nuts or Mexican Chili Dip — and for more serious eating — like the hearty Layered Buffet Sandwich and Crunchy Cabbage Salad. Satisfy a sweet tooth with Bowl Game Brownies and Fudgy Popcorn.

LAYERED BUFFET SANDWICH

- 1 loaf (1 lb./454 g) French bread
- 1 cup (250 mL) chopped green pepper
- ½ cup (125 mL) chopped red onion
- 2 tablespoons (25 mL) butter or margarine
- 2 cups (500 mL) sliced fresh mushrooms
- ¼ cup (50 mL) olive oil
- ¼ cup (50 mL) cider vinegar
- 1 teaspoon (5 mL) Dijon mustard
- ½ teaspoon (2 mL) sugar

- ¼ teaspoon (1 mL) Italian seasoning
- ¼ teaspoon (1 mL) salt
- Lettuce
- ⅓ lb. (175 g) fully cooked turkey, thinly sliced
- ¼ lb. (125 g) salami, thinly sliced
- ⅓ lb. (175 g) fully cooked ham, thinly sliced
- 6 slices (1 oz./30 g each) Provolone cheese
- 6 slices (¾ oz./22 g each) pasteurized process American cheese

6 to 8 servings

1 Slice French bread in half lengthwise. Set aside. In 1½-quart (1.5 L) casserole, combine green pepper, onion and butter. Cover. Microwave at High for 2 minutes. Stir in mushrooms. Re-cover. Microwave at High for 3 to 5 minutes, or until green pepper and onion are tender-crisp. Drain. Set aside. In small bowl, combine oil, vinegar, mustard, sugar, Italian seasoning and salt. Blend well with whisk. Microwave at High for 30 seconds to 1 minute, or until mixture boils. Brush oil mixture evenly over cut sides of loaf.

2 Arrange lettuce evenly over bottom half of loaf. Top with turkey and salami. Spoon drained vegetables over salami. Top with remaining ingredients. Place top of loaf over cheeses. Press lightly. * Wrap in plastic wrap and chill at least 2 hours. Cut diagonally into serving-size pieces. Secure each piece with wooden pick.

Advance preparation: Up to 24 hours in advance, prepare to * above. Wrap in plastic wrap and refrigerate. To serve, cut and secure with wooden picks as directed.

FIERY CHICKEN WINGS
& DIPPING SAUCE →

- 3 lbs. (1.5 kg) chicken wings
- ⅓ cup (75 mL) all-purpose flour
- Vegetable oil
- 2 teaspoons (10 mL) paprika
- 1 teaspoon (5 mL) garlic salt
- ½ teaspoon (2 mL) coarsely ground pepper

Sauce:

- 2 tablespoons (25 mL) finely chopped onion
- 2 teaspoons (10 mL) vegetable oil

- 1 can (8 oz./227 mL) tomato sauce
- 1 tablespoon (15 mL) packed brown sugar
- 2 teaspoons (10 mL) cider vinegar
- 1 teaspoon (5 mL) paprika
- ¼ teaspoon (1 mL) coarsely ground pepper
- ¼ teaspoon (1 mL) garlic salt
- ⅛ teaspoon (0.5 mL) cayenne

10 to 12 servings

Advance preparation: *Up to 1 day in advance, prepare as directed to * below. Cover and refrigerate chicken and sauce in separate containers. To serve, place half of chicken wings on paper-towel-lined plate. Microwave at High for 3 to 4 minutes, or until hot, rotating plate once. Repeat for remaining wings. Microwave sauce at High for 2 to 3 minutes, or until hot, stirring once. Serve sauce with wings.*

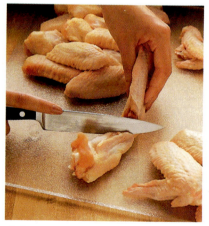

1 Separate each chicken wing into 3 parts, cutting at joints. Discard wing tips. Place flour and wing pieces in large plastic food-storage bag. Shake to coat.

2 Heat ¼" (5 mm) oil in deep 10" (25 cm) skillet over medium-high heat. Fry half of chicken wings at a time for 6 to 8 minutes, or until golden brown, turning once or twice. Drain on paper towel. Set aside.

3 Combine 2 teaspoons (10 mL) paprika, 1 teaspoon (5 mL) garlic salt and ½ teaspoon (2 mL) pepper in small bowl. Sprinkle evenly over wings. Set aside.

CRUNCHY CABBAGE SALAD

- 3 cups (750 mL) shredded green cabbage
- 3 cups (750 mL) shredded red cabbage
- 1 cup (250 mL) shredded carrot
- ⅓ cup (75 mL) salted blanched peanuts (optional)
- 2 green onions, thinly sliced
- 1 package (3 oz./85 g) chicken-flavored Oriental dry noodle soup mix

Dressing:
- ¼ cup (50 mL) vegetable oil
- 3 tablespoons (50 mL) red wine vinegar
- 2 tablespoons (25 mL) sugar
- ¼ teaspoon (1 mL) salt
- ¼ teaspoon (1 mL) pepper

8 servings

4 Combine onion and 2 teaspoons (10 mL) oil in 1-quart (1 L) casserole. Microwave at High for 1 to 2 minutes, or until tender. Stir in remaining ingredients. Microwave at High for 5 to 7 minutes, or until slightly thickened, stirring twice. * Serve with wings.

1 In large mixing bowl, combine cabbages, carrot, peanuts and onions. Sprinkle dry soup seasoning packet over salad. Break dry noodles into small pieces and add to salad. Mix well.

2 In 1-cup (250 mL) measure, combine all dressing ingredients. Mix well. Pour over salad, tossing gently to coat.

Advance preparation: *Up to 4 hours in advance, prepare as directed above. (If softer noodles are desired, prepare salad up to 24 hours in advance.) Cover and refrigerate.*

MEXICAN CHILI DIP

- 1 cup (250 mL) chopped red pepper
- 1 cup (250 mL) chopped green pepper
- 1 pkg. (3 oz./85 g) cream cheese
- 1 cup (250 mL) sour cream
- ⅛ teaspoon (0.5 mL) cayenne
- 1 can (15 oz./426 mL) red kidney beans in chili gravy
- 1 cup (250 mL) shredded Monterey Jack cheese
- ½ cup (125 mL) shredded Cheddar cheese
- 1 pkg. (6 oz./170 g) frozen avocado guacamole, defrosted
- 1 cup (250 mL) seeded chopped tomato
- Round tortilla chips

8 servings

1 Combine red and green peppers in 1-quart (1 L) casserole. Cover. Microwave at High for 4 to 5 minutes, or until tender-crisp, stirring once. Cool slightly.

2 Place cream cheese in small bowl. Microwave at High for 15 to 30 seconds, or until softened. Blend in sour cream and cayenne until smooth.

3 Spoon cream cheese mixture around bottom edge of a 10" (25 cm) deep-dish pie plate, forming ring about 1½" (4 cm) wide.

4 Spoon kidney beans in center and slightly over cream cheese mixture. Sprinkle evenly with peppers. Cover with wax paper. Microwave at 50% (Medium) for 6 to 8 minutes, or until warm in center, rotating dish once.

5 Sprinkle Monterey Jack cheese in circle around edge. Sprinkle Cheddar cheese in center. Cover with wax paper. Microwave at High for 1 to 3 minutes, or until cheese melts.

6 Spoon guacamole on top in wreath shape. Sprinkle tomatoes in center and around guacamole wreath. Place tortilla chips upright around edge of dish.

CHEESE & GARLIC-FLAVORED NUTS

- 2 tablespoons (25 mL) butter or margarine
- 2 teaspoons (10 mL) Worcestershire sauce
- 1 teaspoon (15 mL) garlic salt
- ½ cup (125 mL) whole blanched almonds
- ½ cup (125 mL) whole salted cashews
- ½ cup (125 mL) pecan halves
- ½ cup (125 mL) unsalted dry roasted peanuts
- 1 tablespoon (15 mL) grated Parmesan cheese

2 cups (500 mL)

1 In 2-quart (2 L) casserole, microwave butter at High for 45 seconds to 1 minute, or until melted.

2 Add Worcestershire sauce and garlic salt. Mix well. Add nuts, stirring to coat. Microwave at High for 6 to 9 minutes, or until butter is absorbed, stirring 2 or 3 times.

3 Add Parmesan cheese. Toss to coat. Spread on paper-towel-lined baking sheet to cool.

Advance preparation: *Up to 1 week in advance, prepare as directed above. Store in airtight container.*

↑ FUDGY POPCORN

- 10 cups (2.5 L) popped popcorn
- ½ cup (125 mL) butter or margarine
- ½ cup (125 mL) packed brown sugar
- ¼ cup (50 mL) cocoa
- 2 tablespoons (25 mL) light corn syrup

10 cups (2.5 L)

1 Heat oven to 325°F/160°C. Place popcorn in large mixing bowl. Set aside. In small mixing bowl, microwave butter at High for 1½ to 1¾ minutes, or until melted. Add remaining ingredients. Mix well.

2 Pour butter mixture over popcorn. Toss gently to coat. Spread coated popcorn in an even layer in 15½ x 10½" (40 x 25 cm) jelly roll pan. Bake for 10 minutes, stirring twice. Watch closely to prevent burning.

Advance preparation: *Up to 1 week in advance, prepare as directed above. Store in airtight container.*

BOWL GAME BROWNIES

- 1 pkg. (21.5 to 23.6 oz./600 to 675 g) fudge brownie mix

Frosting:

- 1/3 cup (75 mL) butter or margarine
- 1¾ to 2 cups (425 to 500 mL) powdered sugar
- 2/3 cup (150 mL) cocoa
- 1/3 cup (75 mL) half-and-half
- 1 teaspoon (5 mL) vanilla
- 1 square (2 oz./50 g) white candy coating

2 dozen brownies

1 Making Bowl Game Brownies. Heat oven to 350°F/180°C. Grease 15½ x 10½" (40 x 25 cm) jelly roll pan. Set aside. Prepare brownies according to package directions. Spread evenly in prepared jelly roll pan. Bake for 10 to 17 minutes, or until set and dry on top. Let cool for 2 hours.

2 In large mixing bowl, microwave butter at 30% (Medium Low) for 45 seconds to 1 minute or until softened, checking every 15 to 30 seconds. Beat butter at medium speed of electric mixer until creamed.

3 Add powdered sugar and cocoa alternately with half-and-half while beating at medium speed of electric mixer until of desired consistency. Blend in vanilla. Spread top of brownies with frosting. Using sharp knife, cut brownies diagonally every 1½" (4 cm) in diamond pattern. Melt candy coating and decorate brownies (right).

Advance preparation: *Up to 1 day in advance, prepare as directed above. Store in airtight container.*

1 Decorating Bowl Game Brownies. Place candy coating in small mixing bowl. Microwave at 50% (Medium) for 3 to 4 minutes, or until coating can be stirred smooth. Spoon into 1-quart (1 L) sealable freezer bag.

2 Squeeze coating to one corner of bag. Seal bag. Using scissors, snip corner of bag slightly to form writing tip. Pipe football laces on each brownie.

WINTER WARM-UPS

Outdoor activities — caroling, skating, sledding, sleighing — call for something piping hot when participants pull off their mittens and shake the snow from their boots.

← MIXED FRUIT WARMER

- 1 can (6 oz./170 mL) frozen orange juice concentrate
- 1 bottle (32 oz./1 L) cranberry-raspberry drink
- 2 cups (500 mL) water
- ⅓ cup (75 mL) packed brown sugar
- 4 thin orange slices
- 1 small cinnamon stick

6 to 8 servings

1 Remove metal lid from one end of orange juice. Place orange juice in microwave oven. Microwave at High for 45 seconds to 1 minute, or until defrosted. Pour into 8-cup (2 L) measure.

2 Stir in cranberry-raspberry drink, water and brown sugar. Add orange slices and cinnamon stick. Microwave at High for 11 to 16 minutes, or until hot, stirring once or twice. Before serving, remove cinnamon stick.

RICH ALMOND HOT CHOCOLATE

- 4 squares (1 oz./30 g each) semisweet chocolate
- 2 tablespoons (25 mL) butter or margarine
- 1 can (14 oz./398 mL) sweetened condensed milk
- 4 cups (1 L) milk
- ½ teaspoon (2 mL) almond extract

4 to 6 servings

1 In 8-cup (2 L) measure, microwave chocolate and butter at 50% (Medium) for 3½ to 4½ minutes, or until chocolate is glossy and mixture can be stirred smooth. Add condensed milk. Mix well.

2 Blend in milk gradually, stirring with whisk after each addition. Microwave at High for 9 to 14 minutes, or until mixture is hot, stirring 2 or 3 times. Stir in almond extract. Top each serving with miniature marshmallows, if desired.

HOT BUTTERED RUM

- ⅓ cup (75 mL) butter or margarine
- ¼ teaspoon (1 mL) ground nutmeg
- 4 cups (1 L) apple juice
- ⅔ to 1 cup (150 to 250 mL) dark rum
- ⅓ cup (75 mL) packed brown sugar
- Grated orange peel (optional)

6 to 8 servings

1 In 8-cup (2 L) measure, microwave butter and nutmeg at High for 1½ to 1¾ minutes, or until butter melts. Stir in apple juice, rum and brown sugar.

2 Microwave at High for 6 to 9 minutes, or until hot, stirring twice. Top each serving with orange peel.

HOT SPICED BURGUNDY

- ⅓ cup (75 mL) sugar
- 1 jar (6 oz./170 mL) maraschino cherries, undrained
- 4 cups (1 L) Burgundy wine
- 1 large orange
- 1 large lemon
- 6 whole cloves
- 6 whole allspice

6 to 8 servings

1 Place sugar in 8-cup (2 L) measure. Add cherries with juice. Stir in wine. Set aside.

2 Cut 4 thin slices each from orange and lemon. Add slices to wine mixture. Squeeze juices from remaining portion of orange and lemon. Add juice to wine mixture. Stir in cloves and allspice. Microwave at High for 9 to 12 minutes, or until hot, stirring twice.

MELTED CHEESE ← BREAD

- ¼ cup (50 mL) butter or margarine
- 2 tablespoons (25 mL) Italian dressing
- 2 tablespoons (25 mL) olive oil
- 1 loaf (1 lb./454 g) French bread, sliced diagonally (1"/2.5 cm slices)

Cheese Mixture:

- 1½ cups (375 mL) shredded mozzarella cheese
- 1½ cups (375 mL) shredded Colby cheese
- ½ teaspoon (2 mL) garlic salt
- ½ teaspoon (2 mL) Italian seasoning

6 to 8 servings

1 In medium mixing bowl, combine all cheese mixture ingredients. Toss to coat. Set aside. * In 1-quart (1 L) casserole, combine butter, Italian dressing and oil. Microwave at High for 1 to 1¼ minutes, or until butter melts. Brush butter mixture on one side of each bread slice.

2 To microwave, arrange 4 slices bread buttered-side-up on paper-towel-lined plate. Sprinkle each with about ¼ cup (50 mL) of the cheese mixture. Microwave at High for 1¾ to 2½ minutes, or until cheeses melt, rotating plate once. Repeat with remaining bread slices.

3 To conventionally bake, arrange bread slices buttered-side-up on baking sheet. Sprinkle each with about ¼ cup (50 mL) of the cheese mixture. Place under broiler, 2 to 3" (5 to 8 cm) from heat. Broil until cheeses melt and begin to brown.

Advance preparation: *Up to 1 day in advance, prepare as directed to * above. Cover and refrigerate. To serve, continue as directed.*

QUICK CHICKEN VEGETABLE SOUP ↑

- 4 cups (1 L) hot water
- 2 cans (10¾ oz./284 mL each) condensed chicken noodle soup
- 1 pkg. (10 oz./300 g) frozen mixed vegetables in butter sauce
- 1 cup (250 mL) cubed cooked chicken or turkey (½"/1 cm cubes)

6 to 8 servings

1 In 3-quart (3 L) casserole, combine all ingredients. Cover. Microwave at High for 14 to 20 minutes, or until vegetables are tender and soup is hot, stirring twice.

CREAMY SALMON SOUP →

- ¼ cup (50 mL) butter or margarine
- ¼ cup (50 mL) sliced green onions
- ½ teaspoon (2 mL) grated lemon peel
- ½ teaspoon (2 mL) dried marjoram leaves
- ¼ cup (50 mL) all-purpose flour
- ½ teaspoon (2 mL) salt
- Pinch of white pepper
- 3 cups (750 mL) milk
- 1 pkg. (8 oz./250 g) cream cheese
- 2 cans (6½ oz./184 g each) skinless, boneless salmon, drained
- 1½ cups (375 mL) frozen peas
- 1 jar (2 oz./56 mL) sliced pimiento, drained, divided

6 to 8 servings

1 In 3-quart (3 L) casserole, combine butter, onions, lemon peel and marjoram. Cover. Microwave at High for 2½ to 4 minutes, or until onions are tender. Stir in flour, salt and pepper. Blend in milk. Microwave at High for 9 to 11 minutes, or until mixture thickens and bubbles, stirring 2 or 3 times with whisk.

2 In small bowl, microwave cream cheese at 50% (Medium) for 1½ to 3 minutes, or until softened. Add to milk mixture. Beat well with whisk until smooth. Stir in remaining ingredients, reserving 1 tablespoon (15 mL) pimiento. Cover. Microwave at High for 3 to 5 minutes, or until hot. * Garnish each serving with reserved pimiento.

Advance preparation: *Up to 24 hours in advance, prepare as directed to * above. Cover and refrigerate soup and reserved pimiento in separate containers. To serve, microwave soup at High for 10 to 13 minutes, or until hot, stirring once. Garnish each serving with reserved pimiento.*

CRAB-TOMATO BISQUE

- ¾ cup (175 mL) white wine
- ¼ cup (50 mL) finely chopped celery
- ¼ cup (50 mL) finely chopped carrot
- ¼ cup (50 mL) finely chopped leek
- 2 tablespoons (25 mL) butter or margarine
- ¼ teaspoon (1 mL) ground thyme
- 3 tablespoons (50 mL) tomato paste
- 2 cans (14½ oz./412 mL each) ready-to-serve chicken broth

- 2 cans (6 oz./170 g each) crabmeat, rinsed, drained and cartilage removed
- 1¼ cups (300 mL) half-and-half
- 1¼ cups (300 mL) instant mashed potato flakes
- ½ teaspoon (2 mL) salt
- Pinch of cayenne
- 1 small tomato, seeded and chopped
- Snipped fresh parsley

6 to 8 servings

1 In 3-quart (3 L) casserole, combine wine, celery, carrot, leek, butter and thyme. Cover. Microwave at High for 8 to 12 minutes, or until vegetables are tender, stirring once. Let mixture stand, covered, for 5 minutes.

2 Place mixture in food processor or blender. Add tomato paste. Process until smooth. Return mixture to casserole. Stir in remaining ingredients, except tomato and parsley. Cover. * Microwave at High for 10 to 16 minutes, or until hot and slightly thickened, stirring 2 or 3 times. Before serving, sprinkle with tomato and parsley.

Advance preparation: *Up to 1 day in advance, prepare as directed to * above. Refrigerate. To serve, continue as directed.*

To encourage mingling at your Open House, provide small plates for foods served buffet style, and distribute dips around the room.

SPARKLING GRAPE PUNCH WITH FRUIT ICE RING

- 2 cups (500 mL) crushed ice
- 4 small clusters seedless green grapes
- 1 cup (250 mL) frozen whole cranberries
- 1 kiwifruit, peeled and sliced crosswise (¼"/5 mm thick)
- 4 slices orange (¼"/5 mm thick)
- 1 bottle (64 oz./1.82 L) cranberry juice cocktail
- 1 bottle (25 oz./700 mL) nonalcoholic sparkling grape juice, chilled

Sixteen 6-oz. (175 mL) servings

1 Place ice in 6-cup (1.5 L) ring mold. Arrange fruits over ice. Pour 2 cups (500 mL) cranberry juice cocktail over fruit. Refrigerate remaining cranberry juice cocktail. Freeze ring at least 8 hours, or overnight.

2 Dip mold into warm water for 10 to 15 seconds. Carefully unmold and place ice ring fruit-side-up in punch bowl. Add remaining cranberry juice cocktail and the sparkling grape juice.

SHRIMP PIQUANT ↑

- 1 can (14½ oz./412 mL) diced peeled tomatoes
- 1 cup (250 mL) picante sauce
- ½ cup (125 mL) sliced green onions
- 1 teaspoon (5 mL) sugar
- ¼ teaspoon (1 mL) dried thyme leaves
- 1½ lbs. (750 g) fresh large shrimp, shelled and deveined

8 servings

1 In 2-quart (2 L) casserole, combine all ingredients, except shrimp. Cover. Microwave at High for 8 to 12 minutes, or until onions are tender-crisp, stirring 2 or 3 times.

2 Stir in shrimp. Re-cover. Microwave at High for 4½ to 6½ minutes, or until shrimp are opaque, stirring once. Refrigerate at least 12 hours. Serve cold with wooden picks.

TURKEY PÂTÉ TRUFFLES ↑

- 2 slices soft whole wheat bread
- ¾ cup (175 mL) chopped pecans
- 1 large apple, cored, peeled and chopped (about 1 cup/250 mL)
- ½ cup (125 mL) chopped onion
- ½ cup (125 mL) chopped carrot
- 2 pkgs. (8 oz./250 g each) cream cheese
- 2 cups (500 mL) chopped cooked turkey
- 1 tablespoon (15 mL) Dijon mustard
- ½ teaspoon (2 mL) salt
- ½ teaspoon (2 mL) dried tarragon leaves
- Pinch of pepper

3½ dozen truffles

1 In food processor, place bread and pecans. Process until fine. Place mixture in small mixing bowl. Set aside.

2 In 1-quart (1 L) casserole, combine apple, onion and carrot. Cover. Microwave at High for 5 to 7 minutes, or until mixture is very tender, stirring once. Cool 10 minutes. Place in food processor. Add remaining ingredients, except bread crumb mixture. Process until smooth. Place mixture in medium mixing bowl. Cover with plastic wrap. Chill at least 4 hours, or until firm. Form mixture into 1" (2.5 cm) balls. Roll each in bread crumb mixture. Place on wax-paper-lined baking sheet. Cover with plastic wrap. * Chill at least 4 hours.

Advance preparation: *Up to 24 hours in advance, prepare truffles to * above. Refrigerate.*

MARINATED TORTELLINI & BROCCOLI APPETIZER

- 1 pkg. (10 to 12 oz./300 to 375 g) fresh uncooked tortellini (about 3 cups/750 mL)
- ⅓ cup (75 mL) white wine vinegar
- ⅓ cup (75 mL) olive oil
- ½ teaspoon (2 mL) grated lemon peel
- 1 tablespoon (15 mL) fresh lemon juice
- 1 teaspoon (5 mL) sugar
- ½ teaspoon (2 mL) salt
- ¼ teaspoon (1 mL) dried basil leaves
- 4 cups (1 L) fresh broccoli flowerets or cauliflowerets
- 2 cups (500 mL) cherry tomatoes

8 servings

1 Prepare tortellini as directed on package. Rinse with cold water. Drain. Set aside. In 2-quart (2 L) casserole, combine remaining ingredients, except broccoli and tomatoes. Mix well. Stir in broccoli. Cover. Microwave at High for 3 to 5½ minutes, or until tender-crisp.

2 Add tortellini. Toss to coat. Re-cover. Chill at least 4 hours. Stir in tomatoes. Serve skewered on 3" (8 cm) wooden picks.

Advance preparation: *Up to 24 hours in advance, prepare as directed above. Cover and refrigerate.*

BUFFET MEATBALLS

Meatballs:

- 1½ lbs.(750 g) ground veal
- ½ lb. (250 g) ground turkey
- 2 eggs
- 1 cup (250 mL) soft bread crumbs
- ½ cup (125 mL) apple juice
- ¼ cup (50 mL) finely chopped onion
- 2 tablespoons (25 mL) snipped fresh parsley
- ¾ teaspoon (4 mL) salt
- ¾ teaspoon (4 mL) ground coriander
- ¼ teaspoon (1 mL) dried thyme leaves
- ¼ teaspoon (1 mL) pepper

Sauce:

- 2 carrots, diagonally sliced (½"/1 cm thick)
- 2 tablespoons (25 mL) butter or margarine
- 1 tablespoon (15 mL) snipped fresh parsley
- 1 cup (250 mL) ready-to-serve beef broth
- ½ cup (125 mL) apple juice
- 2 tablespoons (25 mL) cornstarch
- ¾ teaspoon (4 mL) ground coriander
- ½ teaspoon (2 mL) salt
- Pinch of pepper

10 to 12 servings

1 Heat oven to 350°F/180°C. Lightly grease 15½ x 10½" (40 x 25 cm) jelly roll pan. Set aside. In large mixing bowl, combine all meatball ingredients. Mix well. Shape into ninety ¾" (2 cm) meatballs. Arrange in even layer in prepared pan. Bake for 12 to 15 minutes, or until light golden brown. Drain. Cover loosely with foil to keep warm. Set aside. *

2 In 1½-quart (1.5 L) casserole, combine carrots, butter and parsley. Cover. Microwave at High for 2 to 3 minutes, or until butter melts. Add beef broth. Set aside.

3 In 1-cup (250 mL) measure, blend apple juice and cornstarch. Blend into broth mixture. Stir in coriander, salt and pepper. Microwave at High for 7 to 10 minutes, or until sauce is thickened and translucent, stirring 3 or 4 times. Set aside.

4 Place meatballs in 10" (3 L) square casserole. Add sauce. Toss to coat. Garnish with green pepper chunks, if desired. Serve with wooden picks.

Advance preparation: *Up to 2 days in advance, prepare as directed to * above. Cover and refrigerate meatballs. To serve, continue as directed, except microwave meatballs at High for 9 to 15 minutes, or until hot, stirring 2 or 3 times.*

RED PEPPER DIP

← RED PEPPER DIP

- 2 large red peppers
- 1 cup (250 mL) sour cream
- 2 pkgs. (3 oz./85 g each) cream cheese
- ¼ teaspoon (1 mL) salt
- ¼ teaspoon (1 mL) paprika
- ⅛ teaspoon (0.5 mL) cayenne

2½ cups (625 mL)

1 Cut peppers in half lengthwise. Remove the stem, seeds and membrane. Place peppers cut-side-down in 9" (2.5 L) square baking dish. Cover with microwave-safe plastic wrap. Microwave at High for 8 to 10 minutes, or until tender, rearranging pepper halves once. Place peppers in cold water. Remove and discard the skins. Drain skinned pepper halves on paper towel.

2 In food processor or blender, combine peppers and remaining ingredients. Process until smooth. Refrigerate at least 12 hours. Serve with fresh vegetables and bagel chips.

LEMON BRIE DIP

- 2 wheels (8 oz./227 g each) Brie cheese
- ⅔ cup (150 mL) whipping cream
- ½ teaspoon (2 mL) grated lemon peel
- ½ cup (125 mL) sliced almonds, divided
- Red and green apple slices
- Pear slices
- Red and green seedless grapes
- French bread cubes

2 cups (500 mL)

1 Cut rind from Brie. Discard rind. Place Brie in 2-quart (2 L) casserole or serving dish. Add whipping cream and lemon peel. Microwave at 50% (Medium) for 4 to 6 minutes, or until Brie is melted and mixture can be stirred smooth, stirring after every minute.

2 Reserve 1 tablespoon (15 mL) almonds for garnish. Add remaining almonds to dip. Mix well. Pour into serving dish. Sprinkle reserved almonds on top. Serve with fresh fruit and French bread as dippers.

ITALIAN FLAG DIP

- 1 cup (250 mL) finely chopped green pepper
- 1 cup (250 mL) finely chopped mushrooms
- 2 cups (500 mL) shredded mozzarella cheese
- ¼ cup (50 mL) grated Parmesan cheese
- 2 teaspoons (10 mL) dried parsley flakes
- ¾ cup (175 mL) pizza sauce
- ½ cup (125 mL) finely chopped pepperoni (about 2 oz./50 g)

10 to 12 servings

1 In 1-quart (1 L) clear glass casserole or serving dish, combine green pepper and mushrooms. Cover with microwave-safe plastic wrap. Microwave at High for 3 to 4 minutes, or until tender, stirring once. Drain, pressing to remove excess moisture. Spread vegetables evenly in dish. Set aside.

2 In small mixing bowl, combine cheeses and parsley. Layer one-half of the cheese mixture over vegetables. Spoon pizza sauce evenly over cheeses. Top with pepperoni. Sprinkle with remaining cheese mixture. Microwave at 70% (Medium High) for 5½ to 8 minutes, or until cheeses melt, rotating dish once. Serve with crisp bread sticks.

ROASTED GARLIC SPREAD

- 1 whole bulb garlic (2"/5 cm diameter)
- Olive oil
- 2 pkgs. (8 oz./250 g each) cream cheese
- ½ cup (125 mL) mayonnaise
- 1 jar (2 oz./56 mL) sliced pimiento, drained
- 2 teaspoons (10 mL) freeze-dried chives

2½ cups (625 mL)

Advance preparation: *Up to 2 days in advance, prepare as directed below. Cover and refrigerate. Serve with crackers or crisp bread sticks.*

1 Heat oven to 400°F/200°C. Lightly brush outside of garlic bulb with oil. Place in shallow baking pan. Roast on center rack for 30 minutes. Set aside to cool.

2 Place cream cheese in medium mixing bowl. Microwave at 50% (Medium) for 3½ to 4½ minutes, or until softened. Add remaining ingredients. Mix well. Set aside.

3 Remove and discard peel from garlic cloves. Mash garlic, using fork. Add to cream cheese mixture. Mix well. Cover and chill at least 4 hours. Serve with crackers or crisp bread sticks.

DESSERT BUFFET

The dessert buffet is a festive and flexible way to entertain. For eight to ten people, select two or three desserts to provide variety. As your guest list grows, plan another dessert for every eight people. Arrange the desserts on your dining table, reserving one end or a separate table to feature the dessert fondue. Choose one fondue recipe for a small group or all three for a crowd. A coffee buffet completes the party.

CHERRY CHOCOLATE FONDUE

- 2 pkgs. (6 oz./170 g each) white baking bars, broken up
- 1 cup (250 mL) miniature marshmallows
- ¼ cup (50 mL) maraschino cherry juice
- ¼ cup (50 mL) whipping cream
- 2 tablespoons (25 mL) cherry-flavored liqueur (optional)
- 2 drops red food coloring

2 cups (500 mL)

1 In 1½-quart (1.5 L) casserole or serving dish, combine all ingredients, except liqueur and food coloring. Microwave at 50% (Medium) for 5 to 9 minutes, or until baking bars are melted and mixture can be stirred smooth, beating with whisk 2 or 3 times.

2 Stir in liqueur and food coloring. Serve with dippers and condiments (right). Reheat by microwaving at 50% (Medium) for 1 to 2 minutes, stirring once, or keep warm by placing in fondue pot over very low heat.

WHITE CHOCOLATE ALMOND FONDUE →

- ⅓ cup (75 mL) sliced almonds
- 2 teaspoons (10 mL) butter or margarine
- 2 pkgs. (6 oz./170 g each) white baking bars, broken up
- 1 cup (250 mL) miniature marshmallows
- ½ cup (125 mL) whipping cream

2 cups (500 mL)

1 In 9" (23 cm) pie plate, place almonds and butter. Microwave at High for 4 to 6 minutes, or just until almonds begin to brown, stirring every 2 minutes. Drain on paper towel. Reserve 1 tablespoon (15 mL) toasted almonds for garnish. Chop remaining almonds. Set aside.

2 In 1½-quart (1.5 L) casserole or serving dish, combine remaining ingredients. Microwave at 50% (Medium) for 5 to 9 minutes, or until baking bars are melted and mixture can be stirred smooth, beating with whisk 2 or 3 times.

3 Stir in chopped almonds. Sprinkle with reserved sliced almonds. Serve with dippers and condiments (below). Reheat by microwaving at 50% (Medium) for 1 to 2 minutes, stirring once, or keep warm by placing in fondue pot over very low heat.

FONDUE DIPPERS →

- 1 to 2" (2.5 to 5 cm) pieces pound cake or angel food cake

Fresh fruits:
- Whole strawberries
- Banana chunks
- Pineapple chunks
- Apple or pear slices

1 Up to 4 hours in advance, cut cake and fruit. Dip fresh fruit pieces in lemon juice to prevent browning.

2 Arrange fruit on serving platter. Cover with plastic wrap and chill until serving time.

DARK CHOCOLATE FONDUE

- 3 bars (4 oz./114 g each) sweet dark chocolate, broken up
- 1 cup (250 mL) miniature marshmallows
- ½ cup (125 mL) whipping cream
- 2 tablespoons (25 mL) orange-flavored liqueur (optional)

2 cups (500 mL)

1 In 1½-quart (1.5 L) casserole or serving dish, combine all ingredients, except liqueur. Microwave at 50% (Medium) for 4 to 8 minutes, or until chocolate is glossy and mixture can be stirred smooth, beating with whisk 2 or 3 times.

2 Stir in liqueur. Serve with dippers and condiments (above and right). Reheat by microwaving at 50% (Medium) for 1 to 2 minutes, stirring once, or keep warm by placing in fondue pot over very low heat.

FONDUE CONDIMENTS ↑

- ½ cup (125 mL) chopped walnuts, pecans, peanuts or sunflower nuts

- ½ cup (125 mL) miniature semisweet chocolate chips

- ½ cup (125 mL) vanilla wafer crumbs

- ½ cup (125 mL) toasted coconut*

- ¼ cup (50 mL) chocolate or multicolored shot

1 Sprinkle choice of condiments over fondue-dipped cake chunks or fruit pieces.

*To toast coconut, sprinkle ½ cup (125 mL) flaked coconut evenly in 9" (23 cm) pie plate. Microwave at High for 3 to 5 minutes, or until lightly browned, tossing with fork after 1 minute and then every 30 seconds.

FRUIT IN HONEY-LIME SAUCE

- 1½ teaspoons (7 mL) cornstarch
- ¼ teaspoon (1 mL) grated lime peel
- ¼ teaspoon (1 mL) grated fresh gingerroot
- 2 tablespoons (25 mL) fresh lime juice
- ⅓ cup (75 mL) honey
- 2 cups (500 mL) sliced fresh strawberries
- 2 medium bananas, sliced
- 1 can (11 oz./312 mL) mandarin orange segments, drained
- 1 cup (250 mL) seedless green grapes
- 8 individual sponge cake cups
- 1 star fruit, thinly sliced (optional)

8 servings

1 In 2-cup (500 mL) measure, combine cornstarch, lime peel and gingerroot. Blend in lime juice. Stir until smooth. Stir in honey. Microwave at High for 2 to 3 minutes, or until mixture boils, stirring once. Cover with plastic wrap. * Chill until thickened, at least 1 hour.

2 To serve, combine remaining ingredients, except cake cups and star fruit, in medium mixing bowl. Pour honey sauce over fruit mixture. Toss gently to coat. Arrange cake cups on serving platter. Spoon fruit mixture evenly over cake cups. Top each with 1 slice star fruit.

Advance preparation: *Up to 1 day in advance, make honey sauce to * above. Refrigerate. To serve, continue as directed.*

APRICOT-GLAZED APPLE TART →

- 18 slices refrigerated sugar cookie dough (⅛"/3 mm slices)
- 2 cups (500 mL) milk
- ½ cup (125 mL) sugar
- 3 tablespoons (50 mL) cornstarch
- Pinch salt
- 2 egg yolks
- 2 Rome apples, cored and thinly sliced
- ¾ cup (175 mL) apricot preserves
- 1 tablespoon (15 mL) light corn syrup

8 to 10 servings

Apricot-glazed Blueberry Tart:
Follow recipe above, except substitute 1½ to 2 cups (375 to 500 mL) fresh blueberries for apples.

Advance preparation: *Up to 2 days in advance, prepare crust. Cover with wax paper and store in cool, dry place. Up to 1 day in advance, prepare pastry cream. Place plastic wrap directly on surface and refrigerate. To serve, continue as directed.*

1 Heat oven to 350°F/180°C. Arrange cookie slices in even layer in bottom of 10" (25 cm) tart pan. Press cookie dough gently into bottom and up sides of pan. Bake for 10 minutes, or until golden brown. Let cool.

2 Combine milk, sugar, cornstarch and salt in 4-cup (1 L) measure. Mix well. Microwave at High for 6 to 10 minutes, or until mixture thickens and bubbles, stirring with whisk after the first 2 minutes and then every minute.

3 Stir small amount of hot mixture gradually into egg yolks. Blend egg yolks back into hot mixture. Microwave at High for 30 seconds to 1 minute, or until pastry cream thickens slightly, stirring every 30 seconds. Do not overcook.

4 Place plastic wrap directly on surface of pastry cream. Let cool. Remove cooled crust from pan and place on serving plate. Set aside. Dip apple slices in lemon juice to prevent browning. Pour pastry cream into crust. Top with apple slices, slightly overlapping.

5 Combine preserves and corn syrup in small mixing bowl. Microwave at High for 1 to 2 minutes, or until melted. Strain. Discard pulp. Cool glaze and spoon evenly over apples.

CHAMPAGNE TRUFFLES ↑

- 12 squares (1 oz./30 g each) semisweet chocolate
- ¼ cup (50 mL) butter or margarine
- ¾ cup (175 mL) powdered sugar
- ½ cup (125 mL) champagne
- ¼ teaspoon (1 mL) ground nutmeg

Coatings:
- Powdered sugar
- Chopped almonds
- Shredded coconut
- Crushed vanilla wafers
- Cocoa

3 to 4 dozen truffles

1 In 8-cup (2 L) measure, combine chocolate and butter. Microwave at 50% (Medium) for 4 to 5½ minutes, or until chocolate is glossy and mixture can be stirred smooth, stirring twice.

2 Stir in ¾ cup (175 mL) powdered sugar, the champagne and nutmeg. Beat at medium speed of electric mixer until smooth and shiny, about 1 minute. Cover with plastic wrap. Chill until firm, 2 to 3 hours.

3 Place each coating in small bowl. Shape chocolate mixture into ¾" (2 cm) balls. Roll balls in desired coating. Chill at least 24 hours.

Advance preparation: *Up to 1 week in advance, prepare as directed above. Place in airtight container and refrigerate.*

DELUXE CARAMEL BARS ↑

Bar Mixture:
- 1 cup (250 mL) butter or margarine
- 1 cup (250 mL) packed brown sugar
- ⅓ cup (75 mL) granulated sugar
- 2 eggs
- 1 teaspoon (5 mL) vanilla
- 3½ cups (875 mL) quick-cooking oats
- 1 cup (250 mL) all-purpose flour
- ½ cup (125 mL) chopped pecans
- ¼ cup (50 mL) milk
- 1 teaspoon (5 mL) baking soda
- ¾ teaspoon (4 mL) salt

Caramel Filling:
- 1 bag (14 oz./398 g) caramels
- 1 can (14 oz./398 mL) sweetened condensed milk

Topping:
- ½ cup (125 mL) drained maraschino cherries
- 2 squares (1 oz./30 g each) semisweet chocolate
- 2 teaspoons (10 mL) shortening

40 bars

1 Grease 13 x 9" (3.5 L) baking pan. Set aside. Heat oven to 325°F/160°C. In large mixing bowl, microwave butter at 30% (Medium Low) for 45 seconds to 1¼ minutes, or until softened, checking every 15 seconds.

2 Add sugars, eggs and vanilla. Beat at medium speed of electric mixer until mixture is creamed. Stir in remaining bar mixture ingredients. Mix well. Reserve 1½ cups (375 mL) bar mixture. Set aside. Pat remaining bar mixture into bottom of prepared pan. Set aside.

3 In 1-quart (1 L) casserole, combine caramel filling ingredients. Microwave at 50% (Medium) for 10 to 15 minutes, or until caramels are melted and mixture can be stirred smooth, stirring 3 times. Spoon evenly over bar mixture in pan. Drop reserved 1½ cups (375 mL) bar mixture by teaspoonfuls randomly over top of caramel. Bake for 25 minutes, or until top is golden brown.

4 Sprinkle top with cherries. Place chocolate and shortening in 1-cup (250 mL) measure. Microwave at 50% (Medium) for 3 to 4½ minutes, or until chocolate is glossy and mixture can be stirred smooth, stirring once. Drizzle in crisscross pattern over top. Cool completely before cutting.

Advance preparation: *Up to 2 days in advance, prepare as directed above. Cover with foil and store in cool, dry place.*

- 1 pkg. (16 oz./454 g) frozen pound cake
- ⅓ cup (75 mL) strawberry preserves
- 3 cups (750 mL) granulated sugar
- 1½ cups (375 mL) hot water
- ½ teaspoon (2 mL) cream of tartar
- 1¼ cups (300 mL) powdered sugar
- ½ teaspoon (2 mL) peppermint extract
- 1 to 2 drops red food coloring
- Crushed peppermint candies
- Colored sugar
- Fresh strawberry slices

16 servings

Advance preparation: *Up to 24 hours in advance, prepare petits fours. If topping with fresh strawberries, place on petits fours just before serving.*

1 Trim crusts from pound cake. Cut cake lengthwise into 4 layers. Spread 1 layer with one-half of the preserves. Top with second layer. Repeat to make 2 double layers. Cut each into eight 2" (5 cm) squares (16 total). Set aside.

2 Combine granulated sugar, water and cream of tartar in 3-quart (3 L) casserole. Microwave at High for 5 to 7 minutes, or until mixture boils. Stir.

3 Insert microwave candy thermometer. Microwave at High for 7 to 11 minutes, or until mixture reaches 226°F/106°C. Let stand on counter about 1 to 1¼ hours, or until cooled to 110°F/45°C. (Do not stir or cool over water.)

4 Add powdered sugar, peppermint extract and food coloring. Beat at medium speed of electric mixer until smooth.

5 Use 2 forks to dip each layered pound cake square into frosting, coating all sides. Let excess drip off. Place on wire rack over wax paper. Repeat, dipping each square twice.

6 Decorate with crushed peppermint candies, colored sugar or strawberry slices. Let stand until set.

CHEESECAKE TREE

- 3 pkgs. (8 oz./227 g each) individual frozen cheesecakes
- ¼ lb. (125 g) chocolate-flavored candy coating
- 2 teaspoons (10 mL) shortening
- 12 maraschino cherries with stems
- Green colored sugar

12 servings

1 Remove cheesecakes from packages. Arrange in circle on serving platter. Microwave at 30% (Medium Low) for 2 to 3 minutes, or until wooden pick inserted in center meets no resistance, rotating platter once. Let stand for 10 minutes to complete defrosting. Arrange cheesecakes in shape of Christmas tree.

2 In 1-cup (250 mL) measure, microwave candy coating and shortening at 50% (Medium) for 2 to 4 minutes, or until mixture is melted and can be stirred smooth, stirring once or twice.

3 Dip one-half of each cherry into chocolate. Place each dipped cherry on wax paper until chocolate is set. Sprinkle cheesecakes lightly with colored sugar. Top each cheesecake with 1 chocolate-covered cherry.

CINNAMON
COFFEE MOUSSE →

- ¾ cup (175 mL) sugar
- 2 tablespoons (25 mL) cornstarch
- 2 teaspoons (10 mL) instant coffee crystals
- ¼ teaspoon (1 mL) ground cinnamon
- 2 cups (500 mL) half-and-half
- 3 egg yolks, beaten
- 1 cup (250 mL) whipping cream
- Chocolate curls
- Coffee-flavored candy

8 servings

1 In 8-cup (2 L) measure, combine sugar, cornstarch, coffee crystals and cinnamon. Blend in half-and-half. Microwave at High for 6 to 9 minutes, or until mixture thickens, beating with whisk 2 or 3 times.

2 Stir small amount of hot mixture gradually into egg yolks. Blend egg yolks back into hot mixture. Microwave at High for 30 seconds to 1 minute, or until mixture thickens slightly, stirring every 30 seconds. Place plastic wrap directly on surface of pudding. Chill at least 4 hours.

3 In medium mixing bowl, beat whipping cream at high speed of electric mixer until soft peaks form. Fold whipped cream into chilled pudding. Spoon evenly into each of 8 individual serving dishes. * Garnish with chocolate curls or coffee-flavored candy.

Advance preparation: *Up to 2 hours in advance, prepare as directed to * above. Refrigerate. To serve, garnish as directed.*

FLAVORED COFFEES

1 For flavored coffee choices on your buffet, place small bowls of chocolate curls, orange rind and cinnamon sticks to add to individual cups of hot coffee.

2 For flavoring coffee, offer guests an assortment of liqueurs and alcohols, such as orange liqueur, almond liqueur, coffee liqueur, peppermint schnapps and brandy.

3 Top coffee with sweetened spicy whipped cream. To make, whip ½ cup (125 mL) whipping cream. Flavor by stirring in 2 tablespoons (25 mL) powdered sugar, ¼ teaspoon (1 mL) ground cinnamon and dash of ground nutmeg.

AFTER SHOPPING

There are days during the busy holiday season when you can't spare much time for cooking dinner. Shopping, school concerts or holiday preparations call for meals you can make in minutes. Try these main dishes, which you microwave quickly just before serving or prepare the day before for a final, brief reheating.

FIESTA TACO BAKE

- 2 cups (500 mL) uncooked radiatore or elbow macaroni
- 1 lb. (500 g) ground beef
- ½ cup (125 mL) chopped onion
- 1 can (8 oz./227 mL) tomato sauce
- ½ cup (125 mL) mild taco sauce
- 1 can (4 oz./114 mL) chopped green chilies, drained
- ¼ teaspoon (1 mL) ground cumin
- ¼ teaspoon (1 mL) salt
- 1 cup (250 mL) frozen corn
- 1 cup (250 mL) shredded Cheddar cheese
- ½ cup (125 mL) shredded mozzarella cheese

4 to 6 servings

1 Prepare macaroni as directed on package. Rinse and drain. Set aside. In 2-quart (2 L) casserole, combine ground beef and onion. Microwave at High for 4 to 7 minutes, or until meat is no longer pink, stirring twice. Drain.

2 Stir in tomato sauce, taco sauce, green chilies, cumin and salt. Spoon about 1 cup (250 mL) of the meat mixture evenly into bottom of 9" (2.5 L) baking dish. Top with cooked macaroni. Spoon remaining meat mixture over macaroni. Sprinkle evenly with corn. Cover with microwave-safe plastic wrap. * Microwave at High for 7 to 10 minutes, or until center is very hot, rotating dish twice.

3 Sprinkle cheeses over corn in alternating rows to form 3 Cheddar and 2 mozzarella stripes. Re-cover. Microwave at High for 1 to 2 minutes, or until cheeses melt. Decorate with wedges of tomato and avocado, if desired.

Advance preparation: *Up to 24 hours in advance, prepare as directed to * above. Refrigerate. To serve, continue as directed.*

LEMONY SCALLOP SALAD

- ¾ lb. (375 g) fresh spinach, trimmed (about 6 cups/1.5 L)
- 1 cup (250 mL) plus 2 tablespoons (25 mL) water, divided
- 1 lb. (500 g) bay scallops
- 1 tablespoon (15 mL) cornstarch
- 1 teaspoon (5 mL) grated lemon peel
- 2 tablespoons (25 mL) fresh squeezed lemon juice
- 2 medium carrots, cut into julienne strips (2 x ¼"/5 cm x 5 mm)
- 2 tablespoons (25 mL) sliced green onion

4 servings

1 In 3-quart (3 L) casserole, place spinach and 2 tablespoons (25 mL) water. Cover. Microwave at High for 30 seconds to 1 minute, or until spinach is slightly wilted. Drain. Set aside. Arrange scallops in single layer in 10" (3 L) square casserole. Cover with microwave-safe plastic wrap. Microwave at 70% (Medium High) for 5 to 8 minutes, or until firm and opaque, stirring once. Drain. Set aside.

2 In 2-quart (2 L) casserole, combine cornstarch and lemon peel. Blend in remaining 1 cup (250 mL) water and the lemon juice. Stir in carrots. Microwave at High for 6 to 8 minutes, or until sauce is thickened and translucent. Add scallops and onion. Stir to coat. Arrange spinach evenly on 4 serving plates. Before serving, spoon scallop mixture evenly over spinach.

ORANGE-SAUCED FLOUNDER FILLETS

- 2 teaspoons (10 mL) cornstarch
- ⅛ teaspoon (0.5 mL) ground ginger
- Pinch of salt
- ½ cup (125 mL) orange juice
- ¼ cup (50 mL) dry white wine
- ¼ cup (50 mL) orange marmalade
- 1 pkg. (10 oz./284 g) frozen breaded microwave flounder fillets (2 fillets)

2 servings

1 In 2-cup (500 mL) measure, combine cornstarch, ginger and salt. Blend in remaining ingredients, except fillets. Microwave at High for 2 to 3 minutes, or until mixture is thickened and translucent, stirring once. Cover to keep warm. Set aside.

2 Microwave fillets as directed on package. Arrange on serving platter. Top with orange sauce.

VEGETABLE-HAM COMBO OVER NOODLES ↑

- 1 pkg. (10 oz./284 g) uncooked egg noodles
- 2 tablespoons (25 mL) butter or margarine
- ¼ cup (50 mL) sliced green onions
- ¼ cup (50 mL) olive oil
- ½ teaspoon (2 mL) fennel seeds, crushed
- ½ teaspoon (2 mL) salt
- Pinch of pepper
- 2 cups (500 mL) thinly sliced zucchini
- 1 cup (250 mL) frozen corn
- 1½ cups (375 mL) julienne fully cooked ham (1½ x ¼"/4 cm x 5 mm strips)
- 1 large tomato, cut into 16 wedges

4 to 6 servings

1 Prepare noodles as directed on package. Rinse and drain. Cover. Set aside. In 2-quart (2 L) casserole, microwave butter at High for 45 seconds to 1 minute, or until melted. Stir in onions, oil, fennel, salt and pepper. Cover. Microwave at High for 1½ to 2 minutes, or until onions are tender.

2 Stir in zucchini, corn and ham. Re-cover. Microwave at High for 4 to 6½ minutes, or until zucchini is tender, stirring once. Arrange noodles on serving platter. Top with vegetable-ham mixture. Garnish with tomato wedges.

CHICKEN-BROCCOLI PASTRIES

- 1 pkg. (10 oz./300 g) frozen chopped broccoli
- 1 tablespoon (15 mL) butter or margarine
- 1 tablespoon (15 mL) all-purpose flour
- ½ teaspoon (2 mL) dried dill weed
- ½ teaspoon (2 mL) salt

- ¼ teaspoon (1 mL) dry mustard
- ⅛ teaspoon (0.5 mL) garlic powder
- Pinch of white pepper
- ¾ cup (175 mL) milk
- 1 pkg. (3 oz./85 g) cream cheese
- 1 cup (250 mL) chopped cooked chicken

- 1 pkg. (8 oz./227 g) refrigerated crescent rolls
- 1 egg white, beaten
- Dill weed

4 servings

*Advance preparation: Up to 24 hours in advance, prepare filling to * below. Cover and refrigerate. To serve, continue as directed.*

1 Place broccoli in 1-quart (1 L) casserole. Cover. Microwave at High for 4 to 5 minutes, or until defrosted, stirring once to break apart. Drain. Set aside. In 4-cup (1 L) measure, microwave butter at High for 45 seconds to 1 minute, or until melted.

2 Stir in flour, ½ teaspoon (2 mL) dill weed, the salt, mustard, garlic powder and pepper. Blend in milk. Microwave at High for 3 to 4 minutes, or until mixture thickens and bubbles, stirring 2 or 3 times.

3 Place cream cheese in small dish. Microwave at High for 15 to 30 seconds, or until softened. Add to sauce. Beat well with whisk until smooth. Stir in broccoli and chicken. * Set aside.

4 Heat oven to 350°F/180°C. Remove crescent roll dough from package. Separate into 4 rectangles. Press perforations to seal. Press or roll each rectangle to 6" (15 cm) square.

5 Spoon about ½ cup (125 mL) of chicken mixture evenly into center of each square. Bring all 4 corners of each square to center. Pinch to seal. Pinch open edges and corners to seal.

6 Place on ungreased baking sheet. Brush tops of pastries with egg white. Sprinkle lightly with dill weed. Bake for 18 to 24 minutes, or until dark golden brown.

306

TURKEY STIR-FRY

- ¼ cup (50 mL) cornstarch
- 2 tablespoons (25 mL) sugar
- 2 teaspoons (10 mL) instant chicken bouillon granules
- 1 teaspoon (5 mL) ground ginger
- Pinch of white pepper
- 2 cups (500 mL) water
- 2 tablespoons (25 mL) soy sauce
- 1 red pepper, cut into 1" (2.5 cm) chunks (about 1 cup/250 mL)
- 1½ cups (375 mL) cubed cooked turkey (¾"/2 cm cubes)
- 1½ cups (375 mL) sliced bok choy
- 4 cups (1 L) fresh bean sprouts

4 servings

1 In 4-cup (1 L) measure, combine cornstarch, sugar, bouillon, ginger and pepper. Blend in water and soy sauce. Microwave at High for 5 to 8 minutes, or until sauce is thickened and translucent, stirring every 2 minutes.

2 In 2-quart (2 L) casserole, combine sauce and red pepper. Cover. Microwave at High for 2 to 4 minutes, or until red pepper is tender-crisp, stirring once. Add turkey and bok choy. Microwave at High for 3 to 4 minutes, or until hot, stirring once. Serve over bean sprouts.

STOCKING PATTERN

Piece A

Add ½" (1.3 cm) seam allowances.

Grainline

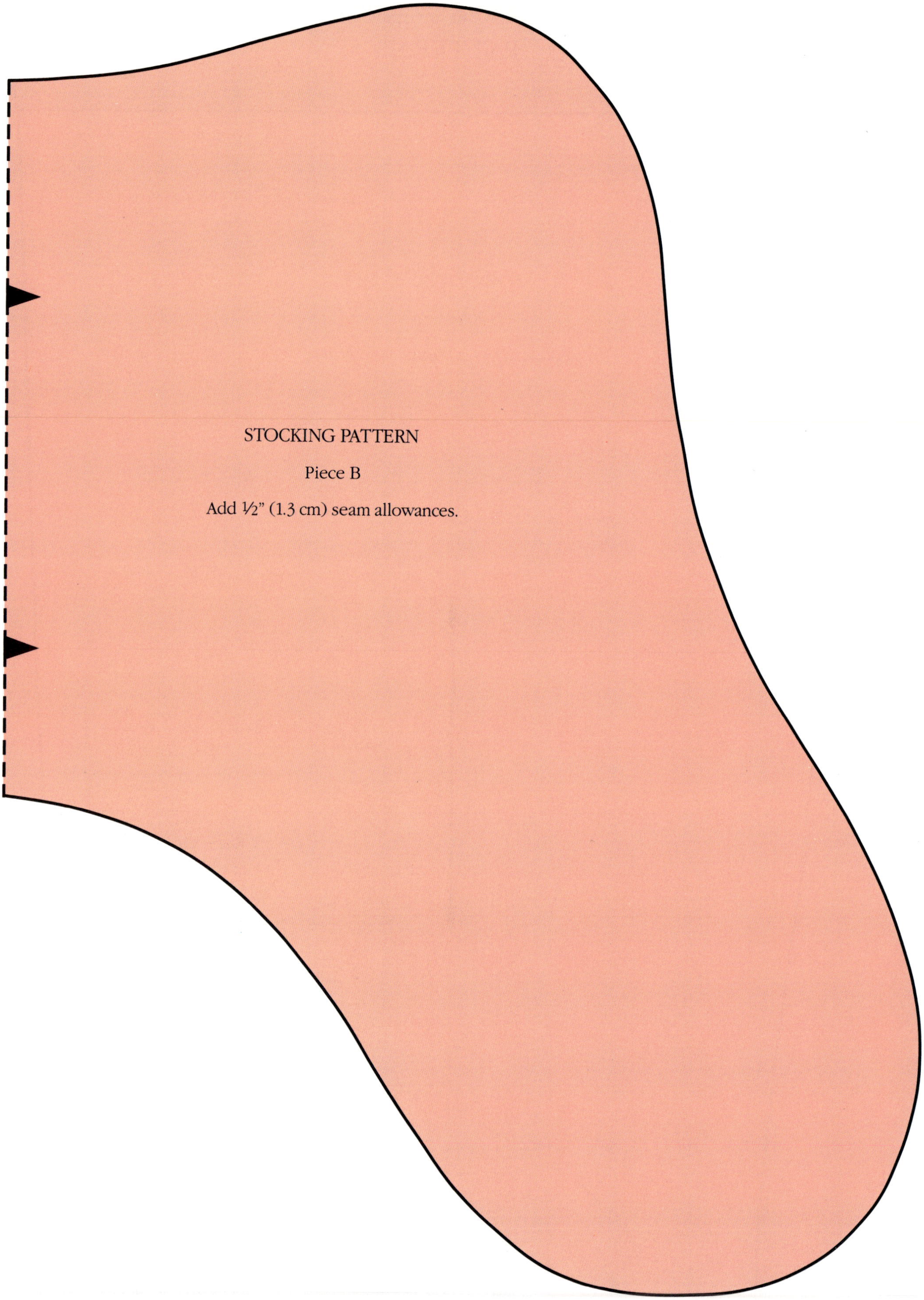

STOCKING PATTERN

Piece B

Add ½" (1.3 cm) seam allowances.

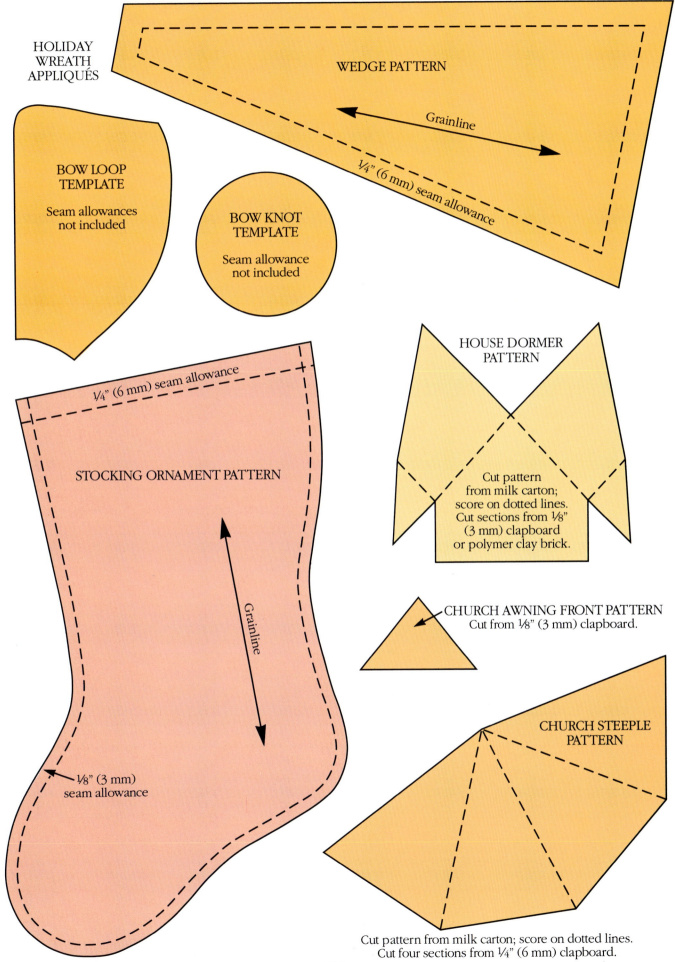

HOLIDAY
WREATH
APPLIQUÉS

WEDGE PATTERN

Grainline

¼" (6 mm) seam allowance

BOW LOOP
TEMPLATE

Seam allowances
not included

BOW KNOT
TEMPLATE

Seam allowance
not included

HOUSE DORMER
PATTERN

Cut pattern
from milk carton;
score on dotted lines.
Cut sections from ⅛"
(3 mm) clapboard
or polymer clay brick.

¼" (6 mm) seam allowance

STOCKING ORNAMENT PATTERN

Grainline

CHURCH AWNING FRONT PATTERN
Cut from ⅛" (3 mm) clapboard.

⅛" (3 mm)
seam allowance

CHURCH STEEPLE
PATTERN

Cut pattern from milk carton; score on dotted lines.
Cut four sections from ¼" (6 mm) clapboard.

311

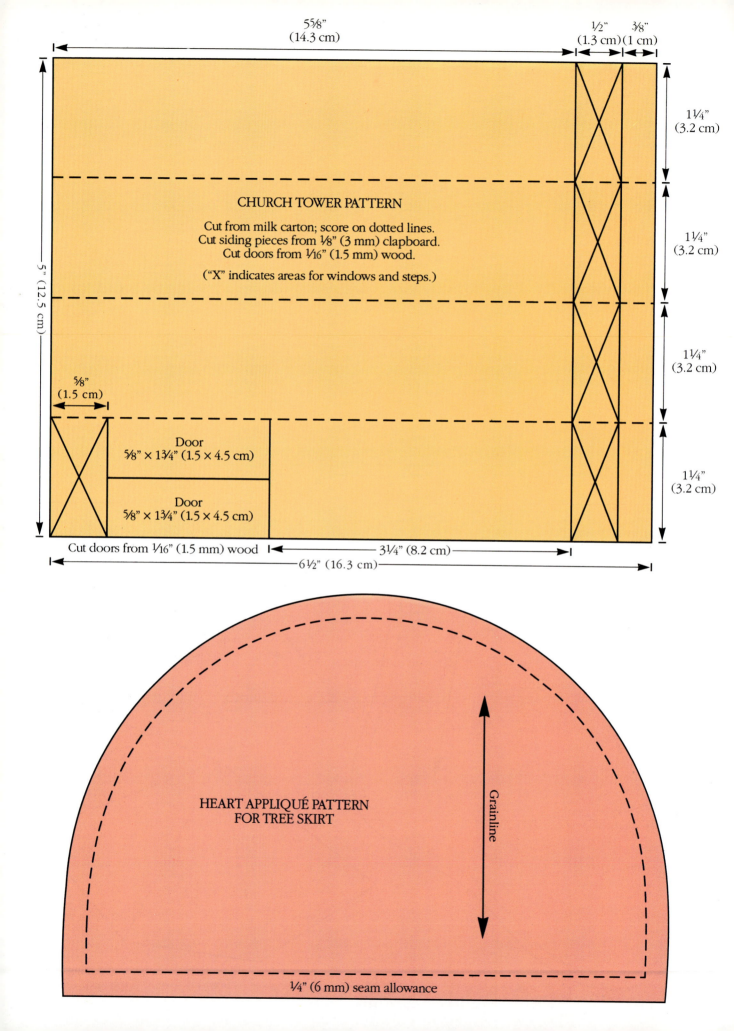

55⁄8"
(14.3 cm)

1⁄2"
(1.3 cm)

3⁄8"
(1 cm)

1¼"
(3.2 cm)

1¼"
(3.2 cm)

1¼"
(3.2 cm)

1¼"
(3.2 cm)

5"
(12.5 cm)

CHURCH TOWER PATTERN

Cut from milk carton; score on dotted lines.
Cut siding pieces from 1⁄8" (3 mm) clapboard.
Cut doors from 1⁄16" (1.5 mm) wood.

("X" indicates areas for windows and steps.)

5⁄8"
(1.5 cm)

Door
5⁄8" × 1¾" (1.5 × 4.5 cm)

Door
5⁄8" × 1¾" (1.5 × 4.5 cm)

Cut doors from 1⁄16" (1.5 mm) wood

3¼" (8.2 cm)

6½" (16.3 cm)

**HEART APPLIQUÉ PATTERN
FOR TREE SKIRT**

Grainline

¼" (6 mm) seam allowance

HELPFUL HINTS

One of the secrets of good cooking is to keep ingredients in their proper proportions. So whenever you use a recipe from this book, measure precisely if you want consistent success.

Measuring is easy with imperial utensils since quantities are listed according to the imperial system. Be aware, however, that U.S. liquid measures, used in these recipes, are not identical to their Canadian namesakes. For example, an American quart is about 8 (Canadian) ounces (1 cup) less than a Canadian quart.

Chances are, however, that imperial measurements on your kitchenware are according to U.S. standards. Since 1954, Canada's cooking industry standards for utensils (and recipes) have followed U.S. imperial measure (see below). As a result, the cooking quart is called the 4-cup quart, and a 5-cup quart is used to measure non-cooking liquids.

Of course metric utensils can also be used in preparing these recipes. Just maintain the proper proportions by measuring *all* ingredients according to the metric system.

GENERAL COOKING GUIDELINES

GRADING MEAT AND EGGS

The inspection marks "Canada Approved" and "Canada" mean the meat carcass was deemed fit for human consumption by a federal meat inspector. Any grade stamp (a colored ribbon) that might appear on the meat indicates the animal's age, color, texture, tenderness of cut and quantity of fat. Red ribbons indicate top quality, followed by blue, brown and black.

Grade A1 beef is the leanest and most tender, although all Grade A beef is well marbled. Grades B and C mean tougher flesh. Grade D is generally sold for processed meats.

Poultry is either Grade A, Grade B or "utility." Grade B and utility birds have imperfections that affect their appearance, or they are less meaty than Grade A poultry. They are best used in pies and stews.

Top egg grades are A1 and A. A1 eggs have a firm, high yolk centered in a clear, thick albumen. Use these for poaching or frying. The thinner albumen of Grade A eggs makes them more suitable for omelets or scrambling. Grade B eggs, occasionally available, are flatter and runnier still, with an off-center yolk, and are best used for baking.

COMMON CREAM VARIETIES

Type of cream	Milk fat (Canadian)	Milk fat (American)
Heavy or whipping cream (cartons)	About 35%	At least 36%
(cans)	18% to 26%	
Table cream	18%	
Half-and-half	About 11.5%	18% to 30%

REFRIGERATION TIME (Raw meat)

Ground meat	1-2 days	Roasts	3-4 days
Poultry	2-3 days	Steaks, chops	2-3 days

TYPES OF MEAT CUTS

Canadian Meat Cuts	American Meat Cuts
Beef	
Beef sirloin tip roast	Beef round tip roast cap off
Beef blade roast boneless	Beef chuck eye roast boneless
Beef shoulder roast	Beef chuck arm pot roast
Beef wing steak	Beef top loin steak
Beef boneless shoulder roast	Beef chuck shoulder pot roast boneless
Beef sirloin steak	Beef pinbone sirloin steak
Beef blade steak	Beef chuck 7-bone steak
Beef inside round; beef top round	Beef top round steak
Pork	
Pork picnic shoulder roast	Pork shoulder arm roast
Pork loin roast, rib end	Pork loin blade roast
Pork cutlets, tenderloin end	Pork loin sirloin cutlets
Pork shoulder butt (or blade) roast	Pork shoulder blade roast
Smoked ham butt end	Smoked ham rump portion
Pork cottage roll	Smoked pork shoulder roll

MEAT DONENESS

Internal Temperatures

Beef	140-170°F	(60-75°C)
Lamb	150-170°F	(65-75°C)
Pork	175-185°F	(80-85°C)
Poultry (thigh)	185°F	(85°C)
Veal	175°F	(80°C)

OVEN TEMPERATURE GUIDE

Celsius	80	100	110	120	140	150	160	180	190	200	220	230	240	260
Fahrenheit	170	200	225	250	275	300	325	350	375	400	425	450	475	500

METRIC & U.S. MEASUREMENTS

COOKING MEASURE EQUIVALENTS

Small Liquid and Dry Measure		Liquid Measure		Dry Measure	
1/4 teaspoon	1 mL	1 fl. oz.	30 mL	1/4 cup	50 mL
1/2 teaspoon	2 mL	2 fl. oz.	60 mL	1/2 cup	125 mL
1 teaspoon	5 mL	3 fl. oz.	100 mL	1 cup	250 mL
1 tablespoon	15 mL	4 fl. oz.	125 mL	2 cups	500 mL
1 coffee measure	25 mL	6 fl. oz.	200 mL	4 cups	1 Liter
		8 fl. oz.	250 mL		

DRY MEASURE

Ounces	Grams
1 oz.	30 g.
1/2 lb. (8 oz.)	220 g.
1 lb. (16 oz.)	450 g.
2 lbs. (32 oz.)	900 g.

LIQUID MEASURE (VOLUME)

Canadian Imperial Fluid Ounces (fl. oz.)	Metric Milliliters (mL)	U.S. Imperial Fluid Ounces (fl. oz.)
8 fl. oz.	235 mL	8 fl. oz.
	475 mL	1 pt.
1 pt. (20 fl. oz.)	570 mL	
	950 mL	1 qt.
1 Liter (35 fl. oz.)	1 Liter	34 fl. oz.
1 qt. (40 fl. oz.)	1137 mL	

EQUIVALENTS FOR COMMON INGREDIENTS

Food	Amount	Approximate Measure
Apples	1 pound (500 g)	3 medium-size
Bananas	1 pound (500 g)	3 medium-size
Bread crumbs, dry	1 slice bread	1/4 cup
Bread crumbs, soft	1 slice bread	1/2 cup
Butter or margarine	1/4 pound (125 g)	1/2 cup
Cheese, Cheddar	4 ounces (125 g)	1 cup shredded
Cheese, cottage	1 pound (500 g)	2 cups
Cheese, cream	3 ounces (90 g)	6 tablespoons
	8 ounces (250 g)	1 cup (16 tablespoons)
Flour, all-purpose	1 pound (500 g)	3 1/2 cups unsifted
		4 cups sifted
Lemon	1 medium-size	3 tablespoons juice
		1 tablespoon grated rind
Orange	1 medium-size	1/3 cup juice
		2 tablespoons grated rind
Potatoes	1 pound (500 g)	3 medium-size
Sugar, brown	1 pound (500 g)	2 1/4 cups (firmly packed)
Sugar, confectioners'	1 pound (500 g)	4 cups unsifted
Sugar, granulated	1 pound (500 g)	2 cups

COOKWARE SIZES

Metric volume	Closest size in centimeters	Closest size in inches or volume	Metric volume	Closest size in centimeters	Closest size in inches or volume
Cake pans			**Pie plate**		
2 L	20 cm square	8 inch square	1 L	22 x 3 cm	9 x 1 1/4 inch
2.5 L	22 cm square	9 inch square	**Skillets or fry pans**		
3 L	30 1/2 x 20 cm rectangular	12 x 8 inch rectangular		30 x 30 x 5 cm	12 x 12 x 2 inch
3.5 L	32 x 21 cm rectangular	12 1/2 x 8 1/2 inch rectangular		33 x 33 x 5 cm	13 x 13 x 2 inch
4 L	33 x 22 cm rectangular	13 x 9 inch rectangular	**Casseroles**		
5 L	35 1/2 x 25 cm rectangular	14 x 10 inch rectangular	500 mL		20 fl. oz.
Loaf pans			750 mL		24 fl. oz.
1.5 L	20 x 12 cm	8 x 4 x 3 inch	1 L		1 qt.
2 L	22 x 12 cm	9 x 5 x 3 inch	1.5 L		1 1/2 qt.
3 L	25 x 12 cm	10 x 5 x 4 inch	2 L		2 qt.
Round layer cake pans			2.5 L		2 1/2 qt.
1.2 L	20 x 3 1/2 cm	8 x 1 1/2 inch	3 L		3 qt.
1.5 L	22 x 3 1/2 cm	9 x 1 1/2 inch	4 L		4 qt.